DENVER

A Pictorial History

Christmas to Dave — 1983
Love,
Dorothy

DENVER

A Pictorial History

from Frontier Camp

to Queen City

of the Plains

William C. Jones
Kenton Forrest

The City is shown looking northwest from Civic Center in 1932. The nearly completed City & County Building is on the left and Broadway stretches to the north along the right of the photo.—*Denver Public Library Western History Collection*

ACKNOWLEDGMENTS

The production of this book was possible because of the generous help provided by numerous individuals, institutions and businesses. Foremost among these were the staff of the Western History Department of the Denver Public Library: Alys Freeze, James H. Davis, Opal Harber, Hazel Lundberg, Kay Kane, Brenda McClurkin, Sandra Turner and Kay Wilcox; and the staff of the Library of the State Historical Society of Colorado: Enid Thompson, Terry Mangan, Kay Pierson and Alice L. Sharp.

The individuals who provided photographs and historical material included Gary Cordray, Henry Couperus, Ronald C. Hill, H. E. Jobes, Robert A. Jones, R. G. Keegan, Richard Kindig (who provided photos from the collection of the late Otto Perry, as well as his own), John Kunz, Ray McAllister, A. D. Mastrogiuseppe of the University of Colorado's Norlin Library, Western Historical Collection, Mrs. E. S. Payne, John Pulliam (Librarian of the Denver Symphony Orchestra), U. T. Reilly, Robert W. Richardson of the Colorado Railroad Museum, Everett Rohrer, Mrs. Henry Sachs, Dieter Sebastion of the City and County of Denver, the late Capt. R. L. Spickelmier, and Jack Willard.

The authors also wish to thank the Amalgamated Transit Union—Division 1001, the Adolph Coors Company, Belleview College, the Colorado Division of Commerce and Development, the Denver Art Museum, the Denver Dry Goods Company, the Denver Planning Department, the Denver Police Department, the Denver Post and the Pat Oliphant-Los Angeles Times Syndicate, the Denver Public Schools, the Denver Urban Renewal Authority, the Denver Water Department, the Elitch Gardens Company, W. W. Clannin of First Federal Savings and Loan Association, the Fairmount Cemetery Association, Fitzsimons General Hospital, Frontier Airlines, the First National Bank of Denver, General Rose Memorial Hospital, the Hilton Hotel, Lakeside Amusement Park, May-D & F Stores, Public Service Company of Colorado, the Rocky Mountain News, Samsonite Corporation, United Air Lines, United Bank of Denver, the United States Army, the United States Navy, the United States Postal Service, and the Wyoming State Archives.

The authors are indebted to F. Hol Wagner, Jr. for the Denver Annexation Map and to Gene McKeever for the 1920 era Denver map.

To a great degree the quality of a book is determined by careful proof reading and for this as well as their constant encouragement the authors are indebted to Mrs. William C. Jones, Mrs. M. A. Forrest, Mrs. S. L. Curry and Mr. Charles Albi.

We wish to thank the many staff members of both Pruett Publishing and Pruett Press for the production of this volume, especially Jerry Keenan, Nikki DeBrouwer and Jim Kifer.

Endsheets—State Historical Society of Colorado Collection.

Library of Congress Catalog Card Number: 72-89020

ISBN: 0-87108-575-5

Paperback Edition Published November 1980
2 3 4 5 6 7 8 9
Printed in the United States of America

INTRODUCTION

Few periods of history have evoked so keen an interest and produced such extensive research and writing as that span of years that witnessed the exploration and settlement of our western lands. The "winning of the West" has been the subject for countless books, theses, magazine articles and television and motion picture plots. Colorado and Denver have shared generously in these chronicles. Strangely, however, little has been accomplished toward publishing the vast photographic record which spans the full history of the Queen City of the Plains. Denver is uniquely fortunate that its pioneer beginnings closely coincided with technological advances in the science of photography, making it practical for the pioneer photographer to leave his studio and capture the changing scene about him. The picture files of libraries, museums, and private collectors provide a continuous visual record of Denver from the earliest settlements along the banks of Cherry Creek and the Platte River, through the building boom of our time which sees the skyline reaching for the clouds.

While numerous works have probed specific points of the city's story and chronicled many of her notable citizens, the occasional tapping of the photographic storehouse has been only to briefly augment the written word. The task here has not been to devote effort and considerable space to again detailing the events of the past in written text, for to do so would be to repeat work already well accomplished and readily available on the library or book store shelf. Rather, here the task has been to cull from many thousands, those few hundred pictures which can each meet the demand to "equal a thousand words." That the process of selecting was often one of difficult choice, is an under-statement; by necessity personal feelings of nostalgia became deeply involved. Hopefully, however, this record will honestly portray the life and times of the city that was and still is Denver.

Here then is presented a panorama of time and place. A city, first seen in its pioneer infancy followed by boom years and then a time of doubtful future. Reassurance arrives with the first railroad train and signals an era of expansion and civic accomplishment that assures the future. The dark days of the Great War and all to soon to the verge of another, and the image of "cow town" is fast fading in the glow of the future. The transformation from the Denver remembered to the metropolis of tomorrow continues today; perhaps with a certain triumph but surely interwoven with a nostalgia for the past.

Kenton H. Forrest—William C. Jones
April, 1973

TABLE OF CONTENTS

THE EARLIEST TIMES 1858-1860's

Throughout human history one of the driving forces behind man's exploration and settlement of new lands has been the lure of riches. In the establishment of pioneer Denver this was surely true; the lure was that of GOLD!

Throughout the eighteenth century, Spanish and French expeditions traversed the land which would eventually become Colorado. During the first half of the nineteenth century, American expeditions more carefully explored the region under such leaders as Zebulon Pike, Stephen Long, John Gunnison and John Fremont.

Settlements appeared at Bent's Fort in 1833, Fort Lupton in 1836, and two years later at Fort St. Vrain. The rush to the California gold fields in 1849, brought a flow of men across the plains and mountains, some of whom remained to establish early settlements.

THE CHERRY CREEK SETTLEMENTS
ARE ESTABLISHED

As the decade of the 1850's opened, the junction of Cherry Creek and the Platte River presented a sylvan scene of sparkling waters amidst towering cottonwoods. This site was soon to be disturbed by the bustling sound of America moving West.

Among those passing through the area in the spring of 1850, was Lewis Ralston and a group of Cherokee Indians. Ralston, exploring the area now known as Arvada, found a small quantity of gold on June 22nd, in the creek that today bears his name. However, after finding no significant amount of gold, the group decided to continue on west.

Some years later, word of the find on Ralston Creek sparked the interest of William Green Russell of Georgia. Having had considerable experience in the California gold mines, Russell was eager to investigate this new gold find and interested his two brothers in organizing a trip to the region. About this same time, John

Beck, a Cherokee preacher, was considering a similar trip. Learning of their mutual interest, Russell and Beck began corresponding and decided to cooperate in a joint exploration.

The Cherokees, led by John Beck, invited a group of white men in Missouri to accompany them West. By late June of 1858, the Cherokees, the Missouri men, and the Russell party, totaling 104 men, had all arrived and made camp at the confluence of Cherry Creek and the South Platte River.

Despite high hopes, only small amounts of gold were found and enthusiasm quickly turned to disappointment, resulting in a number of the men returning eastward. About a dozen men chose to remain and under the leadership of William Green Russell, the small party moved south to present day Englewood where they set up camp on Little Dry Creek. Here they began working a placer which yielded about ten dollars a day per man, but when the gold ran out, the entire group left to prospect eleswhere, returning to the area again in September.

In 1857, an Indian by the name of Fall Leaf, found a few gold nuggets while in Colorado serving as a guide for Colonel Sumner's expedition against the Cheyenne Indians. Returning east, he showed the nuggets in Lawrence, Kansas, evoking considerable interest. From Lawrence, a company of about fifty, including two women, journeyed to the Pike's Peak region in the spring of 1858, but finding no gold, the party divided, with the women and several men heading south into New Mexico and the remainder moving north to investigate rumors of the Russell party's finds on Little Dry Creek. Arriving on September 6th, the Kansas group established Montana City (also known as Montana Diggings) but soon decided no significant gold lay there and moved to the junction of Cherry Creek and the Platte River. It was at this location, on September 24, 1858, that the St. Charles Town Association was formed, claiming the area which is today lower downtown Denver (east of the Platte and to the northeast of Cherry Creek, to about 16th and

JAMES WILLIAM DENVER

Born October 23, 1817, in Winchester, Virginia, James Denver taught school, practiced law, and in 1847 fought in the Mexican War. Moving to California, he served there as a State Senator, Secretary of State, and as a U. S. Congressman. In 1857 he was appointed United States Commissioner of Indian Affairs but interrupted this service briefly to become Governor of Kansas Territory during 1858. Following service in the Civil War, Denver remained active in public life, spending his later years in Wilmington, Ohio, where he died on August 9, 1892. While he visited Denver briefly, he never became a resident of his namesake city.—*State Historical Society of Colorado.*

Larimer Streets). The men decided to return to Kansas for the winter, planning to obtain a legal town charter from the Territorial Legislature before returning in the spring.

While St. Charles was being established, if only on paper, the Russell party returned from their explorations and decided to set up a town across the creek from St. Charles, to the south. On November 1, 1858, the Auraria Town Company was organized, the name being in honor of Auraria, Georgia, home town of the Russell brothers. Work began at once on cabins to house them for the winter, making Auraria the first permanent settlement in what is now Denver.

Only two weeks later, another party of Kansans arrived at Cherry Creek under the leadership of General William Larimer. With Auraria already well established, Larimer's party decided to simply assume the claim of the St. Charles Company, which existed only on paper, and which was now being guarded singly by Charles Nichols who had been sent back to hold the claim when the returning St. Charles men realized others were heading for the area of their town site.

On November 22, 1858, General Larimer and his men met, and voted to establish the Denver City Town Company in the same area which had been already claimed by their predecessors. To placate them, the new company gave shares to Nichols and the others of the St. Charles Company.

To assure themselves of an added advantage in obtaining a charter, General Larimer decided to name the town in honor of the Kansas Territorial Governor, James William Denver. Unknown to Larimer, however, Denver had resigned his position a month earlier to become Commissioner of Indian Affairs. The St. Charles men made an effort to have their claim advanced over that of Denver City, but never succeeded, partially due to the greater concern the Kansas Legislature now held for the problems of John Brown, slavery, and the impending war.

While efforts continued to establish pioneer towns, little concern was voiced for the real owners of the land. The entire area belonged to the Indians, but was taken from them by Congressional action in 1864. Doubtless, there was some

---

AURARIA TOWN COMPANY.

ORIGINAL SHARE, NO.59 CERTIFICATE. NO.1

THIS IS TO CERTIFY, That *A. D. Hooge* is the owner of ONE FOURTH OF ONE ORIGINAL SHARE in the Capital Stock of the AURARIA TOWN COMPANY, which entitles the owner of this Certificate to Four Lots in the Town of Auraria, to be drawn under such Rules and Regulations as may be prescribed by said Company.

No Transfer recognized unless endorsed by the Secretary and recorded in the books of the Company.

Given by Authority, at the office of said Company in Auraria, this 8th day of July A.D. 1859.

Attest: *L. J. Russell* Secretary,

W. A. McFadding President.

An Auraria Town Company lot certificate, shown in actual size.—*State Historical Society of Colorado*

ROCKY MOUNTAIN NEWS.

THE MINES AND MINERS OF KANSAS AND NEBRASKA.

VOL. 1.   CHERRY CREEK, K. T., SATURDAY, APRIL 23 1859.   NO. 1.

concern that the Indians would take hostile action against the white invaders, however, relations remained generally peaceful.

RIVALRY GIVES WAY TO MERGER
AND A CITY IS BORN

As the Denver area prepared to face its first winter, it is estimated that there were some seventy five cabins, two thirds of which were in Auraria. As the pioneers spent a quiet winter in the Cherry Creek settlements, the Missouri River towns were preparing for the springtime rush to the Rockies.

In 1859, several thousand gold seekers arrived but a large percentage quickly became discouraged and headed home. There were, however, signs of permanency: important new gold strikes, such as that of John H. Gregory at what would become Central City, gave new credence to the gold stories; the start of ferry service across the Platte; opening of stores and businesses; and perhaps one of the most notable events during that first spring, the establishment of the *Rocky Mountain News* by William Byers, the first issue of which was partially printed before leaving from Omaha, dated April 23, 1859.

A mild rivalry existed between Denver City and Auraria during these first months, however, it became obvious that one combined town would have many advantages. A dispute arose over the choice of a name for the proposed combined town. The choices of names included not only Auraria and Denver City, but also Highlands. The latter, a small settlement on the west bank of the Platte, is not to be confused with the town of Highlands which later included much of what is today north Denver. At a public meeting on December 26, 1859, the name "Denver City" was selected. Later, in an election on April 3, 1860, the citizens of Auraria voted by 146 to 39 to become part of the combined Denver City. On the evening of April 6th, a moonlight town-

meeting was held on the newly completed Larimer Street bridge over the Platte, and Denver City became a reality.

Many obstacles still faced the young Denver and not the least of these was the lack of government. While Denver was in Kansas Territory, nearby Boulder was in Nebraska Territory. Neither territorial government was capable of administering the law because of the vast distances that separated Denver from the populous areas of the territories. Impatient at this lack of government, a movement developed early in 1859, to form the new state or territory of Jefferson. On September 5th, the voters showed a strong preference for a new territory; however, without the approval of Congress, the new territory had no real authority. For the next two years, neither the unofficial Jefferson Territory nor the official but largely ineffective Kansas and Nebraska Territories, held any great degree of control.

With this obvious necessity to take some action, Congress created the Colorado Territory and an act was signed into law by President Buchanan on February 28, 1861. After assuming office the next month, President Lincoln appointed William Gilpin the first Territorial Governor.

DENVER SURVIVES FIRE AND FLOOD
BUT ALMOST MISSES THE TRAIN

On two occasions the vigor of the youthful community was tested by near disaster. On April 19, 1863, fire spread rapidly through the wooden buildings, destroying much of the business area. The city rallied and quickly rebuilt with brick for better fire protection. Only thirteen months later, on the evening of May 19-20, 1864, heavy rains caused Cherry Creek to overflow its banks and destroy a number of buildings near the stream, resulting in the loss of several lives. While the

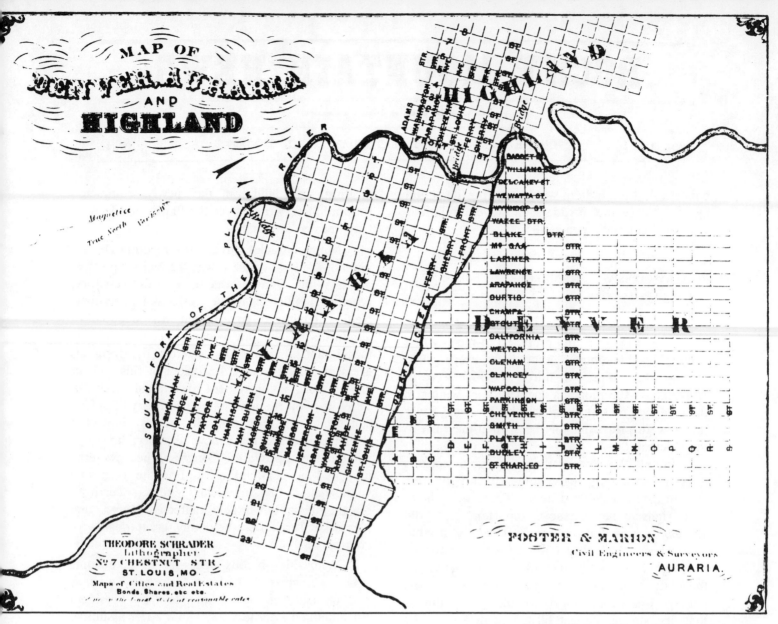

MAP OF DENVER AURARIA AND HIGHLAND

THEODORE SCHRADER
Lithographer
No 7 CHESTNUT STR.
ST. LOUIS, MO.
Maps of Cities and Real Estates
Bonds, Shares, etc etc.

FOSTER & MARION
Civil Engineers & Surveyors
AURARIA.

danger of recurring floods was recognized, the problem remained unsolved until nearly a century later with the completion of the Cherry Creek Dam.

The severest test of the city's determination to survive was yet to come. During the late 1860's, the Union Pacific Railroad was laying its rails westward from Council Bluffs, Iowa, toward a meeting with the Central Pacific which was building eastward from Sacramento, California. The completion of the line at Promontory, Utah, on May 10, 1869, at last provided transcontinental railroad service. However, much to the dismay of its residents, Denver was more than a hundred miles from the nearest station on the new line.

At one time, Denver held hopes the line would build westward through the city but the milder grades across southern Wyoming led to the decision to route the railroad through Cheyenne and Laramie, with the tracks only dipping into Colorado briefly at Julesburg in the extreme northeastern corner of the Territory. Prophets of doom foretold of Denver fading into oblivion but businessmen, under the leadership of John Evans, raised the funds to form a company to construct a railroad between Cheyenne and Denver.

As the 1860's drew to a close, the city could look back at a decade in which its residents faced fire and flood, hordes of disappointed "go backers," and the threat of isolation. With the railroads fast approaching the city, the 1870's held a new promise of a dynamic future for Denver, Colorado Territory.

DENVER PIONEERS

WILLIAM GREEN RUSSELL
1818-1887

In the spring of 1858, Russell led a party of gold seekers from Georgia to the mouth of Cherry Creek and that fall was instrumental in establishing the Auraria Town Company. He led other groups to the area but eventually left to farm in eastern Oklahoma. — *Denver Public Library, Western History Collection*

▲ WILLIAM LARIMER, JR.
1809-1875

General Larimer, heading a group from Leavenworth, Kansas, arrived at Auraria in the fall of 1858. After moving across Cherry Creek, the men organized the Denver City Town Company on the former site of St. Charles. In 1864 Larimer returned to Kansas to serve in the Civil War and later retired to a farm near Leavenworth. — *State Historical Society of Colorado*

WILLIAM GILPIN
1813-1894

Raised in Pennsylvania and graduated from West Point in 1836, Gilpin served in both the Seminole War and the Mexican War. In 1861, he was appointed by President Lincoln to be the first Governor of Colorado Territory. Gilpin remained the rest of his life as a prominent and respected citizen of Denver. —*Denver Public Library, Western History Collection*

THE FRONTIER SCENE

Three pioneer hotels are shown in this series of photos. The Denver House (left), later part of the Elephant Corral, was built in 1859 by A. J. Williams and Charles Blake. The Broadwell House (for a time the Pacific House) was erected at 16th and Larimer Streets by James Broadwell in 1859-1860. A third floor was added in 1870 but the entire structure was razed when the Tabor Building was erected on the site in 1879. The Planter's House was originally built as a depot and post office for the Central Overland, California and Pike's Peak Stage Company in 1860. It survived as a hotel until destroyed by fire in 1875. The site at 16th and Blake Streets was later occupied by the Witter Building, Denver's first apartment house.—*State Historical Society of Colorado*

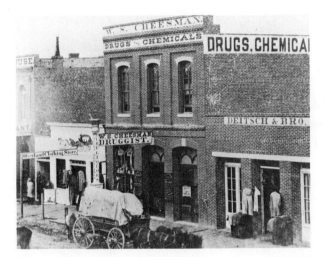

In these scenes on Blake Street between 14th and 16th Streets, can be seen many businesses recently rebuilt following the 1863 fire which swept the area. The Elephant Corral was rebuilt on the site of the Denver House and part of the structure lasted into the 20th Century. The Cheesman Drug Store is visible above and to the left. From this business Walter Scott Cheesman moved into other enterprises and became one of the city's prominent business leaders.—*First Federal Savings Collection*

This is 15th Street as it appeared in the mid-1860's; the scene is looking northwest from Larimer Street toward what is today North Denver.

A close view of business along the southwest side of 15th Street between Larimer Street to the left, and Market Street off the right edge of the photograph. The Lawrence Street Methodist Church is in the background.

The Tappan Building located on 15th Street between Market and Larimer Streets is shown shortly after completion in 1867. For many years the third floor was a Masonic Temple and for a time the building served as the state capitol.
—*All State Historical Society of Colorado*

This scene is very similar to that across the page, however, the date is late in the 1860's. The view is northwest along 15th Street looking toward Market Street.

In a closer view of 15th Street can be seen the Fillmore Block. At this location originally stood the Cherokee House and it was here that the fire began in 1863 that destroyed much of the downtown area.

It is January 20, 1868, and the David Bruce Powers wagon train has just arrived from Leavenworth, Kansas, and is circled in the 1500 block of Market Street.—*State Historical Society of Colorado*

Pioneer Denver thrilled to Mademoiselle Carolista's tightrope walking act over the 1500 block of Larimer Street in 1861.—*State Historical Society of Colorado*

About one year later, at the same location, the tightrope act is gone but the area has continued to expand. In the background the Denver Theater is visible, having recently re-opened in the location of the former Platte Valley Theater. The just arrived wagon train is carrying a steam boiler perhaps to be used in a new building or on its way to a mining camp. One of the city's first post offices has also moved into the block since the earlier photo above was taken.—*Denver Public Library, Western History Collection*

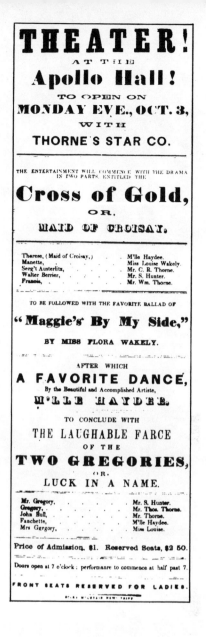

Apollo Hall, Denver's first theater, opened with "Cross of Gold" on October 3, 1859. Located on the north side of Larimer Street, between 14th and 15th Streets, it is the second building from the left in the photo. The first building is the Eldorado Hotel and to the right of Apollo Hall are Brown Brothers Bank, an unidentified store, Greenleaf and Brewer's shop (soon to become the bookstore of C. C. Woolworth and David Moffat) and at the extreme right, the Metropolitan Billiard Saloon.

A pioneer photographer recorded this scene from the tower of the Colorado Seminary building. The view is across Cherry Creek with the Platte River in the background. Beyond are the bluffs which today are part of North Denver. The date is shortly after the 1864 flood and the Lawrence Street bridge has not yet been rebuilt.—*Both State Historical Society of Colorado*

The Earliest Times 1858-1860's

In 1859, William H. Clarke built one of the first cabins in Denver City. Seen here some years later, it was typical of the early cabin homes in the area.

By the late 1860's many fine homes were being built in Denver. This is the home of businessman Hiram Burton, located at 15th and Arapahoe Streets, today the site of the Central Bank.

Hiram Burton's Storage firm can be seen in the foreground of this early 1860's scene on Blake Street, between 15th and 16th Streets. The view is to the northeast with the Platte River in the background.—*All State Historical Society of Colorado*

INDIANS

As late as 1874, the Ute Indians could be seen camped just outside of the Denver area. This scene was taken by pioneer photographer William H. Jackson.—*State Historical Society of Colorado*

On September 28, 1864, Cheyenne, Arapahoe, and other Indian Chieftains held a council with Governor Evans and the Territorial officers. Above, the citizens of Denver wait at 16th and Lawrence Streets to see the arrival of the Indians.—*State Historical Society of Colorado* Below, the Indians are gathered in front of the home of Governor Evans (left of photo) on 14th Street between Larimer and Lawrence Streets.—*Denver Public Library, Western History Collection*

Union Station as seen through the Mizpah Arch (WELCOME on reverse) about 1910.
—*State Historical Society of Colorado*

WAGON WHEELS TO JETS

No single factor is more crucial to a city's orderly and prosperous growth than its access to reliable and affordable transportation. That this has been true historically can be confirmed when considering the location of established cities. The majority of these cities and trade centers have been located either on coastal waters or along navigable rivers and canals.

As the surge westward began, steamboats were regularly plying eastern and southern rivers and moving far up the Missouri River. Likewise, the railroads, already gaining acceptance as viable transportation, were spreading a network of lines across the eastern one-third of the nation and starting to threaten the future of the riverboats. West of the Missouri, however, no rails were yet laid and the would-be pioneer was forced to turn his back on modern transportation.

In the early years of the westward movement, the time tested combination of man and beast proved the only practical transportation. Whether by horseback or by wagon, the journey to Denver was slow, boring, and exacting of human energy and sometimes cost life itself. During its first decade, the city witnessed the arrival of numerous caravans of creaking freight wagons and classic "prairie schooner" covered wagons both pulled by straining horse teams and patient yokes of oxen.

For those able to afford the ticket, the stage coach offered far greater speed, but with only a minimal degree of greater comfort. In addition to carrying passengers, the stages also provided the much needed services of carrying the mail, express, and shipments of gold and other valuables. Needless to say, they were frequent targets for the West's outlaw population.

A very real need of the West in its struggle to obtain a degree of civilization and permanence was for better transportation: time and technology were calling the railroad westward.

WESTWARD THE RAILS

If one event were to be singled out as having the most profound influence in moving Denver from a struggling western settlement to become the gateway to the Rockies, it must be the opening of the Denver Pacific Railroad on June 24, 1871. On that day Denver was tied to the rest of the nation when bands of rails reached to the Union Pacific at Cheyenne—Denver was now part of the transcontinental system. With the completion of the Kansas Pacific from the east in August, and other railroad building projects already planned or under way, Denver was on the way to becoming, as it remains today, one of the major railroad centers of America.

The significance of the railroad on Denver's economy is clearly seen in the population jump from approximately 5,000 in 1870, to 35,000 in 1880. During the same decade Colorado's population rose from 40,000 to almost 200,000 as settlers rushed, not only to the mining regions, but also to tap the wealth of rich farming and ranching lands.

As Denver grew into a hub of railroad activity, Union Station became the travel center of the Intermountain West with trains arriving and departing day and night for near and distant points. Following World War II, the new attractions of flying began to cut deeply into passenger traffic, but for a full century the passenger train continued as a popular and reliable form of transportation, especially attractive to summer tourists and to winter travelers when highways and airports became hazardous. If a date is to be chosen to mark the end of the passenger train era, it would seemingly be May 1, 1971; the assumption on that date of most passenger operations by the Federal Government's Amtrak System brought the discontinuance of over three quarters of the existing service. For the mountains and high plains of the West this meant a strange silence down at the depot from which the express had made its final departure.

MILE-HIGH TROLLEYS

As the city expanded, the need arose for public transit and to fill this void, The Denver Horse Railroad Company constructed a line from 7th and Larimer Streets to 27th and Champa Streets in 1871, with the first horse car service starting on the 17th of December.

During the next twenty years several competing companies worked to cover the city with additional horse car lines, including more than one of which allowed the horse to ride the car downgrade after laboring to the top of a hill. The advent of the cable car caused many lines to be converted to this far speedier and more efficient motive power, and likewise, with the rapid advances in the practical applications of electrical power, electric trolley cars began to replace the cable cars in 1890. By 1900, the various horse, cable and electric railway companies were all consolidated into The Denver City Tramway Company, operating 160 route miles in Denver and the suburbs. This same firm, with the name shortened to the Denver Tramway Corporation, continued to operate until April, 1971, when its bus operations were sold to the City and became Denver Metro Transit.

The trolleys made it possible for new residential areas to develop, since they provided transportation from the outlying areas to the center of the city where the majority of residents were employed. Riding the streetcar became more than just a way to get to work, for before the automobile era, this was the best way to get about the city; to a park, the baseball game, Elitch's, or right to the mountains on the Golden interurban. Until World War II, the big yellow cars of the Denver Tramway were an integral part of life in the Mile-High City.

RUTS TO FREEWAYS—CARS AND MORE CARS

With the 20th Century came the automobile. Almost a toy in its earliest forms, the streets were becoming jammed with cars and trucks even before World War I and the situation demanded attention.

Mayor Robert Speer became the driving force towards improving Denver streets to meet the needs of the automobile age. During his terms of office, from 1904 until 1912 and again between 1916 and his death in May, 1918, numerous projects were undertaken including the paving of many miles of city streets, construction of new bridges over Cherry Creek and the Platte River, and building of the 20th Street viaduct, largely at the expense of the railroads over which it crosses. Perhaps the greatest accomplishment was the construction of the parkway along Cherry Creek which was later named in honor of Speer and remains as one of the vital cross town routes.

After World War I the automobile population climbed at a frantic rate; in 1915 the city registered about 8,300 cars and trucks while in 1925 there were 65,214 cars and 4714 trucks registered. Many street projects were accomplished in a continued effort to keep up with the gas buggies and Denver began to do long range planning as indicated on the 1927 map of the Denver Planning Commission.

Today's freeway system was started after World War II as the Valley Highway. The first segments were in the north and central part of the city, following roughly the route of the Platte, and then north of Denver parallel to North Washington Street. Considerable oppositions arose from residents of the area who feared the highway would eventually ruin their neighborhoods, but just as with the citizen opposition in the 1960's to routing I-70 through North Denver and parts of Rocky Mountain and Berkeley Parks,

the highway planners won and the freeways were built. While our Denver highways are able to provide excellent transportation much of the day, severe congestion often develops during the morning and evening rush hours.

The Denver Tramway ran its last trolleys in the summer of 1950 and converted to an all bus operation in an effort to fight the losing battle against the automobile. As the riders abandoned the buses, service was reduced and the system lost more passengers. The effect of the automobile on the Tramway's buisness is best seen in the ridership figures; reaching a high of 111 million in 1945, by 1960 the number of passengers carried was down to 40 million and in 1970 the buses earned only about 18 million fares. Hopefully, the bottom has now been reached for the public is at last coming to realize the need for quality public transit to take the strain off the streets and highways.

DENVER ENTERS THE AIR AGE

On February 2, 1910, a large crowd waited in the cold at snow covered Overland Park to watch the French aviator Louis Paulham attempt to fly his plane; late in the afternoon the craft sped along the racetrack and then rose in the air. Denverites had witnessed their first flight and the opening of the air age in Colorado.

Many other pioneer aviators flew from Overland Park and later from numerous other makeshift airfields including Sloan's Lake by use of pontoons. After World War I the "aeroplane" began to assume its role as more than a novelty, it became a fast new way to travel. The need now arose for a permanent airport and in 1922, Humphreys Field was opened just a few blocks east of present day Stapleton Field.

In 1929, the Denver Municipal Airport was opened at a cost of over four hundred thousand dollars. Later renamed Stapleton Airfield, in honor of Mayor Benjamin F. Stapleton who served from 1923 until 1931, and again from 1935 until 1947, it has been continually updated and enlarged until today, as Stapleton International Airport, it is one of the nation's most modern air travel centers.

The 1970's find Denver secure in its role as the transportation center of the Intermountain West—a crossroads of rail, air, and highway routes.

Before the advent of the railroad, stagecoaches hauled passengers, mail and express throughout Colorado and the West. An artist's idealized concept of stage travel is captured in this scene of a McClellan & Spotswood Stage. Ben Holladay's Overland Mail & Express Company was located in this building (right) at 15th and Market Streets. The building is still standing in 1972. —*State Historical Society of Colorado; advertisement, Authors' Collection*

Wagon Wheels to Jets

UNION STATION

Several passenger stations have served Denver's railroads in the century since the first train arrived on June 21, 1870. The Kansas Pacific Depot, seen above and left, also served trains of the Denver Pacific and the Colorado Central during the early 1870's. In 1880, the Union Depot and Railroad Company was organized to build the city's first union station which is shown at the upper right, shortly after opening on June 1, 1881. Built at a cost of $525,000, in what has been termed "railroad gothic" styling, the building was connected by a tunnel to the Windsor Hotel and the Denver Omnibus and Cab Company. A fire on March 18, 1894, caused considerable damage (right) but the building was promptly rebuilt with a larger tower as seen in the two photos on page 28. In 1912, a reorganization led to the Denver Union Terminal Railway Company which rebuilt the center part of the station into the present Union Station, as seen in the top and center scenes on page 29. At this time umbrella sheds were also built along the tracks to provide weather protection. One railroad, the Denver & Salt Lake or "Moffat Road", was denied access to Union Station because of a conflict with the powerful Harriman interests and thus built its own station at 15th and Bassett Streets (page 29, bottom) which it used until the line merged with the Rio Grande in 1947. The building still stands, being used for other railroad purposes.—*Bottom, page 27 and center, page 29, Denver Public Library, Western History Collection; bottom, page 28 and upper, page 29, Wyoming State Archives; bottom, page 29, Authors' Collection; others, State Historical Society of Colorado*

Wagon Wheels to Jets

Following the fire of March 18, 1894, Union Station was rebuilt as seen in these two photos. It is interesting to note that the station tracks are laid with three rails to accommodate both narrow and standard gauge trains.

DENVER UNION STATION

The station remains little changed in the 1970's, from its appearance when new in 1912.

THE "MOFFAT ROAD" STATION

The station is busy on this summer morning about 1908, as tourists arrive for the scenic ride into the Rockies on the "Moffat Road."

THE WELCOME ARCH

Denver's famous Welcome or Mizpah Arch, located in front of Union Station, was dedicated on July 4, 1906. Built at a cost of $22,000 which was contributed by several railroads and other businesses, the arch weighed 70 tons and was illuminated by 1,600 light bulbs. At the dedication, Mayor Speer said, "It is to stand here for ages as an expression of the love, good wishes, and kind feeling of our citizens to the stranger who enters our gates." On December 7, 1931, the arch was removed, being termed a traffic hazard. When built, both sides carried the word WELCOME, (see photo on page 22) but by 1908, the word MIZPAH was placed on the side facing 17th Street, biding farewell to travelers. MIZPAH is a Hebrew salutation from Genesis 31:49, "The Lord watch between me and thee, when we are absent one from another."—*State Historical Society of Colorado*

For many years the railroads maintained uptown ticket offices where full travel arrangements could be made. Here are views of the turn of the century offices of the Rio Grande (above) and Colorado Midland (below). The prosperous looking Midland office gives no clue that in 1918, the railroad will be abandoned.—*Denver Public Library, Western History Collection; tickets and advertisements—Colorado Railroad Museum*

Colorado Midland Ry.

UNION PACIFIC — THE OVERLAND ROUTE

THE DENVER LIMITED--WESTBOUND
ELECTRIC LIGHTED
Between Denver and Cheyenne

				Sun.	Mon.	Tues.	Wed.	Thu.	Fri.	Sat.
Lv. St. Louis	No. 3	Wabash	9.01	Sun.	Mon.	Tues.	Wed.	Thu.	Fri.	Sat.
Lv. Kansas City	No. 119	Un. Pacific	0.00	"	"	"	"	"	"	"
Ar. DENVER	"	"	12.20	Mon.	Tues.	Wed.	Thu.	Fri.	Sat.	Sun.
Lv. DENVER	No. 109	"	7.30	"	"	"	"	"	"	"
Ar. Cheyenne	"		11.15	"	"	"	"	"	"	"
Lv. Cheyenne	No. 7	"	12.50	Tue.	Wed.	Thu.	Fri.	Sat.	Sun.	Mon.
Ar. Green River	"	"	9.45	"	"	"	"	"	"	"
Ar. Ogden	"	"	3.35	"	"	"	"	"	"	"
Ar. Salt Lake	"	O.S.L.	4.45	"	"	"	"	"	"	"
Ar. Los Angeles	"	SPLA&SL	4.30	Wed.	Thu.	Fri.	Sat.	Sun.	Mon.	Tue.
Lv. Cheyenne	No. 17	Un. Pacific	12.52	Tue.	Wed.	Thu.	Fri.	Sat.	Sun.	Mon.
Ar. Ogden	No. 67		5.25	"	"	"	"	"	"	"
Ar. Hazen	No. 5	So. Pacific	7.30	Wed.	Thu.	Fri.	Sat.	Sun.	Mon.	Tue.
Ar. Sacramento	"	"	5.00	"	"	"	"	"	"	"
Ar. San Fr'cisco	"	"	8.50	"	"	"	"	"	"	"
Lv. Cheyenne	No. 17	Un. Pacific	12.52	Tue.	Wed.	Thu.	Fri.	Sat.	Sun.	Mon.
Ar. Granger	"	"	12.25	"	"	"	"	"	"	"
Ar. Pocatello	"	O.S.L.	7.15	"	"	"	"	"	"	"
Ar. Portland	"	O W R&N	7.00	Wed.	Thu.	Fri.	Sat.	Sun.	Mon.	Tue.

Observation ten-section Sleeping Car. { Kansas City to Cheyenne. (From Denver on 101.)

Pullman twelve-section Drawing-Room Sleeping Car. { Denver to Salt Lake (west of Cheyenne on No. 7.) { Denver to Portland (west of Cheyenne on No. 17)

Pullman sixteen-section Tourist Sleeping Car. { Denver to Salt Lake (from Kansas City on No. 119.)

Chair Car. { Kansas City to Denver.

Coach. { Denver to Cheyenne.

Dining Car Service. { Kansas City to Cheyenne.

Union Pacific passenger trains have served Denver for over 100 years. Typical of these in the 1930's, was the *Pony Express* seen above or the *Denver Limited* (timetable right) of an earlier time. The U. P. has preserved one steamer, No. 8444, seen below returning to storage in Cheyenne at the head of the *City of Kansas City* on March 29, 1971, following use on an excursion.—*Above, Otto Perry photo, Richard Kindig Collection; below, Ronald C. Hill; timetable, Colorado Railroad Museum*

THREE Dome Cars on the "CITY OF DENVER"
Domeliner
OVERNIGHT between CHICAGO-DENVER

The U.P.'s streamliner *City of Denver* is seen above about to leave Denver on its inaugural run on June 18, 1936. East of Denver, the streamliner is seen as a blur of speed. Operating as part of the Amtrak System, trains such as those seen below still run over the Union Pacific. —*Top, Richard Kindig Collection; center, Charles Albi Collection; Doug Wornom photo; bottom, Ronald C. Hill*

Amtrak

NATIONAL RAILROAD
PASSENGER CORPORATION

Starting again June 6th

— Through Sleeping Car between CHICAGO and OAKLAND - SAN FRANCISCO on the Air - Conditioned ROCKY MOUNTAIN LIMITED TO DENVER

Thence via the James Peak-Moffat Tunnel cut-off—the scenic Denver and Rio Grande Western to Ogden, and Southern Pacific Lines.

New Schedules

Westbound		Eastbound	
Lv. Chicago	10:00 am	Lv. San Francisco	8:20 pm
Ar. Denver	11:45 am	Lv. Oakland	8:55 pm
Ar. Colorado Springs	11:30 am	Lv. Ogden	7:30 pm
Ar. Salt Lake City	7:30 am	Lv. Salt Lake City	10:15 pm
Ar. Ogden	9:00 am	Lv. Denver	2:20 pm
Ar. Oakland	7:55 am	Lv. Colorado Springs	2:20 pm
Ar. San Francisco	8:32 am	Ar. Chicago	5:10 pm

Also New Through Sleeping Car Service between DENVER & ATLANTA Ga.

Air-Conditioned

Via Kansas City, Memphis and Birmingham, providing the most convenient and comfortable service between the Middle and Far West and the Southeast.

Westbound		Eastbound	
Lv. Atlanta	3:40 pm	Lv. Denver	2:20 pm
Lv. Birmingham	11:15 pm	Lv. Colorado Springs	2:20 pm
Lv. Memphis	7:35 am	Ar. McFarland	4:30 am
Lv. Kansas City	8:45 pm	Ar. Kansas City	7:20 am
Lv. McFarland	11:05 pm	Ar. Memphis	9:10 pm
Ar. Denver	11:45 am	Ar. Birmingham	6:50 am
Ar. Colorado Springs	11:30 am	Ar. Atlanta	11:50 am

Via Southern Railway between Atlanta and Birmingham; Frisco Lines—Birmingham and Kansas City; Rock Island Lines—Kansas City and Colorado.

ROCK ISLAND TRAVEL BUREAUS IN ALL PRINCIPAL CITIES

COLORADO CENTENNIAL

1859–1959

"Rush to the Rockies"

on

THE "ROCKY MOUNTAIN ROCKET"

- of course -

The Rock Island vied for the passenger business with its *Rocky Mountain Limited* as advertised in its 1937 timetable. The streamlined era brought the line's *Rockets* to Denver as seen in the two views below.—*Richard Kindig Collection; timetable, Colorado Railroad Museum*

Santa Fe's passenger fleet remains America's most relaxing ride. Even in the Jet Age.

Above—The Santa Fe served Denver on a branch line from La Junta with trains such as this one passing Castle Rock, and on the right, the *Colorado Flyer* caught in this view on August 28, 1937. On May 1, 1971, the line ran the last passenger train to Denver from the south.—*Otto C. Perry photo, Richard Kindig Collection*

While the Missouri Pacific terminated in Pueblo, its trains ran to Denver via the Rio Grande. In the 1940's and 1950's, the *Colorado Eagle* was one of the finest trains between Denver, Kansas City and St. Louis. —*Advertisements on both pages not otherwise credited, Authors' Collection*

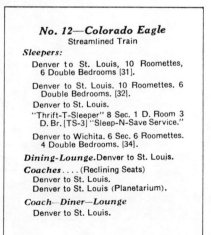

No. 12—Colorado Eagle
Streamlined Train

Sleepers:

Denver to St. Louis, 10 Roomettes, 6 Double Bedrooms [31].

Denver to St. Louis. 10 Roomettes. 6 Double Bedrooms. [32].

Denver to St. Louis.
"Thrift-T-Sleeper" 8 Sec. 1 D. Room 3 D. Br. [TS-3] "Sleep-N-Save Service."

Denver to Wichita. 6 Sec. 6 Roomettes. 4 Double Bedrooms. [34].

Dining-Lounge. Denver to St. Louis.

Coaches . . . . (Reclining Seats)
Denver to St. Louis.
Denver to St. Louis (Planetarium).

Coach—Diner—Lounge
Denver to St. Louis.

MISSOURI PACIFIC LINES

Wagon Wheels to Jets

THE DENVER POST

HOME EDITION

The Paid Circulation of THE DENVER POST Last Sunday Was 277,386

104 PAGES · PRICE FIVE CENTS

THE BEST NEWSPAPER IN THE U. S. A.

Sunday paid circulation of The Denver Post more than 125,000 greater than total paid circulation of all fourteen other Sunday papers printed in Denver and Colorado, Wyoming, New Mexico.

January Paid Circulation
Daily—181,366
Sunday—272,219

DENVER, COLO., SUNDAY MORNING, FEB. 26, 1928

REG. U. S. PAT. OFFICE. COPYRIGHT, 1928. BY THE POST PRINTING & PUBLISHING CO.

FIRST TRAIN THRU TUNNEL SUNDAY WILL OPEN NEW EMPIRE OF RICHES

HISTORY MAKING EVENT AWAITED BY THOUSANDS

Post Bombs Will Signal Start of Train on Epochal Trip.

THE DENVER & SALT LAKE RY — SAFETY FIRST

WHEN DREAMS COME TRUE!

David Moffat's Denver & Salt Lake built only as far as Craig but with the opening of the Moffat Tunnel it became possible to build a connection to the Rio Grande and create a fast new line to the West. One of the three specials to the tunnel opening is seen above, while below is the *Yampa Valley Mail* which served the line to Craig until 1968.—*Above, Otto C. Perry photo, Richard Kindig Collection; bottom, Ronald C. Hill; newspaper, State Historical Society of Colorado*

Rio Grande

The Rio Grande's fine scenery filled such trains as the *Panoramic*, seen above nearing Denver in May, 1935. After the war, new streamliners were inaugurated, including the *Prospector* and *California Zephyr* which are seen in these two views in the front range, an hour out of Denver.—*Top, Otto C. Perry photo, Richard Kindig Collection; center, Richard Kindig Collection; bottom, Ronald C. Hill; advertisements, Authors' Collection*

The South Park Line.
DENVER, LEADVILLE & GUNNISON RAILWAY.

Denver-Cheyenne-Casper-Billings

	READ DOWN			TABLE NO. 2		READ UP	
Bus Daily	Bus Daily	29 Daily	Miles	C. & S. Ry.-C. B. & Q. R. R.	30 Daily	Bus Daily	Bus Daily
AM	PM	PM			AM	AM	PM
*10.00	12.30	8.30	0	Lv....Denver....Ar	7.35	11.20	#3.25
DB	DB	f 8.57	14	"....Broomfield.... "	f 7.07	DB	DB
DB	DB	f 9.05	20	"....Louisville.... "	f 6.58	DB	DB
DB	DB	9.14	28	Lv....Boulder.... Lv	6.46	DB	DB
11.04	1.34	9.39	40	"Longmont(Ry.Mt.Nat'l-EstesPk) "	6.19	10.15	2.20
11.21	1.51	f10.15	51	"....Berthoud.... "	f 5.55	9.57	2.02
11.33	2.03	10.37	57	"Loveland(Ry.Mt.Nat'l-EstesPk) "	5.40	9.45	1.50
11.55	2.25	11.08	71	"....Fort Collins.... "	5.23	9.25	1.30
.....	.....	f11.23	82	"....Wellington.... "	f 4.54	.....	.....
.....	.....	12.06	116	Ar....Cheyenne....{Lv	4.15	.....	.....
.....	.....	12.49		Lv........{Ar	4.01		

Above, a Colorado & Southern Railway (formerly Denver, Leadville & Gunnison) narrow gauge train is ready to embark on the all day run to Leadville about 1900. Train No. 30 is seen (left) doubleheading into Denver on a cold December morning in 1938. The line's last timetable, dated January 22, 1967, still listed the train but by that fall it would make its last run.—*Richard Kindig Collection*

The C.&S. always took pride in its Colorado-Texas service and the scene above is typical of the mid-1930's. In later years the *Texas Zephyr* was the pride of the line and is seen below a few years before being discontinued in 1967. The equipment was that originally used on the Burlington as their first *Denver Zephyr* and was one of the all-time classic trains.—*Above, Otto C. Perry photo, Colorado Railroad Museum Collection; advertisement, Authors' Collection*

The Burlington (now Burlington Northern) has long been famous for its fine passenger trains. During the steam era, trains such as the *Exposition Flyer* (above) and the *Colorado Limited* offered the finest in accommodations. On May 26, 1934, the *Pioneer Zephyr* made an historic dawn to dusk run from Denver to Chicago, covering the 1015.4 miles in 785 minutes. The train captured the public's interest, resulting two years later in the inauguration of the *Denver Zephyr*. A special timed run is seen arriving (right) early in the morning of October 24, 1936, with Mayor Ben Stapleton (right) checking the time with a Western Union timer. In the scene at upper right, the new train is about to leave on its first eastward trip. The *Denver Zephyr* continues to operate today as part of the Amtrak System.—*Above and below, Otto Perry photo, Hol Wagner Collection; upper right, Richard Kindig Collection; right, Denver Public Library, Western History Collection*

Burlington Route

BURLINGTON—RIO GRANDE—WESTERN PACIFIC
EXPOSITION FLYER
Between
Chicago—Denver—Salt Lake City—San Francisco

WESTBOUND—READ DOWN			Table C	EASTBOUND—READ UP	
Via Royal Gorge	**Via Moffat Tunnel**		Detailed schedules between Chicago, St. Louis and Denver in Tables 1 and 6	**Via Moffat Tunnel**	**Via Royal Gorge**
1 Daily (1 day for example)	**1** Daily (1 day for example)	**39** Daily (1 day for example)	Lv...... New York ...... Ar Ar...... Chicago ...... Lv (See Note) BURLINGTON ROUTE	**40** Daily (1 day for example)	**12** Daily (1 day for example)
5.30 Mo	5.30 Mo	12.45 Mo	Lv...... Chicago (C.T.)......Ar	9.45 Th	8.45 Th
4.30 Mo	4.30 Mo	10.20 Mo	Lv......Peoria, Ill.........Ar	10.00 Th	7.30 Th
7.42 Mo	7.42 Mo	3.08 Mo	Lv......Galesburg, Ill.......Ar	6.55 Th	5.52 Th
8.24 Mo	8.24 Mo	3.53 Mo	Lv......Burlington, Ia.......Ar	5.58 Th	5.07 Th
9.32 Mo	9.32 Mo	5.26 Mo	Lv......Ottumwa......Ar	4.30 Th	3.50 Th
1.15 Tu	1.15 Tu	1050 Mo	Lv......Omaha, Neb.....Ar	1155 We	11.50 Th
2.19 Tu	2.19 Tu	1220 Tu	Lv......Lincoln (C.T.).....Ar	1025 We	10.00 We
8.30 Tu	8.30 Tu	8.20 Tu	Ar......Denver (M.T.).....Lv	1.00 We	9.00 We
No. 1	**No. 7**		**RIO GRANDE**		**No. 2**
8.50 Tu	5.30 Tu	2.00 Tu	Lv......Denver (M.T.)......Ar	1150 We	6.30 We
		4.14 Tu	Ar......Moffat Tunnel.....Lv	9.30 We	
10.42 Tu			Ar......Colorado Springs......Lv		4.35 We
11.45 Tu			Ar......Pueblo......Lv		3.30 We
1.28 Tu			Ar......Royal Gorge......Ar		1.46 We
8.05 Tu		8.30 Tu	Ar......Glenwood Springs......Lv	5.35 We	7.30 We
7.05 We	8.15 We	7.25 We	Ar......Salt Lake City (M.T.).....Lv	8.00 Tu	8.50 Tu
No. 39	**No. 39**		**WESTERN PACIFIC**		**No. 40**
8.30 We	8.30 We	8.30 We	Lv...Salt Lake City (M.T.)..Ar	7.30 Tu	7.30 Tu
3.45 Th	3.45 Th	3.45 Th	Ar...Sacramento, Cal. (P.T.)...Lv	10.30 Mo	10.30 Mo
7.50 Th	7.50 Th	7.50 Th	Ar....Oakland......Lv	6.45 Mo	6.45 Mo
8.50 Th	8.50 Th	8.50 Th	Ar....San Francisco (P.T.)...Lv	6.00 Mo	6.00 Mo

Denver: A Pictorial History

40

WORLD RECORD SET BY ZEPHYR ON SPEED RUN

Log of the Zephyr
(The Time Is Denver, or Mtn. Standard)

Station—	Miles from Denver	Time.	Elapsed Time.
Left Denver	....	5:04:40 a. m.	....
Yuma, Colo.	137.5	7:00:08 "	1 hr. 55 min. 28 sec.
Benkelman, Neb.	203.1	7:45:25 "	2 hrs. 40 min. 45 sec.
McCook, Neb.	254.3	8:19:50 "	3 hrs. 15 min. 10 sec.
Holdrege, Neb.	331.2	9:17:20 "	4 hrs. 12 min. 40 sec.
Harvard, Neb.	401.5	11:00:00 "	5 hrs. 4 min. 20 sec.
Lincoln, Neb.	482.6	11:12:15 "	6 hrs. 7 min. 35 sec.
Ashland, Neb.	507.0	11:31:00 "	6 hrs. 26 min. 20 sec.
Malvern, Ia.	556.6	12:23:00 "	7 hrs. 18 min. 20 sec.
Corning, Ia.	603.7	12:56:30 "	7 hrs. 51 min. 50 sec
Average speed	.... 76.8 miles per hour		

TRAIN HITS 112 MILES AN HOUR ON DASH EAST

Passes Half-Way Mark And Streaks On for Chicago.

41

Wagon Wheels to Jets

HORSES, CABLES & TROLLEYS

THE DENVER TRAMWAY

On December 17, 1871, The Denver Horse Railroad Company began operation of the city's first horse car line from 7th and Larimer to 27th and Champa Streets. By 1884, Denver boasted 15½ miles of track, 45 cars and 200 horses and mules. Already, however, the horse cars were being replaced by cable cars and a period of rapid expansion and competition developed between several companies. Eventually the city found itself with one of the most complete cable systems of any city its size and one line is believed to have been the longest single cable line in the world, seven miles long.

In the 1890's, with the refinement of electric trolley systems, the cable cars, like the horses before them, were soon being replaced. In 1899, a consolidation was undertaken which resulted in a number of companies being combined to form the Denver City Tramway Company. This same firm, later reorganized as the Denver Tramway Corporation, continued to operate the city's streetcars until 1950, when all lines were converted to bus operation. In 1971, the City of Denver purchased the Tramway and now operates the system as Denver Metro Transit.

These pages present a record of the transition from horse cars to cable cars to trolleys. The horse cars shown are typical of many that operated about the city. The photo on the left is a very rare scene of a car on the Fort Logan line while on the right is the famous Cherrelyn car. Long after all other cars were retired, the Cherrelyn car continued to operate as a tourist curiosity. Running a short distance south from Orchard Place on South Broadway, the horse pulled the car up the hill and then rode down on the back platform. Today the car, after restoration, is on display in suburban Englewood.

The center photo is the only known view of a Short electric car. A pioneer undertaking, Professor Sidney Short of Denver University, designed the line which began operating on 15th Street on July 31, 1886, making it the second operating electric street railway in the world. The cars drew their power from an underground cable laid in a slot between the rails, a system which was not as practical as the overhead wire system. In 1887, the experiment was dropped but it remains a remarkable achievement for that time.

A typical cable car is shown below, with its conductor and grip man, at the end of the line at Greenwood Avenue (now Tennyson Street) and West Colfax Avenue about 1890. The cable power house (above) is seen at 18th and Lawrence Streets shortly after the end of cable car service. The building has seen various uses over the years but in 1972, was rescued from planned demolition as part of urban renewal and is now being restored to house a restaurant and shops, a colorful link with Denver's past.

The early electric trolleys were small and often towed open air trailers. The car in the center view carries a U.S. Mail sign, denoting it sometimes hauled the mail. In order to avoid crossing numerous railroad tracks, the trolleys used viaducts, in most cases paid for in part or in whole by the Tramway. Here a car is seen about 1905, crossing the original wooden Larimer Street viaduct.

—*Right bottom and extreme upper left, Authors' Collection; upper left, 1st Federal Savings Collection; others, State Historical Society of Colorado*

For many years the Tramway operated trailers behind the trolleys during rush hours. College students were often hired as trailer conductors and for this reason, Denver University gained the nickname "Tramway Tech." The South Division conductors are posed here in 1928: second from the right in the middle row is Phillip Gilliam, today a judge of the Denver juvenile court.—*Above, Amalgamated Transit Union, Division 1001; right, Authors' Collection*

Car 375 (above) was typical of those that served Denver from about 1910 until the late 1940's. The car has just reached the end of the Argo line at W. 48th Avenue and Lipan Street in about 1925. Car 810, seen below at the loop, was one of 50 built by the Tramway in 1922-23. They were the city's newest trolleys and stayed in use until 1950. — *Above, Denver Public Library Western Collection; right, Authors' Collection*

During World War I, the Tramway hired a number of women as both "conductresses" and "motorwomen." The event caused quite a stir but most men felt the idea was good. Sadly, as soon as the manpower shortage was over, the women were placed in other jobs more traditionally suited to them.—*Above, Denver Public Library, Western History Collection*

The Tramway took advantage of Denver's thriving tourist business by operating special "Seeing Denver" trolleys around the city and also on the suburban lines to Golden, Arvada and Leyden. Two trolleys are posed with a new "Seeing Denver" touring car in the scene below, ready to introduce visitors to the city's sights. —*Below, State Historical Society Collection; advertisements and tokens, Authors' Collection*

The Denver Tramway generated its own electricity at a powerhouse on the west bank of the Platte River, at 14th and Platte Streets. Built in 1901, and after an addition in 1911, the plant produced 9,500 kilowatts. The plant closed in 1950, and was used as a warehouse until recently acquired by the Forney Automobile Museum. The Tramway built an office building and car barn at 14th and Arapahoe Streets, seen below while under construction in mid-1911. In the background can be seen the nearly completed Daniels & Fisher Tower. The Tramway Building is now the Denver Center of the University of Colorado.—*Above, Authors' Collection; below, State Historical Society of Colorado*

CENTRAL LOOP

The heart of Denver's trolley network was the Central Loop, seen here at 15th Street between Lawrence and Arapahoe Streets. Adjoining the Central Loop, in mid-block on Arapahoe between 14th and 15th Streets, was the Interurban Loop. Along with Denver Tramway interurbans, cars of the Denver & Interurban Railroad used the loop for their runs to Boulder.—*Authors' Collection*

SCHOOL FARE	From Route		A.M. IF ★ PUNCHED	
HALF FARE	3 N	S	1	15
				30
CAR TO CAR	5 N	S		45
	6 N	S		15
Transfer On Transfer If Punched	8 N	S	2	30
				45
	11N	S	3	15
				30
	13N	S		45
	14N	S	4	15
				30
	28N	S		45
	40N	S	5	15
				30
	50E	W		45
	64E	W	6	15
				30
	72N	S		45
	75E	W	7	15
				30
	DNWN	S		45
	84E	W	8	15
				30
	D			45
	E		9	15
				30
	F			45
	G		10	15
				30
	H			45
	I		11	15
				30
				45
			12	15
				30
				45

VALID ONLY IF PRESENTED WITHIN 15 MIN. OF TIME PUNCHED OR FIRST CAR, COACH OR BUS THEREAFTER

TRANSFER REGULATIONS ON OTHER SIDE

LETTERS AND FIGURES INDICATE DATE

J 7

196148

DENVER TRAMWAY CORPORATION

Globe Ticket Company of Mo., St. Louis

INTERURBAN TO BOULDER

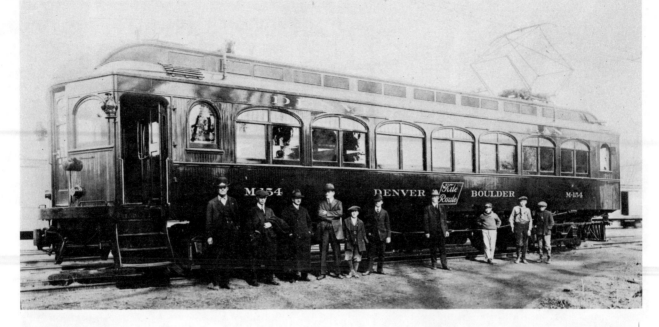

The Denver & Interurban was a high speed electric line owned by the Colorado & Southern Railway which operated to Boulder and Eldorado Springs. For a time the cars ran from the Interurban Loop but later ran from Union Station. A typical car is seen above and the line's yard is seen at right, located near the present 38th Avenue interchange on the Valley Highway. After the line closed in December, 1926, buses assumed the business and Denver & Interurban Motor Company bus No. 829 is seen below ready to leave Boulder for Denver.—*Top, Colorado Railroad Museum Collection; center, University of Colorado Historical Collections; bottom, Authors' Collection*

THE TRAMWAY STRIKE

AUTHORITIES ARE HELPLESS IN ORGY OF TERROR THRUOUT SEVEN HOURS

Tramway Officials Declare Cars Will Be Kept Running—Chief Armstrong and Nine Patrolmen Injured in Melees--Black Jack Jerome Runs Gantlet of Strikers When Detachment of Strikebreakers Arrives From Los Angeles—Firecracker Starts Riot--Barns Stormed

TO THE PEOPLE OF DENVER

Within the past twenty-four hours this city has suffered from the lawless acts of large bodies of men who have brazenly defied the laws of the city and state and the law-enforcing authorities.

Security of life and property is in serious jeopardy. The merits of the controversy between the Tramway company and the strikers now become merged in the greater responsibility upon the citizens of Denver and its executive officers of immediately re-establishing and maintaining law and order.

As mayor of the city of Denver I call upon all law-abiding citizens to give the fullest measure of co-operation in accomplishing this object.

The regularly established police force of the city is inadequate in numbers to cope with the situation as it has developed. To provide immediate reinforcements, I call for 2,000 volunteers to act as special officers until the present crisis is passed and order is restored.

Those responding to this call will report without delay to Manager of Safety Frank M. Downer, city hall.

Your mayor wishes to assure the law abiding of this community that every necessary measure will be taken to restore order and respect for law.

D. C. BAILEY,
Mayor.

Denver, August 6, 1920.

On August 1, 1920, employees of the Denver Tramway went on strike for higher wages. In response, the company hired John "Black Jack" Jerome, a professional strike breaker from San Francisco, to restore service. A series of clashes between the striking Tramway men and the strike-breakers was climaxed on August 5th when a crowd of rioters (including many non-employees) overturned five cars, four of which are shown in these photos, at East Colfax Avenue and Logan Street, in front of the Immaculate Conception Cathedral. That evening the rioters invaded the Denver Post Building and caused considerable damage there, while other trouble broke out around the city. Federal troops were brought into the city to restore peace but the bitterness of the strike lingered for many years.—*Above and newspaper, State Historical Society of Colorado; below, Authors' Collection*

INTERURBANS TO GOLDEN

In 1890, the steam powered standard gauge Denver, Lakewood and Golden Railroad, later the Denver & Intermountain, was completed between its namesake towns. An early commuter train is seen (left) at what is today 12th Avenue and Carr Street in Lakewood. In 1909, the Denver Tramway purchased the line and converted it to electric operation and used cars like No. 24 which is seen below in the Interurban Loop. Car No. 818 is caught in the bottom scene as it was about to leave Golden in 1940, ten years before the line was abandoned. —Left, U. T. Reilly Collection; center, State Historical Society of Colorado; below, Authors' Collection

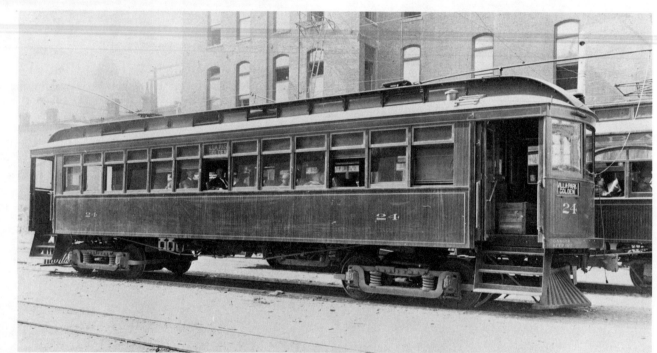

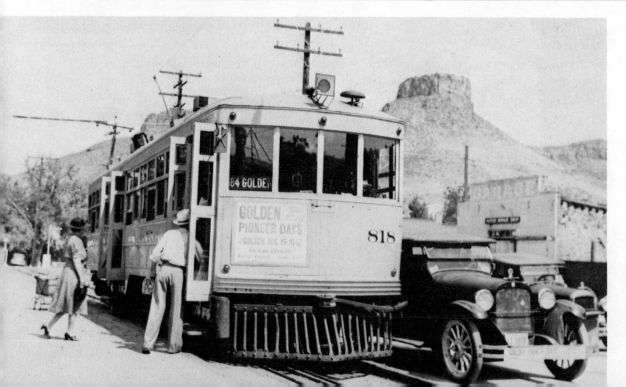

The Tramway's narrow gauge (42 in.—the same as city lines) interurbans ran to Golden, Arvada and Leyden. When seen on a map, the lines took roughly the form of a wishbone and thus the nickname "Wishbone Route." The line left the city at Lakeside and in this scene (right) a car is nearing Harlan Street, inbound to Denver. The line split at Clear Creek Junction which is today just to the northeast of the Wadsworth Interchange on I-70.—*Right and center, Authors' Collection*

Shortly before the interurban was abandoned in 1950, this unusual scene (below-right) was photographed at Oberon Station in suburban Arvada. The new *California Zephyr* is passing the aging Car .03 where the two railroads ran parallel between Arvada and Leyden. The Tramway owned extensive coal mining operations at Leyden from which it hauled coal to its power plant, using the interurban and city line through north Denver. An empty coal train is seen below as it rumbles along West 35th Avenue, bound for the mines, shortly before their closure in 1950.—*Left, Robert W. Richardson; right, Gene McKeever Collection*

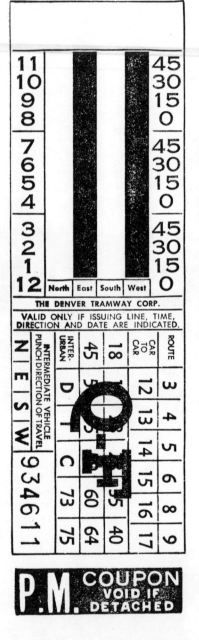

THE DENVER TRAMWAY CORP.

VALID ONLY IF ISSUING LINE, TIME,
DIRECTION AND DATE ARE INDICATED.

P.M. COUPON VOID IF DETACHED

On June 3, 1950, the big yellow trolleys of the Denver Tramway made their final runs (interurbans to Leyden and Golden continued until July 2nd) and a colorful era came to a close. Right—The State Historical Society erected a plaque in Civic Center to commemorate the event and then took a farewell ride to Lakeside Park. Below—In the early hours of June 4th, Car 326 completed its run at the Central Loop and the trolley era was closed.—*Right, Authors' Collection, Below, R. G. Keegan Collection*

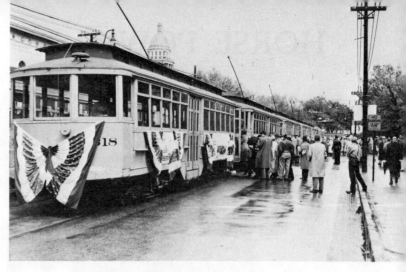

The first trolley line conversion to buses was to Globeville, made necessary by a weakened bridge on the route. On the first day of operation, (upper left) the new bus became stuck in a roadside ditch. The center photo illustrates the newer buses which served in the 1940's, while below is one of the quiet electric coaches which were used between 1940 and 1955, when the entire fleet was converted to diesel operation (right) as it remains today under Denver Metro Transit.—*Left, top and center, Henry Jobes; others, Authors' Collection*

HORSE POWER

The Standard Stables, located at 19th and Curtis Streets, as seen in this 1889 photo (above) was typical of many such facilities around the city. Below, the Kennicott-Patterson Transfer Company displays its fleet of horse drawn freight wagons. The scene is at 15th Street several blocks east of the Platte River.—*Both, State Historical Society of Colorado*

The photos above portray the evolution of cab and touring vehicles. The Denver Omnibus & Cab Company offered service in carriages such as that in the top scene, while early in the 20th Century, motorized "Seeing Denver" buses (center-left) began to tour the city. By the 1930's, several firms operated fleets of taxi cabs such as those above, seen parked at the Brown Palace Hotel. Below—In 1918, city street workers held a "Steam Roller Parade" up 16th Street to display their new paving equipment.—*Top, State Historical Society of Colorado; others, Denver Public Library, Western History Coll.*

THE AUTOMOBILE ERA

$1.00

STATE OF COLORADO

No. _____ 1

BY AUTHORITY OF THE CITY AND COUNTY OF DENVER.

AUTOMOBILE PERMIT.

The Fire and Police Board of the City and County of Denver, to all who shall see these presents, Greeting:

KNOW YE, That Whereas, _Wm A Hover_

of _1507 La Fayette_ Street, has made application for a permit to operate propel and drive an automobile, motor cycle or other similar vehicle within the City and County of Denver, and has otherwise complied with the ordinances of the City and County in this behalf,

THEREFORE, This is to certify that _Wm A Hover_ is permitted to operate, propel and drive an automobile, motor cycle or other similar vehicle within the City and County of Denver, subject to all the ordinances of the City and County now in force or which may hereafter be passed.

IN TESTIMONY WHEREOF, the Fire and Police Board, by its President, has hereunto set its hand this _Eleventh_ day of _July_ 190 _6_

FIRE AND POLICE BOARD,

By _Frank Adams_

President.

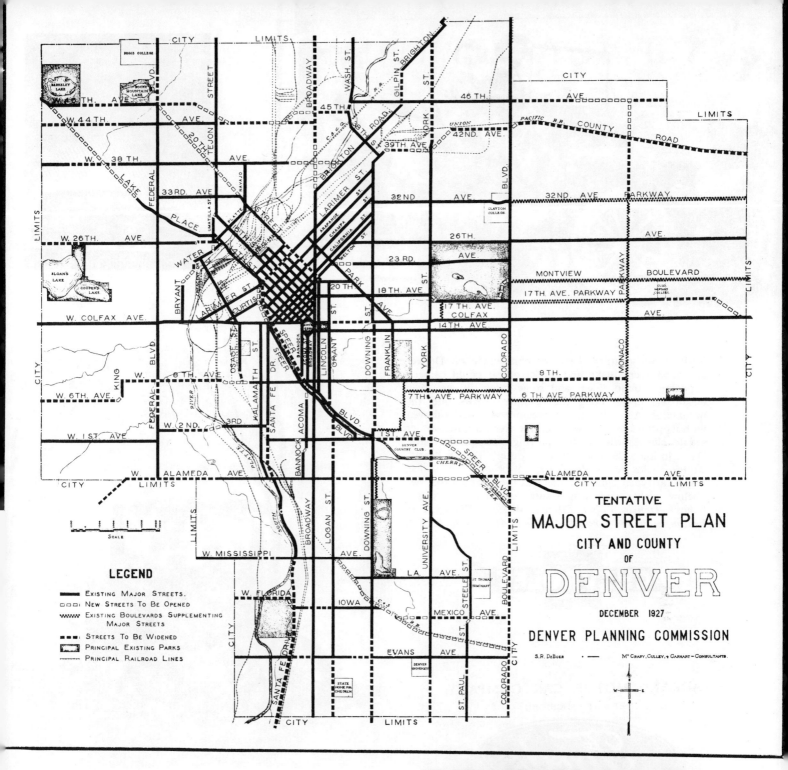

TENTATIVE
MAJOR STREET PLAN
CITY AND COUNTY
OF
DENVER
DECEMBER 1927
DENVER PLANNING COMMISSION

S.R. DeBoer • — McCrary, Culley, & Carhart — Consultants.

LEGEND

— Existing Major Streets.
▫▫▫ New Streets To Be Opened
wwww Existing Boulevards Supplementing Major Streets
▬ ▬ ▬ Streets To Be Widened
▢ Principal Existing Parks
······· Principal Railroad Lines

In 1906, Denver began issuing automobile permits. No. 1 went to William A. Hover who is seen (far left) driving with three Episcopal Bishops—Tuttle, Keates and Olmstead. Some drivers evidently could have used some of the Bishops' divine guidance as witnessed by the pathetic Ford piled up at a street corner. The city was, however, making efforts to improve the safety of the street system, as displayed on the map above.
—*Map, Authors' Collection; others, Denver Public Library, Western History Collection*

57

Wagon Wheels to Jets

Early in the century the automobile craze hit Denver and soon every make and model of car could be seen chugging around town, and some brave drivers even began venturing along the primitive roads into the mountains. A hardy Stanley Steamer is posed (above) with its proud owners, while on the right, a quiet, rather sedate electric car is seen purring through the park. Want to keep the cold out this winter? Try an "Izett" winter enclosure as demonstrated below. The stylish way to arrive at Union Station was in your own roadster (below, right) and it was sure to attract the young ladies.—*Denver Public Library, Western History Collection; emblems, Charles Albi, and Authors' Collection*

THIS IS THE IZETT WINTER ENCLOSURE CAN BE FITTED TO ANY MAKE TOURING

Cars were soon being used for advertising and business, even to help elect Robert Speer as Mayor; this is probably prior to the 1908 election. In the center scene, three young ladies are learning the joys of changing a tire out in the country with no men around. Taking a ride in the family car became a national pastime and even the dog (below left) seems to be enjoying the trip. The brave souls in the scene below (right) have equipped their car with tire chains and driven out to Morrison. They are parked at the Colorado & Southern Station about 1909.—*Denver Public Library, Western History Collection*

In 1910, Denverites thronged to the auto show and found the latest in automobiles and accessories. The shows eventually became so popular that they were held in the City Auditorium or Stockyards Stadium. Below, a racer is stripped for display, probably at Overland Park about 1909.—*Denver Public Library, Western History Collection*

CROSS-COUNTRY RACES

Denver took part in several cross-country endurance races as seen in these three photos. The middle scene records a common event and frequent cause for delays —a flat tire. The two cars are near the Kansas-Colorado border on a race to Denver early in the century.
—*Denver Public Library, Western History Collection*

PIONEER AVIATORS

On February 2, 1910, Louis Paulhan made the first flight of an airplane in Colorado. These two photos were taken at Overland Park on that cold winter afternoon as the Frenchman's plane made several flights, the longest lasting five or six minutes. To the skeptics, the reality of flight had been proven.—*Denver Public Library, Western History Collection*

On November 17, 1910, Arch Hoxsey, (above) along with Walter Brookins and Ralph Johnstone presented an air show at Overland Park. During the afternoon performance Johnstone's plane crashed, killing him. Hoxsey continued the show but later that winter he was killed when his own plane crashed during a show in Los Angeles. The strange contraption seen below is believed to be the work of the Davidson Flying Machine Company, which was located at the home of George Davidson in suburban Montclair. The photo dates to the fall of 1907. The following spring the boiler for the plane's steam engine exploded and brought the project to an end.—*Denver Public Library, Western Collection*

MUNICIPAL AIRPORT

The Denver Municipal Airport is seen in this aerial photo shortly after opening in 1929. During the early years of the air age the arrival of a new plane was a big event. In the 1930 scene below, the crowd is out to see the new Fokker F.32, one of five purchased by Western Air Express (later Western Airlines). These unusual planes, of which only ten were built, featured four tandem-pair mounted engines and were considered spectacular for their day. The model number "32" was used to indicate daytime seating for that number while berths slept 16 at night. Persistent problems with the cooling of the rear engines forced Western to retire the planes after a few years but they were surely a major step forward in aircraft evolution.—*Denver Public Library, Western History Collection*

By 1930, many businesses were purchasing planes such as the Travel Air Three-place Biplane (left) owned by Phillips Petroleum Company. Western Air Express began air mail service between Denver and Pueblo on December 10, 1927 and soon used planes such as the 1929 Stearman Biplane seen below.—*Denver Public Library, Western History Collection; sketch by Robert A. Jones*

Between 1926 and 1931, the Ford Motor Company produced their famous Ford Tri-Motor plane, often affectionately called the "Tin Goose." Eventually 199 of the planes were built in seven models and their use of metal instead of wood in construction was an important step forward. The plane below, the "Queen of the Rockies," belonged to the Curtiss Flying School and is seen posed with a group of salesmen from the Oakland Motor Car Company. A number of Ford Tri-Motors are still in flying condition and flown on occasion by antique airplane enthusiasts.—*D.P.L., Western History Collection*

UNITED AIR LINES

United Air Lines was formed in 1931, by the consolidation of four small lines: Varney Air Lines, National Lines, Boeing Air Transport, and Pacific Air Transport. Service to Denver began in 1931, and the line's first ticket counter in the main terminal is seen at the left when opened in 1937. Agent Tom Dawson (far left) handles a reservation while Stewardess Evelyn Carpenter chats with a passenger. On May 15, 1937, the line inaugurated twice daily transcontinental flights to San San Francisco, Chicago and New York, using DC-3 planes such as the *City of Denver* seen in the center photo. By the late 1940's, United was using larger planes such as the DC-6 seen in the lower photo about to take off from Denver.—*Top, United Air Lines Photo, courtesy Captain R. L. & Mrs. Evelyn Spickelmier; center, United Air Lines Photo; bottom, Denver Public Library, Western History Collection*

Frontier Airlines began in November, 1946, as Monarch Air Lines flying a route from Denver to Monte Vista. In 1950, Monarch, Arizona Air Lines and Challenger of Wyoming, merged to form Frontier Airlines which in turn merged with Central Airlines in 1967. The photo above is of a Monarch DC-3, typical of the planes used to serve Colorado during the line's early years.

Continental Air Lines was formed in 1939, from segments of several other lines and today is among the nation's major carriers. A Continental 747 is seen below a moment after takeoff on May 16, 1971. The heat of the jet exhaust blurs the view of the Stapleton International Airport terminal in the background.—*Above, Frontier Airlines, courtesy Gary Cordray; below, Ronald C. Hill*

ALL AROUND THE TOWN

The face of a city is always changing. From a cluster of crude cabins along Cherry Creek, Denver was transformed, in little more than a century, into a city of half a million population with burgeoning suburbs more than doubling that number.

The changes have been constant, the result of countless causes and forces. Man and his machines have dug and cut the earth reshaping it to hold homes and great industrial complexes, flattened and smoothed it to accommodate great airliners, formed it into long serpentine freeways and railroads; never complete, the building continues at a feverish pace. Nature, too, changes the city: the surging flood waters of Cherry Creek and the Platte River have time and again displayed their awesome power in defiance of man's attempts to control them; howling blizzards of winter lash the land, foiling almost every mechanical device under the smothering blanket of white.

POPULATION—CONSTANT PRESSURE FOR CHANGE

Perhaps the greatest force for change has been the relentless pressure of population growth. The census reports provide considerable insight to Denver's growth pattern, but must be viewed with regard to the many annexations that have changed the corporate limits of the city from the 3.52 square miles of 1864, to a giant, surpassing 100 square miles in the 1970's.

Following an initial growth during the great rush to the Rockies in the years 1858-1860, the city remained almost static in population until the early 1870's. The arrival of the railroad and the boom in mining launched a pattern of continual growth for the area. Bursts of annexation, however, account for the apparent explosion in the population of Denver City itself. The apparent slow growth from the 1910 annexation-swelled population figure, until 1940, is due to

the rapid expansion into the suburbs, while not a single change was made in the boundaries of the City of Denver from December 1, 1902 until December 2, 1941. Thus, the 1940 metropolitan population had expanded at a far faster rate than that of the city itself. The numerous annexations of the 1940's, brought the city and the metropolitan population totals closer together. By the early 1960's, the City and County of Denver was reaching the limits of expansion as it was confronted with the boundaries of incorporated suburban cities along virtually its entire length except directly to the north along Adams County.

CENSUS FIGURES OF DENVER

Year	City Of Denver	Denver Metropolitan Area*
1860	4,749	—
1870	4,759	—
1880	35,629	—
1890	106,713	—
1900	133,859	—
1910	213,381	—
1920	256,491	—
1930	287,861	—
1940	322,412	445,206
1950	415,786	495,513
1960	493,887	858,300
1970	514,678	1,227,529

*Prior to 1940, Metropolitan area not reported.

Often discussed, dreamed of, and perhaps someday to be a reality, it would seem that some form of metropolitan government must eventually be devised to serve one united city stretching from Littleton on the south, to Northglenn on the north and from Aurora on the east, beyond Golden to the mountains on the west.

Left—A panorama of Denver at the turn of the century, looking northwest from Broadway, along 16th Street.—*State Historical Society of Colorado*

THE SURGING FLOOD WATERS

In June, 1965, Denver suffered severe flooding along the Platte River; it had been over thirty years since the last such threat to the city. Much of the population was too young to remember or had long forgotten that the same stream which trickled through the city during the long dry summers could, on rare occasions, swell to many times its usual size and bring death and destruction to the very heart of the town. History contradicts the notion that the Platte or Cherry Creek are always placid and well behaved.

The Indians had warned the first settlers of their foolishness in building close to the Creek and the flood of April 19, 1864, proved the red man's wisdom on matters of nature. During the ensuing century both waterways would time and again display their strength. Cherry Creek floods struck the city on May 22, 1876, and exactly two years later on the 22nd of May in 1878. Again, on July 26, 1885, July 14, 1912, and July 28, 1922, the waters of the Creek flooded the lowlands and washed out bridges. The Creek saved its greatest show of force, and perhaps its last, for August 3, 1933. In 1890, a group of promoters had constructed Castlewood Dam about thirty miles southeast of Denver near Parker, in an effort to establish an irrigated farming colony and resort community. The effort never was very successful, but the dam remained despite continued fears for its long range safety. The dam failed during the night of August 3, 1933, releasing a wall of water which reached Denver early in the morning, causing widespread flooding in the lowlands. The need for protection from Cherry Creek flooding was now obvious and became a reality with the completion of the Cherry Creek Dam by the United States Army Corps of Engineers in 1950.

The Platte has been just as severe a violator of its banks as Cherry Creek and in fact it was sometimes the Creek's flood waters that brought the river to flood stage in the Denver area. Early records indicate a major flood in the spring of 1844, and flooding occurred again in 1864 and 1867, with major floods coming on May 31, 1894, and again on June 2, 1921. Prior to 1965, the Platte reached its maximum flood reading on September 9 and 10, 1933, only a month after the Cherry Creek flood, causing widespread

All Around the Town

flooding in the lower downtown area for the second time that summer.

For more than thirty years the city was spared any major flooding. The spring of 1965, however, was unusually wet and with many streams and the Platte River already running full, a series of heavy storms hit the entire area and brought the Platte to its all time record flow. Early in the evening of June 16th, the river swept over its banks washing away countless low lying homes and businesses and destroying several bridges. The city was left with a new respect for the Platte and also a firm resolve not to let history be repeated. Work is well under way on the Chatfield Dam being constructed south of Littleton. With the completion of this dam will hopefully be written the last chapter in the Platte's flood history.

SNOW!

Winter in Denver is crisp and pleasant. Snows are frequent but usually amount to only a few inches. The dry air and bright sun make fast work of the white blanket. The occasional heavy snow provides the motorist with long traffic lines and dented fenders, but generally the city is safe in the knowledge that the real storm is up on the mountain passes or out on the plains. Twice, however, nature has gone berserk and temporarily changed the city into a cluster of immovable humanity buried under a mountain of white.

Now almost legendary, the blizzard of 1913 paralyzed the entire city for more than two days. Several days of light snows during the first week of December were not at all unusual, but on Thursday the 4th, the storm hit in full force and dumped 20.9 inches on the struggling city. The life line of transportation was, of course, the trolley and the Denver Tramway made a valiant effort to keep the cars running, but to no avail. By 7:30 P.M. the entire trolley system was shut down and almost all railroad traffic also had come to a standstill. Thousands walked home or stayed in downtown buildings. Friday saw another 16.5 inches of snow with almost no movement across the city. Finally, on Saturday the storm ran its course with a final few inches of snow to bring the storm's total to 47.6 inches. The job of digging out began at once and required days to bring life back to normal.

The development of modern snow removal equipment has provided Man with better weapons to deal with winter storms, and perhaps the 1913 winter had grown faint in the memory of most Denverites, but the blizzard of November, 1946, served to remind all that winter in the West was still a mighty force with which to reckon.

Saturday, November 2, 1946, didn't start as an unusual day in Denver. Snow was falling at dawn but this was quite normal for the season. By Sunday the city was paralyzed under a blanket of white with the storm continuing in full force. By mid-day on Monday, two feet of snow had fallen and with a final total of 28 inches by Tuesday, the storm ranked second only to the 1913 blizzard. Just as in 1913, despite the best efforts of man and snow fighting equipment vastly improved since that earlier storm, the city literally shut down and then began to dig out of the drifts.

Denver winters since 1946 have been rather ordinary as regarding snow falls, but the odds are high that "Ole Man Winter" will once again decide to visit us with the best he has to offer.

THE CHANGING FACE OF THE CITY

The city has experienced endless change. Now in the 1970's, one of the mightiest forces for such change has come in the form of urban renewal. Steeped in controversy, the largely federally-funded programs seek to remove worn, old, run-down buildings from slum areas and replace them with functional and pleasing homes, stores, and businesses. While the program has resulted in much worthwhile renewal, this "progress" has not been made without some very questionable sacrifices of historical landmarks. Especially sad has been the demolition of numerous pioneer buildings in lower downtown Denver, once the heart of the city. The roll call of losses is a literal panorama of history; the Tabor Grand Opera House, the Cooper Building, the Tabor Building, the Windsor Hotel, and the Daniels and Fisher Store, of which only the tower has been spared.

Thankfully, Larimer Square has been successful to the extent that it is now cherished by the people of Denver and appears safe as a small reminder of our exciting past.

A pioneer photographer climbed the electric light tower at 18th Avenue and Grant Street (one of several in the area) to capture this scene of Denver in 1881. Grant Street runs from lower right to upper left and the vacant lot near the center of the photo is today the site of the State Capitol Building.—*State Historical Society of Colorado*

Above—Broadway was still a tree lined street when this picture was taken in 1878. 17th Street is on the left and 18th Street on the right, with the triangle lot in the lower left now the site of the Brown Palace Hotel. Below—19th Street is in the center of this early 1880's view and 20th Street is on the right. The intersection at lower left is 19th Avenue and Lincoln Street (Lincoln running left to right), and the old St. John's Episcopal Church is located in the center right.—*State Historical Society of Colorado*

DENVER - 1873

These eight scenes comprise a 360° panoramic view of Denver in 1873. The photos were taken from the roof of the Arapahoe School in the block bounded by 17th, 18th, Lawrence, and Arapahoe Streets. From the top and moving left to right, the view is due west to north, the middle row is from north to southeast. and the bottom row is from southeast to west. The streets include: on the top row, 17th running from lower left to upper right and intersecting Lawrence Street in front of the steeple; on the middle row, 18th Street running full width (roughly center) and intersecting Lawrence Street on the left and Arapahoe Street on the right: on the bottom row, Arapahoe Street running from the lower left margin of the photos to the upper right, intersecting 18th Street on the left and 17th Street on the right.

—*State Historical Society of Colorado*

BROADWAY

Above—Looking south from 19th Avenue early in the 20th century, Trinity Methodist Church is on the left with the Hotel Metropole (now part of the Cosmopolitan Hotel) behind it at 18th Avenue. The Brown Palace Hotel is on the right. Below—The Capitol grounds are to the right of this scene, and on the left is the old Tramway cable car power house (by this time being used for stores and a warehouse) and beyond it is Fire Station No. 1, on the site of which the Pioneer Monument now stands.—*Authors' Collection*

15th STREET –
CIRCA 1905

This view at 15th and Curtis Streets is markedly changed today, for by the early 1970's every building in this photograph had been razed.

On the right of this scene at 15th and Lawrence Streets, the tower of the Mining Exchange Building is visible; on this site the Brooks Towers is now located.

An interurban electric car arriving from Leyden was captured in this scene on Lawrence Street between 15th and 16th Streets. As with the other photos on this page, the buildings have succumbed to urban renewal. On the right is the Interstate Trust Building and beyond, at 16th Street, is the Daniels and Fisher Store. On the left is the Moffat and Kassler Building, built in 1880, and the Golden Eagle Department Store which until recently housed the Miller Western Wear Company.—*Authors' Collection*

Above—Taken at 16th Street and Broadway looking northwest toward the Rockies, this mid-1920's view includes the Majestic Building and the Brown Palace Hotel on the right and the old Arapahoe County Courthouse on the left. The courthouse site is now the location of the May-D & F Store.

Right—Downtown Denver in the 20's. In the distance looms the tower of the D & F Store while in the foreground are two landmarks which have survived until the present; the Kittridge Building (now housing the Paramount Theater) and next to that the Masonic Temple.—*Historical Collection, University of Colorado*

During the winter of 1887-88, Denverites faced a sea of mud on the countless streets which were still unpaved. This scene at 16th and Welton Streets is just a block short of the location on the right—but some 35 years earlier.—*State Historical Society of Colorado*

Above—At the heart of downtown Denver: 16th and California Streets looking northwest about 1915. The Denver Dry Goods Store is on the extreme left while on the right is the May Company at Champa Street and behind it is the D & F tower at Arapahoe Street.—*State Historical Society of Colorado*

Below—Just one block from the scene above, this view at 16th and Stout Streets dates to 1950 and includes several of the pollution free electric trolley buses which served from 1940 until 1955, when replaced by diesel buses.—*Denver Public Library, Western History Collection*

Above—This 1900 view from 16th and Champa Streets includes many landmark buildings, most of which have been razed in recent years. On the left is Joslin's Store (still
at this location), and beyond is the Tabor Theater. The May Company will soon be
built on the site of the Mayer Jewelry Store and the D & F tower building will be
added ten years later at Lawrence Street.—*Authors' Collection*

Below—Looking from 16th and Boulder Streets towards downtown, this scene reveals
recent grading to lower the street, resulting in the high embankments still evident today.
The photo dates to about 1905.—*State Historical Society of Colorado*

17th STREET

17th Street at the start of the 20th Century. Above—Taken from in front of Union Station, looking towards Broadway; on the left is the old Denver City Railway horse-car barn which until recently was occupied by Hendrie and Bolthoff Company. On the right is the Oxford Hotel which still operates at that location.—*1st Federal Savings Collection*

Below—From 17th and Champa Streets, looking in the direction of the depot. On the left is the Ernest and Cranmer Building, dating to 1891; the entire block is now occupied by the Colorado National Bank. The eight story building on the right is the Cooper Building which opened in 1892. It was demolished in a massive 8 second explosion staged by the Denver Urban Renewal Authority on April 5, 1970.—*Authors' Collection*

TO THE OUTSKIRTS

Top—On April 10, 1900, Roy Kent caught this scene of fresh snow near his home in suburban Highlands, in the 2700 block of Federal Boulevard (then Blvd. F).—*State Historical Society of Colorado*

Middle—Edgewater was far out in the country in this 1890's view of Sloan's Lake from just east of present day Sheridan Boulevard.—*Denver Public Library, Western History Collection*

Bottom—Today in the center of a busy suburban area, on November 16, 1936, Sheridan Boulevard, near 12th Avenue, looked peaceful as a lone automobile approached the interurban station which had a short time before been struck by a careless driver.—*State Historical Society of Colorado*

All Around the Town

A PANORAMA OF YESTERDAY!

These views were taken from the Capitol Building by L. C. McClure in 1911. The scene begins at due west on the right, near 16th Street and Broadway, with the lower row of photos continuing to Colfax and Sherman Street, facing due north.—*Denver Public Library, Western History Collection*

Foreground—Old Cable Power House; to

Left to right—D & F Tower, Majestic Bldg., and Brown Palace Hotel.

Left to right—Y.M.C.A. (corner only), East High School.

rear, Denver Public Library and U.S. Mint.

The large domed building in center right is the old Arapahoe County Courthouse.

Trinity Church steeple, and close by, old

Left-center—Central Presbyterian Church and behind, the Scottish Rite Masonic Temple.

All Around the Town

DENVER: BIRDS-EYE VIEWS

Four panoramic views of Denver. On the lower right the city is seen as it appeared in the late 1960's, looking northwest from just east of the capitol. The other three photographs date to the late 1920's or very early 1930's. The view on the upper left is toward the southwest with the area between the Colfax Viaduct, (left) and the Larimer Street Viaduct, (right) now part of the Auraria Urban Renewal project. The scene at lower left faces due north along Broadway from Mississippi Avenue; Gates Rubber Company is in the foreground. The photo at upper right is toward the southeast from about 16th and Larimer Streets.—*Lower left, Denver Public Library Western Collection; others— State Historical Society of Colorado*

IN THIS PAPER YOU WILL FIND DAILY THE TELEGRAPHIC SERVICES OF THE ASSOCIATED PRESS, NEW YORK TIMES, CHICAGO TRIBUNE, UNIVERSAL SERVICE AND THE INTERNATIONAL NEWS SERVICE. NO OTHER NEWSPAPER IN THE WORLD HAS ALL OF THESE GREAT WIRE SERVICES

LOWER SECTION OF DENVER FLOODED
AS CASTLEWOOD DAM RIPS OUT AND
SENDS DELUGE DOWN CHERRY CREEK

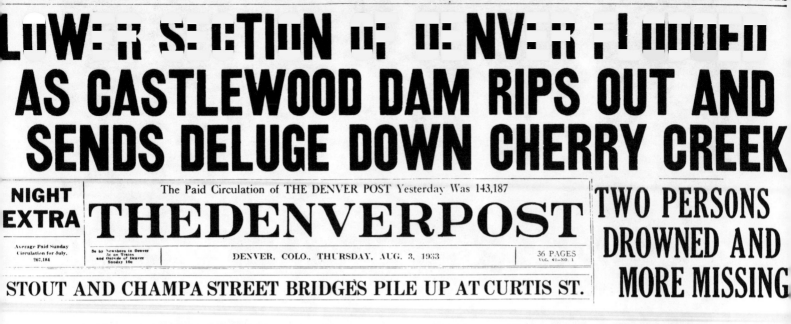

NIGHT EXTRA

Average Paid Sunday Circulation for July, 267,184

The Paid Circulation of THE DENVER POST Yesterday Was 143,187

THEDENVERPOST

3c by Newsboys in Denver
5c on Trains and Outside of Denver
Sunday 10c

DENVER, COLO., THURSDAY, AUG. 3, 1933

36 PAGES
Vol. 42—No. 1

TWO PERSONS DROWNED AND MORE MISSING

STOUT AND CHAMPA STREET BRIDGES PILE UP AT CURTIS ST.

On the morning of August 3, 1933, the Castlewood Dam broke and released a flood of water into Cherry Creek. On the opposite page the dam is seen in its better days, while across the bottom are two scenes of the Creek at flood stage along Speer Boulevard. Much of lower downtown Denver was flooded as seen in the view in front of Union Station, and in the photo below of the Colorado & Southern Railway yards at 7th Street, just southwest of the Speer Viaduct.—*Headline and lower right photo, State Historical Society of Colorado; others—Denver Public Library, Western History Collection*

DENVER'S FIRST FLOOD – 1864

The flood of 1933 was by no means the city's first, for in the night of May 19-20, 1864, Cherry Creek flooded pioneer Denver, sweeping away the City Hall, the Rocky Mountain News office, and several other buildings. Above, the flood is viewed down Larimer Street on May 20th, while below, the location is looking west from 14th and Larimer Streets.—*State Historical Society of Colorado*

... AND AGAIN IN 1878!

On May 2, 1878, Cherry Creek again flooded and this time carried out most of the city's bridges. Above, the damage is visible along Larimer Street looking southwest, while below, the view is from Larimer Street facing northwest; the Platte River is along the trees in the background.—*State Historical Society of Colorado*

HISTORY REPEATS ITSELF!

Again, on July 26, 1885, Cherry Creek repeated its past performances and this time threatened the recently completed City Hall, seen on the right behind the Larimer Street bridge.—*State Historical Society of Colorado*

Below—On June 17, 1965, Mother Nature proved that modern man is still very vulnerable to her power. The scene is at West 6th Avenue and the Platte River on the morning after the devastating flood in which the river reached its highest recorded level. Many of the bridges across the Platte River, as in this photo, caught debris and acted as dams, compounding the damage to low lying areas.—*Denver Public Library, Western History Collection*

THE BIG SNOW

On Thursday, December 4, 1913, Denver was struck by its all-time worst snow storm. In these two scenes the city is seen struggling in a losing battle with the blizzard. In the top photo, a young man is seen displaying a bit of practical initative as he takes to skis on a downtown street.—*State Historical Society of Colorado* In the scene below, a Denver Tramway snow sweeper forges its way down 16th Street near Welton Street, in a vain attempt to maintain trolley service as the storm gained in intensity.—*Denver Public Library, Western History Collection*

CLEAN YOUR ROOF
Of the snow to prevent loss of life and collapse of your building.

THE DENVER TIMES

Home Edition

VOL. 43: 297.   Weather Forecast—Snow This Afternoon and Tonight.   FRIDAY EVENING, DECEMBER 5, 1913.   —12 PAGES.   Saturday Clearing, Not Much Change in Temperature.   PRICE 2 CENTS On Streets On Trains, a Cent

MANY MISSING, TRAINS SNOW-TIED, BUILDINGS COLLAPSE, ALL BUSINESS HALTS

RECORD-BREAKING STORM HOLDS CITY AND STATE IN ICE-BOUND GRIP

SCORE OF CITIES BURIED UNDER GIANT DRIFTS; ROOFS CRUSHED IN; ZERO GALES SWEEP OVER HILLS

1,000 MEN ARE DIGGING TRAMWAY TRACKS FREE

Company Hopes to OpeN Fifteenth Street by Night and Possibly Sixteenth and Seventeenth; 48 Hours to Restore Service.

WHOLE DENVER BATTLES GIANT DRIFTS; ROOFS THREATEN CAVEIN AS SNOW WEIGHT HOURLY PILES

Above—A line of trolleys is stranded on East 17th Avenue at Broadway during the height of the storm. Below—Even the Denver Fire Department finally was forced to give up when their horse drawn trucks became bogged down in the mounting drifts. —Both, *Denver Public Library, Western History Collections; newspaper, State Historical Society of Colorado*

A moment of humor in the midst of the storm; a snowman is erected with the familiar slogan, long used by the Denver Post, " 'Tis a Privilege to live in Colorado." For most Denverites the storm meant more struggle than "privilege," and a lot of walking as the streetcars became hopelessly snowbound as seen in the center photo, taken at East 17th Avenue and Lincoln Street, looking towards Broadway, and in the bottom scene at Colfax and Broadway.—*State Historical Society of Colorado*

Snow removal is still a big problem in the city, but in this scene following a mid-1920's storm, the trap door in the Speer Viaduct provides a simple way to dispose of the "white stuff." At the time of the 1913 storm, however, the tremendous volume of snow made it necessary to haul much of it to Civic Center where the huge piles lasted almost until the summer of 1914. — *Top and bottom, Denver Public Library, Western History Collection; center, State Historical Society of Colorado*

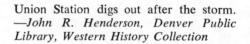

Union Station digs out after the storm.
—*John R. Henderson, Denver Public Library, Western History Collection*

Almost no deliveries were possible during the storm or for several days afterward, so to provide heat for Denver General Hospital, the Tramway brought cars of coal from its Leyden mines, using the city trolley tracks. — *State Historical Society of Colorado*

In the suburbs the storm was, if anything, even more severe, as witnessed by this half buried Route 83 Golden interurban which was marooned for several days west of Lakeside. Rescue came with the arrival of a Tramway plow.—*Authors' Collection*

All Around the Town

THE CHANGING SCENE

FROM TEPEE TO SKYSCRAPER

The city is ever changing; the contrasts of a century and a quarter are brought into focus with such scenes. The historic lithograph is the work of pioneer artist J. Y. Glendinen, and portrays the pioneer settlements along Cherry Creek at its confluence with the Platte River as they appeared in the summer of 1858. A city soon arose where tepees and Conestoga wagons had once stood, but man in his yearning to build ever bigger and better, must also tear down to make way for the future. The sequence of three photos, from left to right, tell of the death of a building which had served well but stood in the way of progress. Great quantities of explosives were placed at strategic points in the Interstate Trust Building at 16th and Lawrence Streets and on November 15, 1970, it was brought down in a matter of seconds. The first explosions shook the foundation and moments later the building writhed in its death struggle; then there was only rubble. On April 21, 1972, lower downtown Denver appeared as seen at the upper left, looking west from the roof of the University Building at 16th and Champa Streets. A magnificent link with the Denver of yesterday, the Daniels and Fisher tower looms in the midst of vacant lots where numerous other old buildings have been removed; most of those within two blocks of the tower would be removed before the year's end. At the right of the photo the new Prudential Plaza offers a clue of what the entire area will look like before the end of the decade of the 1970's, yet someday even such a fine structure will be razed in the name of ever continuing progress.—*Above, State Historical Society of Colorado; upper left, Ronald C. Hill, others, Denver Urban Renewal Authority*

All Around the Town

GOVERNMENT OF AND FOR THE PEOPLE

On April 8, 1881, the voters of Colorado gave formal approval to what had long been an accepted fact—Denver would be the capital city of Colorado. While only a formality, the vote signaled the final round in a long struggle to locate the capital elsewhere.

The first session of the Territorial Legislature was called by Governor William Gilpin in November, 1861, at Denver with the two legislative houses meeting in separate buildings in what is now the lower downtown area. At its first session, the Legislature selected Colorado City, now a part of Colorado Springs, as the capital; however, at the second session, after meeting in Colorado City briefly, the legislators decided to move back to Denver in July of 1862. The third session chose to meet in Golden City during February, 1864, but returned to Denver to complete its work. The fourth session met in Golden, but the fifth, while opening there, returned to Denver for the balance of the session. Late in 1866, the sixth session was opened back in Golden and early in 1867, the seventh session also opened in Golden, only to move back to Denver after one week. That return trip to Denver was the final move for the Territorial Legislature. Following statehood on August 1, 1876, the capital has remained in Denver.

THE COLORADO CAPITOL—
AND REAL GOLD ON THE DOME

During the territoral days and early years of statehood, the functions of state government were carried out in several rented facilities around the city, in spite of continuing talk regarding the need for a permanent capitol building. The present site of the gold domed Colorado capitol was presented to the state as a gift by Henry C. Brown, well remembered as the builder of the Brown Palace Hotel. He owned other real estate in the area and hoped that his donation of ten acres between Grant and Lincoln Streets and Colfax and 14th Avenues would bring an early start on construction of a capitol building and eventually enhance values on his other holdings.

Finally, eighteen years after Brown's gift, and following long heated discussions and attempts by Brown himself to regain his land due to the state's failure to proceed with construction of a capitol, on April 1, 1885, a bill was passed providing for construction of the present Capitol building. Delays continued and numerous changes were made in construction plans, wisely including a change from the use of sandstone to granite as the basic building material. Finally, on July 4, 1890, the cornerstone was laid. The 10th Session of the State Legislature occupied the capitol in January, 1895, but finishing touches continued past the turn of the century bringing the total cost to almost three million dollars.

With its magnificent gold dome, the Colorado capitol remains today among the most striking such structures in the nation. The ever expanding State government has required additional buildings in the area and today the State of Colorado is among the major employers in the Denver area.

CHANGING PATTERNS OF
DENVER CITY GOVERNMENT

Denver's pioneer residents realized the urgent need for organization of effective local government. Centralized government was far across the plains and the territorial governments of Kansas, Nebraska and Jefferson Territories lacked any real organizational power during the earliest days of the Cherry Creek settlements, making a viable local government the best hope of the settlers.

The first attempt to organize a local government came under the charter granted by Jefferson Territory, itself of questionable legal status. Chartered as the "City of Denver, Auraria and

Highland," the first election was held on December 19, 1859, at which John C. Moore was elected as the first Mayor, with other city officers and council members also being chosen, as well as the first law officer, Marshall W. E. Sisty. These men were picked to serve only while a city constitution was in preparation. The constitution was adopted as "The People's Government of the City of Denver," on October 1, 1860, with an overwhelming 1,112 votes cast in favor and only 40 opposed. The next April, additional city positions were filled by election and these men all continued to serve while the territorial government was being organized. Finally, on November 7, 1861, the First Legislative Assembly of Colorado Territory passed an act granting a city charter. For the first time, legal status was given to the combined towns of Denver, Auraria, and Highland to be known as "The City of Denver." On November 18th, an election was held selecting a Board of Aldermen, the first City Mayor, C. A. Cook, and other city officers, including the first Police Magistrate, P. P. Wilcox.

In following years, the Legislature made several changes in the law affecting Denver's government. Among these changes was the addition of a Board of Supervisors to act as an upper house to the Board of Aldermen. The most important additions were the creation of both a Board of Public Works and the Fire and Police Board, both of which were to be appointed by the governor and which together controlled the vital functions of the city's government. In effect, the city was now under the control of the state. Widespread demand for change caused the city to call for a charter convention in 1898, in order to frame a new *home rule* charter. After much political haggling, the Legislature finally agreed and submitted the issue to the people in the 1902 election. With its passage it became Article XX of the Constitution of the State of Colorado. The city held a charter convention, the second charter draft of which was approved by the voters in February, 1904.

MAYOR ROBERT W. SPEER

Denver's first home rule mayor was elected in May, 1904, and the city entered one of its most colorful and progressive, but also most controversial eras—the reign of Mayor Robert W. Speer. Speer continued in office until 1912, when in a move for governmental reform the people elected Henry Arnold for his pledge to drop the mayor-council system and replace it with a board of commissioners. At the election of February, 1913, the voters accepted Arnold's proposal for the creation of such a board, the members of which were to be elected the following May. In fulfilling his campaign pledge, Arnold caused his own position as Mayor to be abolished.

While the five commissioners undertook some fine improvements, including the placement of most city employees under civil service and also made a start on the Denver Mountain Parks system, the overriding weakness of the system proved to be the lack of a single executive head to steer the direction of the city government. Gradually, public sentiment developed for the return of the mayor—council system and at a special election on May 9, 1916, the electorate chose to drop the commission government. At the same election Robert Speer was returned to office but with a unicameral council instead of the old two-house body.

Speer continued in office until his death on May 14, 1918, and while he used a political machine to accomplish his ends, he must be given the credit for many capital improvements of lasting value; among them the start on the new Civic Center, completion of embankments on Cherry Creek and construction of many miles of parkway, both along the Creek and elsewhere. His tree-planting campaigns and park improvements, and work which led to eventual purchase of the privately owned water company, all did much to give us the beautiful city of today.

MEN IN BLUE—
THE DENVER POLICE DEPARTMENT

Denver's police history began with the election of W. E. Sisty as Marshal in 1859, and for several years after that, policing was handled by a marshal and several deputies. In 1874, the city created the position of "Chief of Police" and J. C. McCallin became the first in a long line of men who have held the post. Most chiefs served for only a short time, since for many years it was

Government Of and For the People

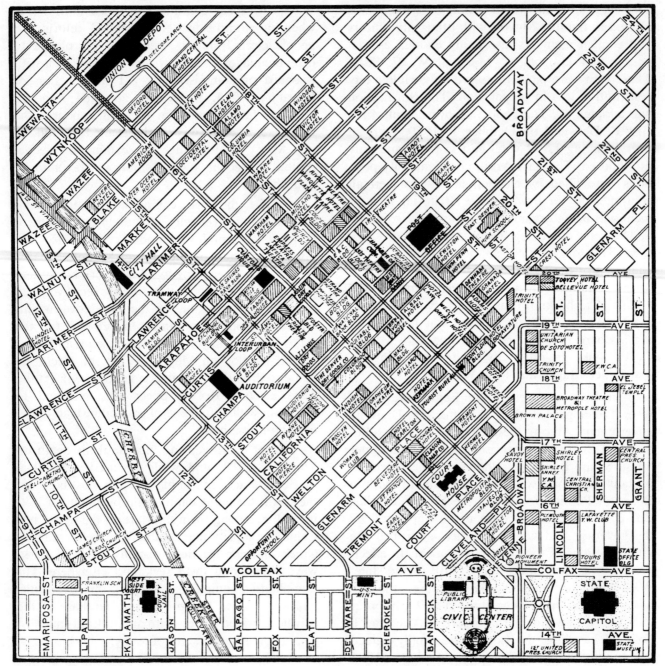

DENVER STREET NAMES

The earliest Denver streets, those in the downtown area, were laid out parallel to Cherry Creek and the Platte River. Those beyond downtown, however, were generally laid out to run north-south and east-west. To add to an already confused system, little coordination was used in naming streets and thus by the turn of the century, there were over 800 names for Denver's more than 400 streets; many had two names and some three, within a short distance.

The present system of street names and numbers was developed by Howard C. Maloney, a water company employee, in his spare time. It was adopted by the city in 1904, and was so well planned that the only change has been to add new streets as the city grew.

Excluding the downtown area, all thoroughfares running north-south are "Streets" and those running east-west are "Avenues." All streets are numbered east and west of Broadway, while all avenues are numbered north and south of Ellsworth Avenue.

Avenues begin as 1st, one block north of Ellsworth, and continue as far north as required by the city's expansion. South of Ellsworth, are a series of avenues named for states, but not in alphabetical order, followed by a series named for colleges and universities and partly in alphabetical order.

Streets running west of Broadway include first a set in alphabetical order that are named for Indian tribes and nations (Acoma, Bannock, Cherokee, etc.) This is followed by a set named for prominent Americans (Alcott, Bryant, Clay, etc.) and one named for Senators and Justices of the Supreme Court (Ames, Benton, Chase, etc.).

To the east of Broadway, the early street names were retained between Lincoln and Colorado Boulevard, but beyond is a double alphabetical set, the first being the name of a place followed by the name of a tree, fruit or flower (Albion and Ash, Bellaire and Birch, etc.). To both the east and west it has been necessary to add new names as the suburban areas have grown.

Within the downtown area, the numbered streets meet the same numbered avenues at Broadway. Thus 17th Street (downtown) runs into East 17th Avenue at Broadway, 16th Street meets 16th Avenue, and 15th Street meets Colfax (actually 15th) Avenue, which is the first avenue south of 46th Avenue that is not divided by a downtown street. The downtown numbered streets run from 1st through 44th Streets, although in reality both the low and high numbered streets are not actually in existence or are only a few blocks in length. In the city's earliest years the numbered streets carried alphabetical names. "A" Street corresponded to the present 10th Street and the series continued north through "Q" Street. The named streets in the downtown area run northeast-southwest but are spoken of as running east-west, while the numbered streets are spoken of as running north-south but actually run in a northwest-southeast direction. Many of the named streets date to the city's early years and a full list follows, numbered from east to west.

1 Cheyenne Place (originally Parkinson Street)
2 Cleveland Place (originally Wapolla or "Wasoola" Street)
3 Court Place (originally Clancy Street)
4 Tremont Place

5 Glenarm Place
6 Welton Street
7 California Street
8 Stout Street
9 Champa Street
10 Curtis Street
11 Arapahoe Street
12 Lawrence Street
13 Larimer Street
14 Market & Walnut Streets (originally McGaa St. and later Holliday St.)
    Note: Market St. is between 14th and 25th Streets and Walnut on either end.
15 Blake Street
16 Wazee Street
17 Wynkoop Street
18 Wewatta Street
19 Delgany Street
20 Chestnut Place (originally Williams Street)
21 Bassett Street
22 Water Street
23 Platte Street
24 Central Street
25 Boulder Street
26 Erie Street

Four additional streets, Smith, Platte, Dudley and St. Charles, were planned to run east of Cheyenne Place but were never actually constructed.

MUNICIPALITIES BORDERING DENVER

ARVADA—Northwest of Denver in Jefferson County predominately, but also small area of Adams County. Founded in 1880 and incorporated August 21, 1904.

AURORA—East of Denver in both Adams and Arapahoe Counties. Area originally known as Fletcher but incorporated as Aurora on May 1, 1891.

CHERRY HILLS VILLAGE—South of Denver in Arapahoe County. Incorporated in October, 1945.

COMMERCE CITY—Northeast of Denver in Adams County. Incorporated as Commerce Town in December, 1952; became Commerce City in 1960.

EDGEWATER—West of Denver in Jefferson County. Founded in 1870's and incorporated August 18, 1901.

ENGLEWOOD—South of Denver in Arapahoe County. Incorporated May 13, 1903.

GLENDALE—Located within the southeastern part of the City of Denver but is part of Arapahoe County. Incorporated May, 1952.

LAKESIDE—Northwest of Denver in Jefferson County. Population less than 20 persons but includes both Lakeside Amusement Park and Lakeside Shopping Center. Incorporated November 25, 1907.

LAKEWOOD—West of Denver in Jefferson County. Area known as Lakewood since the 1880's, but was incorporated as Jefferson City on June 26, 1969. Within a year the name was changed to Lakewood.

LITTLETON—South of Englewood in Arapahoe County and is the county seat. Incorporated March 13, 1890.

MOUNTAIN VIEW—West of Denver in Jefferson County. Incorporated October 11, 1904.

SHERIDAN—South of Denver in Arapahoe County. Incorporated April 16, 1892.

WHEAT RIDGE—West of Denver in Jefferson County. Area settled in 1880's, but not incorporated until August 20, 1969.

NOTE: Neither Arvada or Littleton border on Denver but intervening distances are less than one-half mile.

an elective position. Eventually, the office became appointive under the control of the mayor.

Among the more colorful early chiefs was David J. Cook who held the post during 1880 and 1881. He began his police career in 1866, as a City Marshal, and remained on the Denver force until 1905, spanning almost forty years of law enforcement activities. Perhaps best remembered of the later chiefs was Hamilton C. Armstrong who gained the position first in 1894, and then went on to serve a total of twelve years in non-consecutive terms until his death in 1921.

The first Denver jail was in a log building near 15th and Blake Streets. Built in 1861, it was destroyed by fire shortly after construction and several other locations served until erection of the City Hall in 1883. The Hall housed the city jail and the fire and police headquarters and even after other city departments moved to the new Civic Center, the fire and police departments remained in the old City Hall until it was razed following opening of the Police Building at 13th and Champa Streets in 1940.

It should be pointed out, that prior to becoming a home rule city, Denver was a part of Arapahoe County and thus after creation of Denver County the city gained certain Arapahoe County facilities located within the city limits. These included the county jail and criminal court building. In 1874, the block bounded by Colfax and 14th Avenues, Santa Fe Drive, and Kalamath Street was set aside for a jail. Later that jail became the Criminal Court Building following construction of the new Arapahoe County Jail on the same block in 1891. This jail served Denver until replaced by the modern facility now in use on Smith Road near Stapleton International Airport.

When Chief McCallin took control of his department in 1874, it consisted of just thirteen men. From this small beginning, the growth was continued steadily, with 121 men in the department at the turn of the century. The Denver Police have kept abreast of technological advances; radios were placed in patrol cars early in the 1930's, at first one-way radios only, soon two-way radios were being used to vastly extend the effectiveness of the police. Modern methods were brought to the crime laboratory and by the 1970's the police took to the air, using helicopters to aid in fighting crime from above the city.

By the Centennial Year of 1959, the department had swelled to 856, of which 701 were officers, and in 1972, the force numbered 1456 men and women including 1206 police officers.

Denver's Police Department has had a colorful history in its role of bringing law and order to a growing western town; legal hangings were once held in the streets, several murder cases shocked the city over the years, and perhaps the most famous was the so-called Mint Robbery which was in fact actually a robbery of the Federal Reserve Bank truck parked in front of the Mint. In recent years, the city was given a jolt when it was discovered that crime had crept inside the police ranks and a number of officers were removed from their jobs and several tried and sent to prison. After this house cleaning, the rest of the force worked to regain their department's honor and once again have reason to demand the respect of the city's honest citizens.

WHITE FIRE ENGINES

"Attention is directed to the call for a meeting to organize fire companies . . . The necessity for prompt action and thorough organization of hook and ladder and bucket companies, is apparent to every home reader." *The Rocky Mountain News, March 21, 1860*

Despite good intentions, there was no viable fire department when the city faced destruction on April 19, 1863; the fire which burned much of the downtown area still did not bring about more than weak efforts at organization. During the winter of 1865-66, however, a series of small fires occurred and were believed to be the work of an arsonist. A small group of citizens resolved to take action and on Sunday afternoon, March 25, 1866, they met in the Davis and Curtis grocery store and organized the Denver Hook and Ladder Company No. 1. George W. McClure was made Foreman and the first piece of equipment, a small home-made hook and ladder cart, was obtained from the United States Quartermaster. Later in the year, the Company received a large hook and ladder truck from a firm in Cincinnati.

The city soon built a two story brick fire station on Lawrence Street between 15th and 16th Streets and then purchased a 2,100 pound bell which when rung to signal a fire, could be heard far beyond the city limits.

Denver's first hose company was the James

Archer Company No. 2, which was organized in April, 1872, and housed at 1714 Curtis Street. The Company was named in honor of the President of the Denver City Water Company, the firm which first brought the city a reliable water supply. Only a month later the Joseph E. Bates Fire and Hose Company No. 3, opened as the "West Denver" company and finally, in July, the Woodie Fisher Hose Company began to operate out of the Lawrence Street firehouse. The Fisher Company was named in honor of fireman Fisher who had recently been killed while attempting to stop a runaway team of horses.

In 1872, Phillip Troustine was appointed Chief Engineer of the Fire Department and was placed over all volunteer operations. In 1881, the end began for the volunteers; the city saw the need to begin a paid professional department and gradually the volunteer departments were placed under the direction of the first paid Fire Chief, George Duggan. The end of the volunteers brought to a close a colorful era. To be a volunteer was considered an important honor and the various companies carried great civic pride in their equipment, uniforms and fire-fighting ability. The social activity of the volunteer departments was of importance to the entire community and included summer picnics, ball teams, and of course, the annual Fireman's Ball. Today, several of Denver's suburban neighbors still have active volunteer fire departments carrying on these proud traditions.

Denver's professional firemen soon gained the reputation of being among the nation's finest and thus the city has very favorable fire insurance rates. The department early decided to use powered equipment and received their first steam pumper in August, 1881. Since that time, the fleet has always been well maintained but in one respect different from almost all other fire departments: Denver fire engines are painted white instead of red, a strange sight to many visitors. While the reason for this color choice is lost in the past, it seems certain to remain the company color in the future.

One of the most unusual fire companies in the city was the Negro Company which for many years was housed in east Denver. It is said that a keen rivalry existed between the black company and its white neighbor companies when they would be called to fight the same fire. Tragedy struck the company while fighting the St. James Hotel fire on March 23, 1894; the three man company and their white Captain lost their lives when a floor gave way in the burning building.

By 1900, the city had 107 firemen and 12 fire stations. In the Centennial year of 1959, this had grown to 552 men working in 24 stations and by 1972 the department staffed 27 stations (including the airport) with 902 firemen.

DENVER'S CITY HALL WAR

It is difficult to imagine a more bazaar series of events striking any city than those which threw Denver into turmoil during March, 1894 —the City Hall War. Governor David H. Waite held the power of appointment to Denver's Fire and Police Board and the Board of Public Works. He decided to replace two members of the Fire and Police Board who had been acting contrary to his will. The two men, Jackson Orr and D. J. Martin, refused to resign and claimed loudly that they were being replaced simply because they refused to cooperate in the governor's plan to control the city police force. In a rage, Governor Waite called out the First Regiment of Colorado Infantry and the Chaffee Light Artillery to surround the City Hall while inside Orr and Martin were barricaded with the backing of the police force and a large number of deputy sheriffs. A citizens group called upon the governor to refrain from this course of action, but the governor reacted by then requesting federal troops from Fort Logan and ordering the National Guard to assemble, while the seige continued at City Hall. Finally, after a flurry of court injunctions and an appeal from a quickly formed "Committee of Safety," which included most of the civic leaders, the Governor agreed to request a ruling from the Supreme Court of Colorado. The ruling upheld the removal of Orr and Martin but denied the Governor had the authority to call up troops to enforce their removal. Eventually, Orr and Martin quietly left their offices. At the next election Governor Waite lost in his bid for re-election, ending his brief and controversial term.

WATER—LIFEBLOOD OF THE CITY

To the Mile-High City, water is perhaps the single most coveted natural resource. Had it not been for the farsightedness of a few men, it is doubtful that water resources would today be available to support the sprawling Denver metropolitan area.

As early as 1859, a company was formed to bring water by ditch to Auraria, while a few months later a similar plan came forth in Denver City. Neither firm seems to have accomplished anything, but finally in 1865, the Witter Ditch was completed from a point on the South Platte River near Littleton to the Capitol Hill area. The ditch eventually was extended to the present City Park and became known as the City Ditch. Now it became possible for home owners to irrigate their lawns, to plant trees and begin to develop Denver into the beautiful city it is today.

The first company to actually bring domestic water to the city was organized in October, 1870, as the Denver City Water Company. The leadership of the company rested with the President, Colonel James Archer and the Board of Directors, including such notable citizens as David Moffat and Walter Cheesman. Over the next twenty years this company built a water system drawing upon both Cherry Creek and the Platte River. It also built Lake Archer, a storage reservoir which is no longer in existence, but for many years a long, narrow lake lying east of the Platte River and running north and south approximately between 1st Avenue and 8th Avenue, just west of the present Denver and Rio Grande Western Railroad yards.

A rival water company was organized in 1889, as the Citizens' Water Company and promptly constructed the huge Marston Lake Reservoir to the southwest of Denver. The rivalry of the two firms became so intense that for a short time some residents were actually supplied water free of charge. Naturally, the competition did not permit either company to operate very profitably and in 1894 the battle was concluded by a merger into the Denver Union Water Company.

The new firm undertook the important project of building the Cheesman Dam, vastly increasing the city's water reserve. However, by the turn of the century, the continuing demand for water rate increases caused a public outcry and brought attempts by the city to purchase the water company. As early as 1899, efforts were made by the city to set a purchase price but no compromise could be reached. For almost twenty years the City and the Denver Union Water Company continued a running argument over a sale price but finally, on August 6, 1918, the people of Denver voted to purchase the system for $13,970,000, and it continues today under the control of the Board of Water Commissioners.

Since 1918, the Denver Water Board has continued to develop water resources designed to provide the city with an abundant supply of high quality water.

BUILDING THE CAPITOL

On July 4, 1890, (below-left) a large crowd came out in the rain to witness the laying of the cornerstone of the Colorado Capitol Building. As the work progressed, it became necessary to hire 200 stonecutters, many coming from as far away as Maine, Vermont and California. A number of the men posed for the picture at the right. The center photo provides a close-up view of the framework of the building's huge dome. The large round holes provided space for the stained glass windows which portray Colorado pioneers. In the 1894 photo below, the building is nearing completion and was occupied by the legislature in January, 1895. Many finishing touches were added and work continued until about 1901.—*State Historical Society of Colorado*

The chambers of the House of Representatives (above-left) and the Senate (below-left) are seen as they appear in the mid-1970's. Some changes have been made over the years, including replacement of the original roll-top desks, but the general atmosphere remains as when built.

The State Capitol is seen at right, shortly after completion, about 1900. The 24k gold dome required the use of 200 ounces of gold and another 50 ounces were applied in 1950. A typical office in the new building is that of the State Treasurer, seen below at the turn of the century.

As state government expanded, it became necessary to acquire new office space and on June 20, 1920, the cornerstone was laid (bottom) for the State Office Building at the corner of Colfax Avenue and Sherman Street.—*State Historical Society of Colorado*

Denver Municipal Facts

ISSUED EVERY WEEK BY THE CITY OF DENVER

Vol. IV	SATURDAY, AUGUST 3, 1912	No. 31
Free on Request of Taxpayers	(*Read—Then Pass It On.*)	Office, Room 208, City Hall

TOWN OF HIGHLANDS.

INCORPORATED 1875.

DEDICATION CITY HALL.

JULY 11. 1890.

The old Denver City Hall, as it appeared about 1930, is seen above (right) in this painting by Herndon Davis. Built in 1886, it was used by the Police Department and Fire Department after other offices moved to the new City and County Building in 1932, and was finally demolished in the late 1940's. Above, the Board of Supervisors is shown meeting in the City Hall in 1901, with William A. Hover, President of the Board. For many years, the city published "Denver Municipal Facts" (above) to keep its citizens informed of the workings of their government.

On July 11, 1890, suburban Highlands dedicated its new City Hall, but less than ten years later the town would annex to Denver and the building be converted to Fire Station No. 12 and a Police sub-station. The building was razed in 1969 and replaced by a new Fire Station No. 12.

The Arapahoe County Court House (right) was built in 1883, and remained in use until 1934, when demolished and the land converted to Court House Square Park. The May-D&F store was built on the site in 1958.—*Right and above, State Historical Society of Colorado; others, Denver Public Library, Western History Collection*

ROBERT W. SPEER

Robert Walter Speer was Mayor of Denver from 1904 until his death in 1918, except for the period 1912-1916. There is no question that he ran the city government with a powerful political machine, but this does not alter the fact that the "Speer Years" had a profound beneficial effect on Denver that is still enjoyed today. Speer moved from one project to another in his efforts to attain a beautiful city: the Civic Center, the City Auditorium, the Cherry Creek beautification, new parks and boulevards; these and many other projects were undertaken during his tenure in office. Each spring the city distributed free maple and elm trees and Mayor Speer is seen above inspecting the trees in the spring of 1905.

In the spring of 1918, Speer came down with a cold that turned into pneumonia and after a brief illness, he died at 3:00 P.M. on May 14, 1918. His death was felt as a personal loss by many of Denver's citizens and quite fittingly, his funeral service was held in the auditorium he had helped bring to reality. Seen below, the funeral was attended by more than 10,000 men, women and children who came to bid farewell to Denver's most colorful leader, Mayor Robert Speer.—*Denver Public Library, Western History Collection*

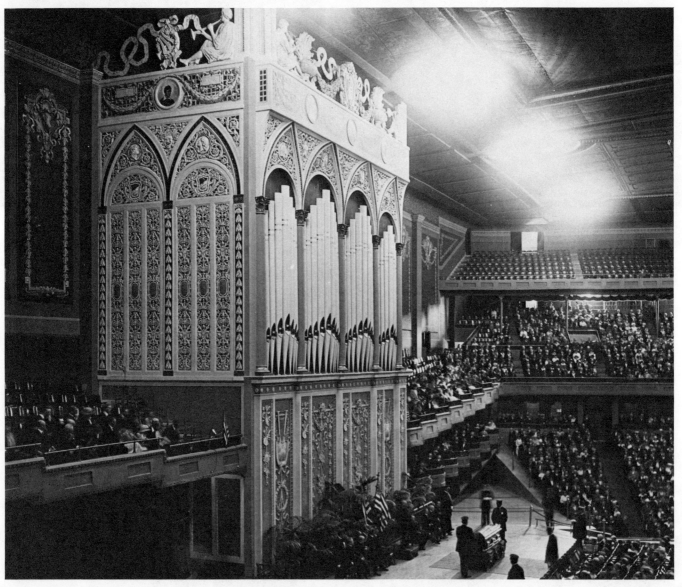

THE
CITY
AUDITORIUM

On May 17, 1904, voters approved a bond issue for the construction of a new municipal auditorium, as seen in these three photographs. The building, on 15th between Curtis and Champa Streets, is seen above soon after completion in 1908, just in time to accommodate the Democratic National Convention which opened that July. The magnificent auditorium organ is seen being installed (left) while the completed instrument is visible in the bottom scene of the auditorium with a full house. An unusual feature of the auditorium was its ability to be converted from a 3,300 seat theater to a 12,000 seat hall, as seen below. This was made possible by an elaborate system of moveable walls. The auditorium was almost always busy with a convention, entertainment, sports events, or the always popular Sunday afternoon free concerts, another idea instituted by Mayor Speer. After construction of the Auditorium Arena adjoining on Curtis Street, the auditorium was converted into a large theater which continues to host large road shows and is the home of the Denver Symphony.—*D.P.L., Western History Collection*

Each Christmas since the early 1920s Denver has decorated the Civic Center. The 1922 decorations are seen below, while the much more elaborate decorations shown above (1939) have been a typical scene since the 1930s.—*Denver Public Library, Western History Collection*

CIVIC CENTER

Mayor Robert Speer's great dream was the development of Civic Center, and at one time consideration was given to extending the Civic Center west as far as Speer Boulevard. In 1913, work began on clearing all buildings except the library, from an area bounded by Colfax and 14th Avenues, Broadway and Bannock Street. The top photo, taken in 1915, shows the land cleared and a lawn planted. Work on the City and County Building began in 1924 and by the time of the center photo, 1932, the building was complete except for installation of the Speer Memorial clock and chimes, donated by Mrs. Kate A. Speer, and completed on October 23, 1932. The Voorhies Memorial Entrance, seen below shortly before completion in 1918, was a gift of J. H. P. Voorhies. This construction necessitated placing the only curve in Colfax Avenue.—*Top and center, D.P.L., Western Hist. Coll.; bottom, State Historical Society of Colo.*

DENVER'S
FROM 1859

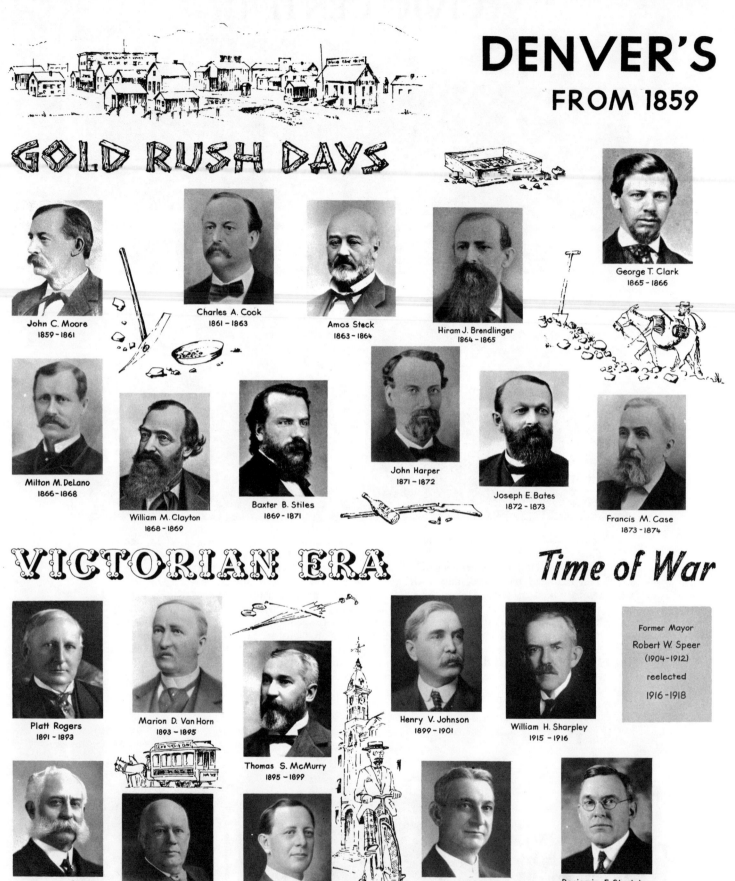

GOLD RUSH DAYS

John C. Moore
1859–1861

Charles A. Cook
1861–1863

Amos Steck
1863–1864

Hiram J. Brendlinger
1864–1865

George T. Clark
1865–1866

Milton M. DeLano
1866–1868

William M. Clayton
1868–1869

Baxter B. Stiles
1869–1871

John Harper
1871–1872

Joseph E. Bates
1872–1873

Francis M. Case
1873–1874

VICTORIAN ERA

Time of War

Platt Rogers
1891–1893

Marion D. Van Horn
1893–1895

Thomas S. McMurry
1895–1899

Henry V. Johnson
1899–1901

William H. Sharpley
1915–1916

Former Mayor
Robert W. Speer
(1904–1912)
reelected
1916–1918

Robert R. Wright
1901–1904

Robert W. Speer
1904–1912

Henry J. Arnold
1912–1913

James M. Perkins
1913–1915

Benjamin F. Stapleton
1923–1931

MAYORS

TO PRESENT

TAMING THE WILD WEST

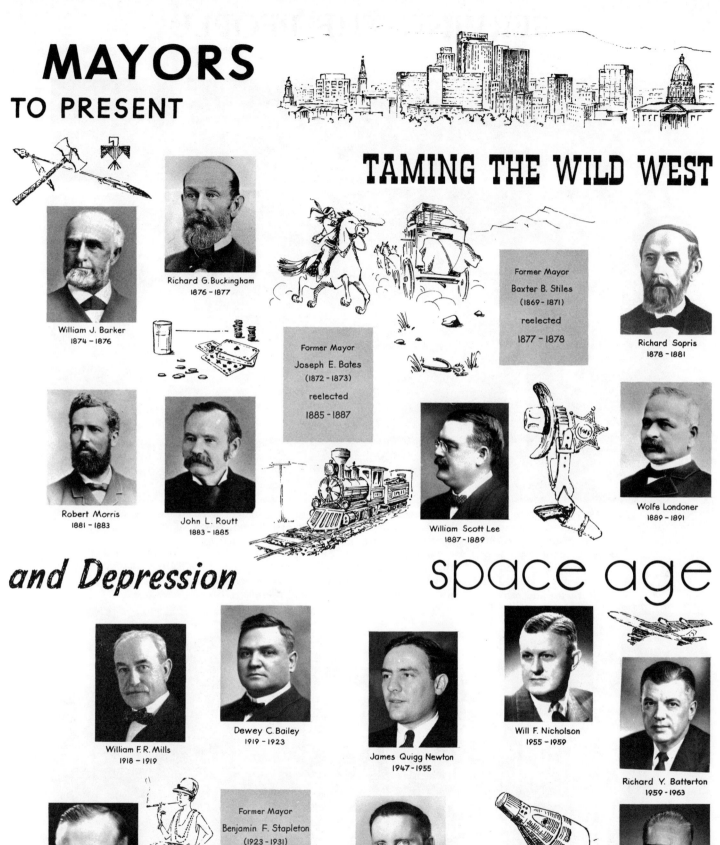

Richard G. Buckingham
1876 – 1877

William J. Barker
1874 – 1876

Former Mayor
Baxter B. Stiles
(1869 – 1871)
reelected
1877 – 1878

Richard Sopris
1878 – 1881

Former Mayor
Joseph E. Bates
(1872 – 1873)
reelected
1885 – 1887

Robert Morris
1881 – 1883

John L. Routt
1883 – 1885

William Scott Lee
1887 – 1889

Wolfe Londoner
1889 – 1891

and Depression

space age

William F. R. Mills
1918 – 1919

Dewey C. Bailey
1919 – 1923

James Quigg Newton
1947 – 1955

Will F. Nicholson
1955 – 1959

Richard Y. Batterton
1959 – 1963

George D. Begole
1931 – 1935

Former Mayor
Benjamin F. Stapleton
(1923 – 1931)
reelected
1935 – 1947

Thomas G. Currigan
1963 – 1968

William H. McNichols, Jr.
1969 –

Dieter Sebastion, City & County of Denver

SERVING THE PEOPLE

For many years, prior to development of our modern welfare system, Denver cared for its aged and destitute at the Denver Poor Farm near Henderson, north of the city. The residents lived and worked on the farm, producing much of their own food.

The Public Bath House was built at 20th and Curtis Streets in 1908, and included a gymnasium in addition to the bathing facilities. The need for public bathing facilities gradually dwindled and in the mid-1960's, the building was given over entirely to use as a gym and recreation center.—*Denver Public Library, Western History Collection*

Many vital city services remain almost unknown to the general public until a need for the service suddenly arises. The Denver Dog Pound, at E. 52nd Avenue and Columbine Street, is seen above as it appeared about 1950. After a rabies outbreak hit the city in the late 1940's, a program of mass rabies vaccination was undertaken and resulted in Denver having one of the most progressive programs of dog care and control.

The Dead Animal Collector, regretfully a constant necessity in the city, boasted one of the finest trucks in the city fleet.

With the coming of the automobile, Denver embarked on an extensive program of street improvement, using equipment such as the "modern" street oiler, seen below, hard at work.—*Denver Public Library, Western History Collection*

LAW AND ORDER

On December 1, 1868, Samford Dougan was hung by the "Vigilance Committee" from a tree near 12th and Market Streets, and is seen in the photo at right just before being removed for burial the following morning. The crime which led to Dougan's execution occurred less than two weeks earlier but was the last in a long series of crimes listed to his credit by the age of 23. On November 20th, Dougan, along with Ed Franklin, robbed Judge Orson Brooks, an elderly and respected Denverite. City Marshal D. J. Cook attempted to capture Franklin at his hotel room but was forced to shoot him in self defense. Dougan was captured just south of the Wyoming border and taken to Denver, but Marshal Cook, fearing an attempt would be made to "snatch" him, was taking Dougan to a safer location when intercepted by the Vigilance Committee on the Larimer Street bridge. The hanging took place a short time later that night.—*State Historical Society of Colorado*

One of Denver's earliest jails is shown at left. Located in the former Butterick Meat Market building at 1355 13th Street, it served from 1866 through 1883. In 1891, the new Arapahoe County Jail (above) was opened in the block bounded by Colfax and 14th Avenues, Santa Fe Drive and Kalamath Street. The new jail could accommodate 350 prisoners and replaced a much smaller jail which had been within the same block in 1874, and which continued in use as a court. In 1956, Denver opened a new county jail on Smith Road at Havana Street and the 1891 facility was razed in July, 1963.

On February 19, 1886, the Denver Police Department began using its first horse drawn patrol wagon, seen at the left, posed a block from City Hall. It is interesting to note, that until 1921, the Police Department had small round booths, called kiosks, placed around the city on street corners. A prisoner could be locked in one of these until the officer could arrange for the necessary help or transportation to bring the man to the police station.

Hamilton Armstrong was one of the longest serving Chiefs of Police. He held the position in 1894, again in 1901, 1908-1912, and from 1919 until his death on January 10, 1921. Armstrong also served in the state legislature during part of the time that he was not the Chief of Police. One of his greatest challenges came at the end of his career, when the city was torn with strife during the Tramway strike of August, 1920. The Chief was caught in the midst of some of the demonstrations but eventually the city was brought under control.
—Right, State Historical Society of Colorado; others, Denver Public Library, Western History Collection

HAMILTON ARMSTRONG

Government Of and For the People

CHIEF AUGUST HANEBUTH

The Denver Police Department received its first motorized patrol wagon on March 16, 1909. At the time, the force still relied on both a bicycle patrol, which continued until 1920, and on the mounted patrol (seen above) just prior to being disbanded in July, 1931. The motor fleet grew quickly and by 1920, included the fine new patrol wagon at lower left, and thirteen motorcycles with side cars, such as seen below at the Capitol Hill Station at 2239 East Colfax Avenue. The most unusual vehicle is seen above (left), Denver's "Auto Bandit Chaser." The car had a Cadillac engine and chassis, and the many special features included a T-guard rail for crowding cars into the ditch, bullet-proof armor plate and windshield and a mounted machine gun. On the right of the car, front to rear, stand Chief Williams, Manager of Safety Downer and Captain Carter. Bandits Beware!

Chief August Hanebuth headed the department from January 1, 1938, until his retirement in May, 1947, having served the longest continuous time of any chief. He died in March, 1958.—*Denver Public Library, Western History Collection*

Government Of and For the People

On May 4, 1940, the new Police Headquarters opened at 13th and Champa Streets, replacing the facility in the old City Hall which included the City Jail seen above, shortly before the move to the new building.

The seal of the Denver Police Department is symbolic of the men and women who serve the goals of law and order, not only in Denver, but in the suburban areas as well. In the Denver Police Department alone, 47 officers have given their lives in the line of duty, the first being John C. Phillips who was shot on July 16, 1889, at 15th and Platte Streets; the case remains unsolved. —*Denver Public Library, Western History Collection*

THE BARNES DANCE

Henry Barnes, Denver Traffic Engineer from 1947 until 1953, is perhaps best remembered for his startling idea of allowing pedestrians to walk in all directions at downtown intersections, while all traffic was stopped. Quickly nick-named the "Barnes Dance" or "Shuffle," Denverites enjoyed watching the dismay of out-of-towners when the traffic light flashed to WALK. Barnes began his career in Flint, Michigan, and after leaving Denver he became Traffic Engineer in Baltimore and later in New York City where he died on September 17, 1967. While in Denver he spent 3 million dollars to install 20,000 traffic signs, developed the one-way street systems and installed a "traffic brain" in City Hall to control the traffic light system.—*Denver Public Library, Western History Collection*

JUSTICE IN ACTION

BENJAMIN BARR LINDSEY

PHILIP S. VAN CISE

One of Denver's most notable judges was Ben Lindsey. Appointed a judge of the County Court in 1901, he soon began to work for reform in the handling of minors. In 1907, he was appointed by Mayor Speer to the city's first Juvenile Court, (below) one of the first in the nation. Lindsey became involved in many reform movements and left the state after a long hate campaign led to his being disbarred. Moving to California he was admitted to its bar and rose to be a California Superior Court Judge.

Philip Van Cise was elected Denver District Attorney in 1920, and is credited with cleaning the corruption from the Police Department and gaining the conviction of twenty underworld figures including Lou Blonger. —*All photos this page, Denver Public Library, Western History Collection*

DENVER'S ROGUES' GALLERY

LOU BLONGER

MIKE ROSSI

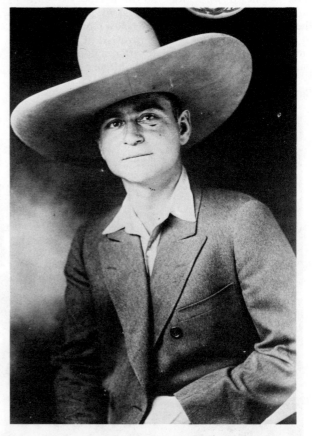

"DIAMOND JACK"

Presented here is a selection of the personalities in some of Denver's more interesting criminal cases.

Lou Blonger controlled Denver's gambling and confidence operations from the late 1880's until 1922, when District Attorney Philip Van Cise finally obtained a conviction for him and 19 associates.

Mike Rossi operated the Moonlight Ranch on Morrison Road and was also in the wholesale liquor business during prohibition. On November 8, 1926, his wife Caroline was murdered and Rossi was tried for the crime. Found guilty, he was sentenced to life but was paroled in 1934. He died in 1938. Mrs. Rossi had herself been tried and acquitted for murder after killing Norman Gould with a baseball bat in 1921. She claimed self defense. The Rossi's daughter was later married to Diamond Jack.

Diamond Jack, alias Louis Alteria, (real name Leland Varain) had been a member of Dion O'Banion's gang in Chicago but retired to Colorado. He was a colorful figure, becoming involved in the rodeo business, and also retaining an interest in underworld activities. While in Chicago on July 18, 1935, he was the victim of a gangland killing.

Isabelle Patterson Springer committed no crime but was the cause of two murders. She was married to John W. Springer but also enjoyed a relationship with Frank Henwood and Tony Von Phul who became involved in an argument over her at the Brown Palace Hotel on May 23, 1911. Henwood killed Von Phul and a bystander. Receiving a life sentence, he obtained a retrial, this time receiving the death sentence which was later reduced to life, from which he was paroled, only to get into trouble and was returned to prison where he died in 1929.

Mr. and Mrs. Charles Patterson appear happy in their photo but Charles had a habit of beating Gertrud and for this she killed him on September 25, 1911, with four shots, leaving his body on the grounds of Baron von Richthofen's castle. After a long and controversial trial, she was acquitted on the basis of his treatment of her and his very poor health. She went to Europe and is believed to have booked passage home under an assumed name on the ill-fated Titanic.

On October 15, 1930, 10 year old Leona O'Loughlin was reported missing by her parents, Denver Detective Leo O'Loughlin and step-mother Pearl. The girl was found in Berkeley Lake on the 18th but evidence indicated she had received a blow on the head. Pearl was tried and convicted of the murder and sentenced to a life term but was paroled in 1951.—*All—D.P.L. Coll.*

ISABELLE PATTERSON SPRINGER

MR. & MRS. CHARLES PATTERSON

PEARL O'LOUGHLIN

DENVER'S FIRE FIGHTERS

Two of Denver's earliest volunteer fire companies are shown here. Above, is the Woodie Fisher Hose Company No. 1, organized in July, 1872, and named in honor of Fireman Woodie "Redwood" Fisher who was killed on May 12, 1870, attempting to stop a runaway team of horses. The Fisher Company shared the Central Fire Station at 1534 Lawrence Street, with Hook and Ladder Company No. 1, which had been organized in March, 1866. The Joseph E. Bates Fire and Hose Company No. 3, is seen below in 1881. Named in honor of Mayor Bates who had helped the company get started in April, 1872, they were housed at 1714 Curtis Street and often referred to as the "West Denver" company.—*Above, Denver Public Library, Western History Collection; below, State Historical Society of Colorado*

TURN OF THE CENTURY FIREFIGHTERS

During the 1880's, Denver began to establish a paid Fire Department and these photos portray the department in the period of 1890 to the early 1900's. Above, the crew of Engine No. 5, (1) Harry Johns, engineer, (2) Mark Blake, assistant engineer, and (3) Louis Goodman, driver, pose in front of the City Hall Station. At the right are the men and equipment of Engine Co. No. 8, at E. 16th Avenue and Marion Street. The station, built in 1890, served until 1971, when replaced by a new building on the same site. The two bottom scenes are of Highlands Hose Co. No. 1, on West 26th Avenue just west of Federal Blvd. Highlands had annexed to Denver on July 24, 1896, but Roy S. Kent photographed the company on what likely was one of its last runs.—*Bottom right, State Historical Society of Colorado; others, Denver Public Library, Western History Collection*

Early in the 20th Century Denver built several new fire stations, including the three shown here. Station No. 15, at East 11th Avenue and Clayton Street, is seen at the top, a few years after opening in 1925. The center photo is of Station No. 3, at East 25th Avenue and Washington Street, when new in 1931. This was known as the "Negro Company," having been originally organized in 1893 and manned by Negroes until 1962, when fully integrated with the rest of the department. Station No. 1, at 1326 Tremont Street, was built in 1909, to replace the original Engine Company No. 1, at Broadway and Colfax, now the site of the Pioneer Monument. The Station is seen at the right in the mid-1920's.
—*Denver Public Library, Western History Collection*

These two scenes are behind the old City Hall, on the Market Street bridge at Speer Boulevard. Above, in 1924, the pumpers are being tested, a task which is still necessary but which is now generally done at a lake in one of the city parks. Below, at about the same year, the department's men and equipment are proudly on display, perhaps for an annual inspection.—*Denver Public Library, Western History Collection*

CHIEF ALLIE FELDMAN

Allie Feldman became Fire Chief in May, 1946, succeeding John F. Healy who had served since 1912. Under both Healy and Feldman, who retired in June, 1964, the department became one of the nation's finest, as displayed in responding to two typical fires: the old Denver Post Building on Champa Street in the 1940's, and the Mining Exchange Building on February 16, 1939.—*Denver Public Library, Western History Collection*

THE CITY HALL WAR

In March, 1894, Governor Davis H. Waite (lower right) became embroiled in a bitter fight with city officials and eventually he called out the Colorado Infantry in a threat to storm the City Hall where a large number of police and deputy sheriffs were barricaded in protest of the governor's control over appointments to the Fire and Police Board. The crowds are seen above, at City Hall on March 15th, awaiting arrival of the troops, seen below, as they march up Lawrence towards 15th Street. The Colorado Supreme Court resolved the matter but Governor Waite did not gain another term in office, having received considerable criticism for his handling of the matter.—*Denver Public Library, Western History Collection*

Government Of and For the People

JAMES ARCHER

WATER!

In 1870, James Archer (left) organized the Denver City Water Company and became its president. Early in 1872, the firm began delivering the city's first piped water and by 1880, increased demand caused the company to build a reservoir, Lake Archer, named for the company founder. Located directly east of the Platte River, the lake and pumping station (below) are seen in 1899; the lake is gone but the buildings, located at 12th Avenue and Shoshone Street, are now part of the Denver Water Department's West Side Storage Yard. In 1882, the company reorganized as the Denver Water Company, with Archer continuing as president, and opened offices in this building (bottom-left) at 17th and California Streets.

Many Denverites could not afford or did not want piped water and instead purchased it from delivery wagons such as these (center-left) belonging to the Union Artesian Water Company. The "water wagons" are posed with company proprietor Frank C. Timson at far left, near 6th Avenue and Galapago Street.—*Below, courtesy Denver Water Department; others, Denver Public Library, Western History Collection*

In 1882, the High Line Canal was dug from Kassler, on the South Platte River, to a point east of the Rocky Mountain Arsenal. Designed to irrigate farmland east of the city, it has lacked sufficient water rights to be fully utilized. The scene at right is typical of numerous canals in the area.—*Denver Public Library, Western History Collection*

Walter Cheesman came to Denver in 1860, and for a time operated a drug store where he sold water by the bottle or draught. He soon became involved in banking, railroads and the water business, serving as a director of the Denver City Water Company. In 1894, he became president of the Denver Union Water Company and under his leadership the Cheesman Dam was built—his most fiitting memorial.

The Capitol Hill Pump Station and adjoining reservoir are located in Congress Park. The station was completed in 1899, and is seen below (left) in 1905, while on the right is the huge Barr pump as seen in the same year. In the picture on the left, taken on June 22, 1912, the crew building conduit No. 8 is shown banding a 60 inch wood stave line in southwest Denver. Such lines remained in use until the mid-20th Century.—*Right, Denver Public Library, Western History Collection; others, courtesy Denver Water Department*

WALTER SCOTT CHEESMAN

In 1896, the Denver Union Water Company began planning the construction of the first major segment of our modern Denver water system. The dam, on the South Fork of the South Platte, near Deckers, was begun in 1898, and built of granite blocks quarried near the dam site. Work was already well along when the photo above was taken in July, 1902, and the dam is seen below as it appeared shortly after completion in 1905. Named in honor of Walter Cheesman, the dam continues in use today.—*Above and right, courtesy Denver Water Department; below, D.P.L., Western History Coll.*

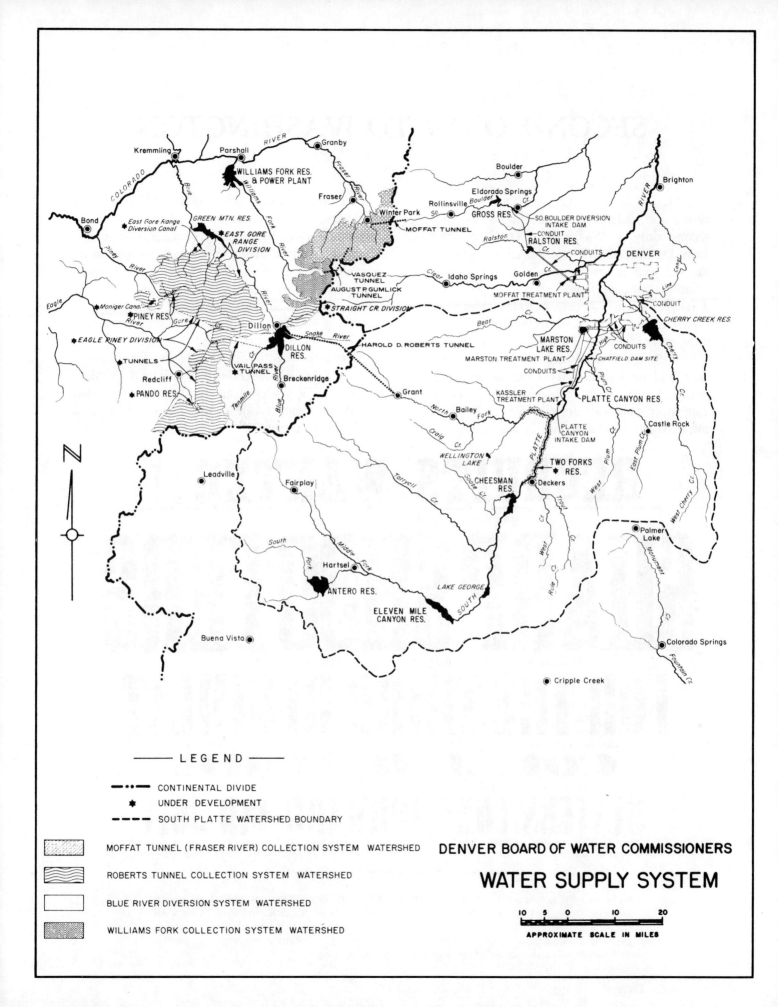

Kremmling
Parshall
Granby
RIVER
Boulder
Brighton
WILLIAMS FORK RES. & POWER PLANT
Eldorado Springs
Bond
COLORADO
Fraser
Rollinsville
Boulder Cr.
GROSS RES.
SO. BOULDER DIVERSION INTAKE DAM
East Gore Range Diversion Canal
GREEN MTN. RES.
Winter Park
So.
CONDUIT
Piney River
EAST GORE RANGE DIVISION
MOFFAT TUNNEL
Ralston Cr.
RALSTON RES.
DENVER
CONDUITS
Eagle
VASQUEZ TUNNEL
Clear Cr.
Idaho Springs
Golden
Moniger Canal
AUGUST P. GUMLICK TUNNEL
MOFFAT TREATMENT PLANT
PINEY RES.
Gore Cr.
Dillon
STRAIGHT CR. DIVISION
Snake River
CONDUIT
EAGLE PINEY DIVISION
Bear Cr.
CHERRY CREEK RES.
MARSTON LAKE RES.
TUNNELS
DILLON RES.
HAROLD D. ROBERTS TUNNEL
CONDUITS
VAIL PASS TUNNEL
MARSTON TREATMENT PLANT
CHATFIELD DAM SITE
Redcliff
Breckenridge
Tenmile Cr.
Blue River
Grant
CONDUITS
PANDO RES.
KASSLER TREATMENT PLANT
PLATTE CANYON RES.
North Fork
Bailey
Craig Cr.
Castle Rock
Leadville
WELLINGTON LAKE
PLATTE CANYON INTAKE DAM
Fairplay
Tarryall Cr.
CHEESMAN RES.
TWO FORKS RES.
Deckers
Goose Cr.
Palmer Lake
South Fork
Middle Fork
Hartsel
ANTERO RES.
LAKE GEORGE
West Plum Cr.
West Cherry Cr.
ELEVEN MILE CANYON RES.
SOUTH
Colorado Springs
Buena Vista
Cripple Creek
Fountain Cr.

N

LEGEND

- ·—··— CONTINENTAL DIVIDE
- ✶ UNDER DEVELOPMENT
- - - - SOUTH PLATTE WATERSHED BOUNDARY

MOFFAT TUNNEL (FRASER RIVER) COLLECTION SYSTEM WATERSHED

ROBERTS TUNNEL COLLECTION SYSTEM WATERSHED

BLUE RIVER DIVERSION SYSTEM WATERSHED

WILLIAMS FORK COLLECTION SYSTEM WATERSHED

DENVER BOARD OF WATER COMMISSIONERS

WATER SUPPLY SYSTEM

10   5   0   10   20

APPROXIMATE SCALE IN MILES

SECOND ONLY TO WASHINGTON

Metropolitan Denver stands today as a major center for Federal Government offices, ranking second only to Washington, D.C. In contrast, early Denver, and in fact the entire West, knew the national government in a far different and detached manner from the role it plays in the daily life of every American today. Almost every aspect of our lives is controlled, affected or perhaps encouraged, by the far flung workings of the United States Government; by contrast the pioneer had no choice but to handle most of his needs through local or territorial government. The sheer weight of distance denied Washington the privilege of greater involvement.

Certain needs could be handled only with the resources and control of the Federal Government and Denver gradually became a center for numerous departments and agencies operating throughout the West. One of the earliest major undertakings of the government, and one very often overlooked today, was the mapping and detailing of the resources of the vast western lands. Known as the "Great Surveys" and carried out between 1867 and 1879, four surveys led by John Wesley Powell, Ferdinand Hayden, Clarence King, and Montague Wheeler, provided for the first time a true picture of these lands and their future potential.

RECRUITS WANTED!!

Having been appointed to raise a Company of

SHARP SHOOTERS

from the Hunters of the Rocky Mountains and the Arkansas Valley.

FOR THE THIRD REGIMENT

Colorado Volunteers, to proceed to the States as soon as organized, under command of

COL. J. H. FORD.

I am now ready to receive recruits at my head quarters at Canon City.

HUNTERS COME FORWARD AND JOIN

The Crack Company of the Crack Regiment. As this is to be picked Company none but good able bodied men need apply.
DAVID P. WILSON, Recruiting Officer.

Commonweal' & Republican Steam Press Print, Denver.

Colorado did not become involved in the Civil War fighting. The Colorado Volunteers, however, took part in the battle at Apache Canyon in New Mexico, and this, along with Major Chivington's victory at nearby La Glorieta Pass, ended Southern hopes of moving into the West. Volunteers were recruited with posters such as this one which appeared in Denver in 1861.—*State Historical Society of Colorado*

In this scene, typical of the expeditions of the Great Surveys, the Hayden Party pauses at Yellowstone Lake (now in Yellowstone Park) in 1871. The surveys succeeded in mapping much of the West including Colorado, and led to the establishment of the U. S. Geological Survey in 1879.—*W. H. Jackson photo, State Historical Society of Colorado*

THE MAIL MUST GO THROUGH

No government service is of so great an importance to the average citizen as that of the post office. To the pioneer it was a link to civilization and as such of vital concern. Doubtless, Denver considered it a major event when on January 18, 1858, the United States Post Office authorized the establishment of an office at Auraria, Kansas Territory. However, it would be more than a year until an actual post office was established and to provide mail service to the Cherry Creek Settlements, a contract was arranged with the Leavenworth & Pike's Peak Express Company to haul the mail from Leavenworth to Denver. Known as Coraville, Kansas Territory, this office continued into mid-1859 when the regular postal operations began.

With the approach of the railroad the mail service improved and the arrival of the Denver Pacific Railroad assured fast and reliable service. Beginning May 31, 1926, the airplane joined in moving the mail. From the pioneer air mail service of that date, the priority mail has gradually been shifted from surface transportation to the airplane.

Denver's postmasters have included some of the city's most notable citizens, among them William Byers, Rocky Mountain News founder, who took office in 1864, future Mayor Robert Speer who became Postmaster in 1885, Horace Tabor in 1896, and another future mayor, Benjamin Stapleton, who gained the postal position in 1915.

From an office in a frame building at 14th and Larimer Streets in 1860, the Denver Post Office eventually moved into its own new building at the corner of 16th and Arapahoe Streets in 1886. The present main Denver Post Office Building at 18th and Stout Streets was constructed of Colorado Yule marble and opened in 1916. Today it is supplemented by numerous branch stations.

THE MILITARY—INDIAN FIGHTERS TO JET PILOTS

The fear of Indian attack was present in pioneer Denver as in much of the West and thus

Second Only to Washington

the United States Army was early on the scene in Colorado to keep the red man under control. Denver, however, had no military base until the establishment of Camp Weld in 1861. Located at what is today 8th Avenue and Vallejo Street, the camp was named in honor of Lewis Weld, first Secretary of Colorado Territory, and was the base for the First Regiment of Colorado Volunteers organized by Governor William Gilpin. In the spring of 1862, the volunteers took part in the Battle of La Glorieta which spelled doom for Confederate hopes of moving into the West. While Indians were involved in numerous skirmishes across Colorado, Denver was never attacked.

Today, Fort Logan is both a National Cemetery and a Mental Health Center. For many years, however, it served as a military base, being established in the fall of 1887 and named in honor of General John Logan, a native of Illinois who had spent much time in Denver. Fort Logan remained in active service until after World War II when its facilities were converted to their present uses.

In the spring of 1898, in preparation for the Spanish American War, a tent camp was set up near City Park and named in honor of Governor Alva Adams. Camp Adams lasted only a brief time, but served to gather the First Regiment Colorado Infantry, United States Volunteers, which took part in the capture of Manila in August, 1898, under the command of Colonel Irving Hale.

With the prospect of war looming close on the horizon, America entered a period of rapid military buildup prior to the Second World War. Lowry Air Field was established in 1937, on the site of the Agnes Memorial Sanitarium, and nearby Buckley Field was opened in 1942. In 1941, the Denver Ordnance Plant was opened in Lakewood and operated under contract to the Remington Arms Company. The next year the Rocky Mountain Arsenal was established on land to the northeast of the city and continues its operation to the present. Fitzsimons General Hospital had opened in 1918 and was enlarged for its role in World War II.

In a short time Denver had become a major military and defense center which it remains to this day. Such modern plants as the Rocky Flats Atomic Plant and the Martin Marietta Corpora-

tion's aerospace facilities have continued to spur the economy of Denver.

NO SAMPLES PLEASE!—THE DENVER MINT

To tourists and local folk alike, the Denver Branch of the United States Mint holds a strange fascination. It is here that a major share of our nation's coins are produced, with visitors welcome to observe the massive operation. While the present mint building dates to 1906, the mint story had its beginning more than a century ago. In July, 1860, the banking firm of Clark, Gruber and Company began to mint gold coins in order to avoid the costly and risky transportation of the metal to eastern markets. At that time it was legal to mint private coins and they soon became very popular in the area. In 1863, however, Congress authorized the purchase of the minting operation and also prohibited any other private minting in the future. The government maintained an office to assay and purchase gold but waited 43 years before resuming minting operations in Denver. Today the Clark, Gruber & Company minting equipment is preserved in the Colorado State Museum, more than a century after purchase by the government.

IKE AND MAMIE EISENHOWER

Denver has one special claim to fame in the realm of national political life. During his terms in office as President, Dwight David Eisenhower often came to Colorado to vacation and also to work away from the pressures of Washington. It was here that Ike's political career was launched from headquarters in the Brown Palace Hotel. On their many return trips, Mamie Eisenhower enjoyed visits to the Doud family home, and together the President and First Lady were often seen about the city and on Sunday mornings frequently attending Corona Presbyterian Church. On one of these visits, September 24, 1955, the President suffered a heart attack, and for many tense days Denver was the focal point of both national and world attention. In later years the Eisenhowers returned several times, usually arriving by train, always to be warmly received by a city which would never lose its special feeling for them.

Above—Ferdinand V. Hayden, whose surveys spanned the years 1873-78, examines a soil sample while on expedition.

Left—George M. Wheeler, while an Army Lieutenant, directed an extensive survey of the West between 1872 and 1879. The surveys were undertaken to provide the War Department with information relative to transportation routes.—*Denver Public Library, Western History Collection*

Above—John Wesley Powell led expeditions which explored the Colorado River and surveyed much of Colorado during the period 1869 to 1879. Between 1881 and 1894, Powell was Director of the U.S. Geological Survey.—*Author's Collection*

Lower left—In 1867, Clarence King led the 40th Parallel Survey which for the first time mapped much of northern Colorado. In 1879 King was made the first Director of the U.S. Geological Survey, serving until 1881.—*Denver Public Library, Western History Collection*

Second Only to Washington

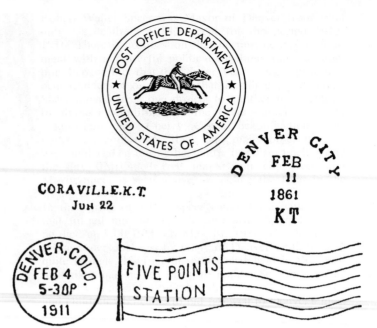

POST OFFICE DEPARTMENT
UNITED STATES OF AMERICA

CORAVILLE.K.T.
JUN 22

DENVER CITY
FEB
11
1861
KT

DENVER, COLO.
FEB 4
5-30P.
1911

FIVE POINTS
STATION

The old Denver Post Office (opposite page) was begun in 1884, requiring several years to complete. Long a conspicuous landmark at 16th and Arapahoe Streets, it was inadequate for postal purposes even when new. The new Denver Post Office (left) was constructed of Colorado Yule marble and opened on January 2, 1916, in the full block bounded by 18th, 19th, Champa and Stout Streets. At that time the old post office became the U.S. Customs House and continued to serve various Federal offices until demolished in 1965, to make way for the new Federal Reserve Branch Bank.—*Left, Denver Public Library, Western History Collection; others, State Historical Society of Colorado; postmarks, John H. Willard*

For almost 90 years, from 1880 until 1967, Railway Post Offices operated throughout Colorado in cars like this one being loaded at Union Station. Each route had its own postmark, such as those above, and identified the end points of the mail run. Despite the efficiency of the system, air and truck routes gradually replaced the RPO cars; often this resulted in actually slowing mail delivery to many towns.—*State Historical Society of Colorado; R.P.O. postmarks, Colorado Railroad Museum*

Second Only to Washington

THE COLORADO VOLUNTEERS

"CAMP—WELD" C.T.

Camp Weld is seen in this artists' sketch as it appeared in 1862, one year after being established at what is now West 8th Avenue and Vallejo Street. Built to house the 1st Regiment of Colorado Volunteers, it was closed in 1865, after a fire destroyed much of the camp.—*State Historical Society of Colorado*

Officers of the Colorado Volunteers pose here in the early 1860's, during the Civil War. On the bottom row, third from the left, is Major Edwin W. Wynkoop and to the right is Colonel James H. Ford whose name appears on the 1861 recruiting poster on page 138. —*State Historical Society of Colorado*

In 1873, the Guards Hall was built at 15th and Curtis Streets to house the Governor's Guards, a forerunner of the National Guard. In later years the building was used for stores and a theater.—*State Historical Society of Colorado*

THE SPANISH AMERICAN WAR

The Colorado Volunteers played a vital role in the Spanish American War. Fort Logan (seen above as it appeared in later years) was established in 1887, and became a key facility for the war effort.

On September 14, 1899, the troops returned home victorious from the Battle of Manila, in the Philippines, and are seen (below) parading up 16th Street, past Lawrence Street, en route from the depot to the capitol grounds. Later that same day, (left) the regiment's battle flag is presented to Governor Charles S. Thomas. *Top and bottom, Denver Public Library Western Collection; middle, State Historical Society of Colorado*

CITY AND COUNTY OF DENVER
WAR RISK INSURANCE
DENVER PAYS THE PREMIUM ON $1000 WAR RISK INSURANCE
FOR EVERY CITIZEN ENGAGED IN THE WAR

No. 1

Denver, Colo., Feb. 28 1918

Pay to the Order of   Major Harold G. Garwood

Ten and 08/100 - - - - - - - - - - - - - dollars $10.08

COMMITTEE ON WAR INSURANCE

TO THE COLORADO NATIONAL BANK

DENVER, COLORADO.

CHAIRMAN

TREASURER

Denver took great pride in its fighting men and provided each with a free insurance policy such as the one above. The Red Cross established a reception center in Union Station (right) to provide help and relaxation for servicemen awaiting their trains. Camp George West, (below) located just east of Golden, was typical of camps across the nation during this era. Originally known as Rifle Range, when opened as a gun club in 1903, it was renamed in 1934 to honor Brigadier General George "Give 'Em Hell" West. The camp remains in use by the National Guard, State Patrol and Colorado Law Enforcement Training Academy.—*Denver Public Library, Western History Collection*

THE HOME FRONT

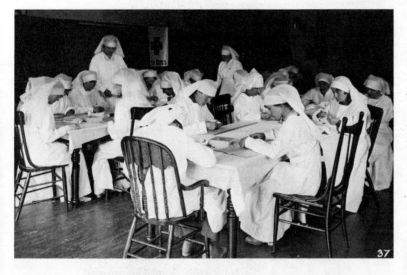

Denverites did their part to support their men in action. The Loretto Heights "service camp" (above) was set up behind the college buildings and provided many opportunities for women to join the war effort. A constant activity (left) at the camp was the rolling of bandages as these ladies are doing under the watchful eye of Red Cross instructors.

Shortly after the war, citizens were allowed to purchase military surplus food. In the scene below, Mayor Dewey C. Bailey (far right) lends a hand with the distribution in the City Auditorium.—*Denver Public Library, Western History Collection*

Denver celebrated the end of the Great War with a parade on 16th Street, seen here between Champa and Stout Streets. All too short would be the peace they were celebrating!—*Denver Public Library, Western History Collection*

PEACE SHATTERED!

As Denver moved full swing into the effort for victory in World War II, the Denver Tramway painted car 833 in red, white and blue to spur bond sales. Posing with Tramway, military, and bond drive officials is Mayor Ben Stapleton, on far left, and Governor John C. Vivian on the far right.—*Denver Post photo*

In 1941, the Denver Ordnance Plant was established eight miles west of the city. Built and operated by the Remington Arms Company, the plant enhanced Denver's status as a defense center. After the war in 1946, the facility became the Denver Federal Center as seen in this early 1950's aerial view.—*General Services Administration, courtesy Everett Rohrer*

A sign of the times—Americans learned to live by their ration books, using the coupons for everything from shoes to gasoline.

The war brought a need for new military bases and thus in 1937, the city purchased the Agnes Memorial Sanatorium (middle), and turned it over to the Federal Government to become Lowry Field. KLZ Radio is seen covering the dedication (below) as the field was named for Francis Brown Lowry, the first Colorado airman lost in World War I.—*Denver Public Library, Western History Collection; ration book, Authors' Collection*

THE U.S.S. DENVER

Mayor Ben Stapleton was on hand for the launching (right) of the city's namesake ship, the *U.S.S. Denver,* on April 4, 1942. Below, the ship is seen just outside Havana Harbor, New Hebrides Islands, in the South Pacific Ocean. The *U.S.S. Denver* spent much of her time in Pacific waters and there earned ten battle stars during World War II. The statistics of the ship's construction are listed below.—*Denver Public Library, Western History Collection; below, Official U.S. Navy Photograph*

U.S.S. Denver—No. CL-58, Cleveland Class of Light Cruiser

Keel laid December 26, 1940

Launched April 4, 1942

Commissioned October, 1942

Displacement—10,500 tons—light; 13,755 tons—loaded

Crew—916 (peacetime); 1200 (wartime)

Scrapped—1959

NOTE: Two other ships have been named for the city. The first *U.S.S. Denver* was a cruiser (1902-1930) and the third *U.S.S. Denver*, an amphibious transport dock, was commissioned October 26, 1968.

THE U.S. MINT

After the Federal Government purchased the private mint of Clark, Gruber and Company in 1863, no minting took place until 1906, although an assay office was operated in the building (left) at 16th and Market Streets. Construction of the new mint began in 1898, and was well along when the middle photo was made on May 30, 1900. The completed U. S. Mint at Cherokee Street and Colfax Avenue is seen below shortly after coinage began on February 2, 1906. Additions were made to the facility in 1936, 1946, and 1965; plans now call for an entirely new mint to be built by the late 1970's.
—*State Historical Society of Colorado*

THE ROCKY MOUNTAIN NEWS
COLORADO'S GREATEST NEWSPAPER

A FEW LINES OF TYPE
...d a man discovers his life work—a
...siness is revealed—a lost valuable is
...covered. Such are the effects of News-
...mes Want Ads.

SATISFACTION
That's what you are entitled to and that's
what you'll get if you report any inef-
ficiencies to Main 6840.

. LXIII: NO. 353   DENVER, COLO., TUESDAY, DECEMBER 19, 1922—16 PAGES

ALL CLEWS FAIL IN $200,000 MINT HOLDUP

Federal Bank Guard Is Killed in Wildest Gun Battle of Denver's History

The infamous Denver Mint robbery was more correctly a robbery of a Federal Reserve Bank truck in front of the mint. One guard was killed, $200,000.00 in five dollar bills was taken, and the case remains today never fully solved nor was all the money recovered. One of the members of the robbery gang, which included five men and two women, Nicholas Trainor (alias J. S. Sloan) is seen in the photos below along with the car in which his frozen body was found, in a garage at 1631 Gilpin Street, eighteen days after the robbery.—*Both, Denver Public Library, Western History Collection; newspaper, State Historical Society of Colorado*

ATTACK OF DESPERADOES TOOK LESS THAN MINUTE, WITNESSES OF ROBBERY SAY

Bandits Lay Down Barrage of Lead on Door of Mint to Shield Transfer of Currency From Truck to Waiting Automobile.

Federal Cashier Will Offer Reward For Mint Bandits

OUTLAWS COVER UP TRAIL IN DASH FOR OPEN COUNTRY WITH FORTUNE IN PLUNDER

Bloody Fingerprints on Stock of Shotgun Have No Duplicates in Bertillon Records of Police Department; Eva Lewis Is Questioned; First Arrest Proves Fruitless.

WEATHER INDICATIONS
For Colorado Fair Wednesday, warmer in south and west portions. Thursday fair.

METAL QUOTATIONS
Silver, ...
Copper, ...
Lead, ...
Spelter, at ...

THE DENVER REPUBLICAN.

16 PAGES. DENVER, COLORADO, WEDNESDAY, MORNING, JULY 8, 1908. 16 PAGES. PRICE FIVE CENTS.

Ever Swelling Chorus of "Bryan, Bryan, Bryan," Rises and Falls to Rise Again in Every Quarter of Denver

Interior View of Denver's Splendid Auditorium at the Opening Session of the National Democratic Convention.

JUGGERNAUT CAR OF BRYAN CRUSHES DOWN HIS FOES

Commoner Makes Known at Opening Session of Convention That He Is the Only Lord of Democracy and Absolute Dictator of All Proceedings—Battle Over Dead Cleveland Taken Up on Floor and Calls Forth Show of Prowess—Parker ...

PLATFORM TO GO IN TOMORROW

RESOLUTIONS COMMITTEE HEARS LABOR LEADERS

HUMILIATION OF PARKER TO CROWN BRYAN IN THE EAST

First Day's Session of Convention Shows Nebraskan Sage in Zenith of His Power and Commoner Rides Rough Shod Over All Opponents in Cleveland Resolution ... With ... ffey and Naming P... ... Ch... —Hobso...

Crowning the Queen of Convention Cities

1908 DEMOCRATIC CONVENTION

Denver's City Auditorium was completed just in time to accommodate the Democratic National Convention in July, 1908. As the headlines indicate, William Jennings Bryan won the nomination for President; in November, however, he went down in defeat to William Howard Taft.—*Political cartoon, Denver Public Library, Western History Collection; ticket and newspaper, State Historical Society of Colorado*

VISITING ROYALTY

Among the royalty that visited Denver, was Queen Marie of Rumania. During her stay of November 10-11, 1926, one of her activities was a trip up Lookout Mountain to place a wreath on the grave of Buffalo Bill. The Queen is seen above at Union Station which in that era was the travel center of the city.

The Crown Prince (the late King Frederick) and Crown Princess Ingrid of Denmark and Iceland visited Denver and were honored with a dinner (below) held at the Brown Palace Hotel on April 17, 1939.—*All, Denver Public Library, Western History Collection*

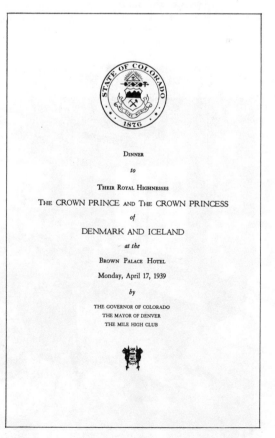

STATE OF COLORADO
1876

DINNER

to

THEIR ROYAL HIGHNESSES

THE CROWN PRINCE AND THE CROWN PRINCESS

of

DENMARK AND ICELAND

at the

BROWN PALACE HOTEL

Monday, April 17, 1939

by

THE GOVERNOR OF COLORADO
THE MAYOR OF DENVER
THE MILE HIGH CLUB

Second Only to Washington

On September 6, 1901, President William McKinley was mortally wounded by an assassin's bullet while attending the Pan American Exposition in Buffalo, New York. Following his death eight days later, the nation was plunged into mourning and an estimated 40,000 persons gathered on the capitol grounds (above) to join in nationwide memorial services on September 19th; thus, Denver bid farewell to the 25th President of the United States.

On May 4, 1903, President Theodore Roosevelt visited Denver and is seen below just prior to delivering a speech at the Colorado Capitol Building.—*Above, State Historical Society of Colorado; below, Denver Public Library, Western History Collection*

President "Teddy" Roosevelt loved the rugged Colorado outdoors and thus made several trips to the state and Denver. On his visit of May 4, 1903, (see opposite page and right) "T.R." delivered a stirring speech to a large audience gathered on the capitol grounds. After his presidency he continued to enjoy Colorado and is seen below (right) sharing a chuckwagon lunch with Mayor Robert Speer (center), and Governor John Shafroth (right), in Overland Park on August 29, 1910.—*Above, 1st Federal Savings Collection; below, Denver Public Library, Western History Collection*

President William Howard Taft came to Denver on October 3, 1911, and delivered a speech to a large audience gathered at the University of Denver. This was the first time a president visited D. U. and was an important event in the school's history; the Chancellor, Henry A. Buchtel, is the man wearing the large badge and seated behind and to the left of the President in the photo below.—*State Historical Society of Colorado*

"Any man who tries to excite class hatred, sectional hate, hate of creeds, any kind of hatred, in our community, though he may effect to do it in the interest of the class he is addressing, is that class's own worst enemy."—*President Theodore Roosevelt at Denver, Colorado, May 4, 1903*

Second Only to Washington

Mamie Doud, the future Mrs. Dwight David Eisenhower, is sitting on the porch of her girlhood home at 750 Lafayette Street (top photo, opposite page) with her sisters behind her and their parents in the family automobile. In the scene below, taken in 1938, Mr. Eisenhower has just enjoyed a spin in the Doud's 1912 Ranch-Lang Electric car. When "Ike" decided to enter the presidential race, he opened his campaign headquarters at the Brown Palace Hotel. He is seen above arriving at his new headquarters on June 15, 1952. The President and First Lady enjoyed numerous visits to Denver and often worshipped at Corona Presbyterian Church. Below, they are seen chatting with the pastor, Reverend Robert Lutz.—*D.P.L., Western History Coll.*

BUSINESS HUB OF THE WEST

From the beginning, Denver's economy has been closely tied to that of the rest of Colorado and the adjoining areas of the Intermountain West. The vast area that stretches from western Kansas and Nebraska to Utah and from northern New Mexico to Wyoming and even to Montana, is the region in the center of which lies mile-high Denver.

This empire of mountains and plains depends in large measure on Denver. It is not only the center for retail and wholesale merchandising, banking and financial services, but also the consumer of the region's rich supplies of raw materials. The city is the communications and transportation center for this vast region of our nation and quite literally the gateway to the Rockies for tourists and skiers who today are the basis for the rapidly expanding leisure industry.

It may be said that the city's economy is geared to serving the entire area but conversely it exists in large measure only because of the vast empire which is the source of supply for many raw materials. At the same time the area is a market for the goods and services which the city offers in return.

The economy and prosperity of Denver and this entire region have gone through four distinct periods during the one hundred plus years since gold fever brought the first settlers to Cherry Creek.

THE MINING ERA: 1860's-1890's

The lure of gold brought the first pioneers to our city and set its economy in motion. The movement of men from back east into the mountains presented the need for conveniently placed supply centers. Close on the heels of the gold seekers came the pioneer merchants. In October, 1858, Charles Blake and Andrew Williams arrived at the Cherry Creek settlement with four freight wagons containing general merchandise. The two men from Crescent City, Iowa opened the firm of Blake and Williams in a cabin near 12th and Wewatta Streets and became Denver's first merchants.

During the following few months, a wide array of businesses sprang up to serve the needs of the growing ranks of settlers and gold seekers. Uncle Dick (Richens L.) Wootton arrived with two wagons of merchandise from New Mexico just before Christmas of 1858, and his stock of "Taos Lightning" whiskey most certainly helped to make the holidays merry. In short order the first blacksmith, Thomas Pollock, opened shop,

RICHENS L. "UNCLE DICK" WOOTTON
—First Federal Savings Collection

Henry R. Reitze and E. Karczewsky opened the first bakery, J. D. Ramage opened the first jewelry and watch repair shop, and of certain interest to the citizenry, the first saloon opened its doors in January of 1859.

From these pioneer ventures grew many of the businesses which became the retail establishments of today. In the remaining years of the nineteenth century and into the start of the twentieth, such men as W. B. Daniels, W. G. Fisher, David May, James Cash Penney, John Jay Joslin, Dennis Sheedy (pioneer beginnings of The Denver Dry), Meyer and Max Neusteter, Leopold Henry Guldman (founder of the Golden Eagle Department Store), and Merrit W. Gano Sr., entered the retail field and established the merchandising patterns which are continued in modern Denver's fine stores.

The rapid extension of mining brought a continual and growing demand for all manner of tools and heavy equipment, with the result that the city became and remains today a major supplier of mining equipment.

While not an oil state of the same importance of some other areas of the West, the second oil field in America was established near Florence, Colorado, and from that start we today find numerous oil and oil exploration companies having offices in Denver.

The gold and silver boom eventually died but the state has continued as an important producer of other minerals and of coal. Its prominence in mining and petroleum is evidenced by the worldwide fame of the Colorado School of Mines in Golden where the enrollment includes students from many states and foreign countries.

THE FARMING AND RANCHING ERA: 1900-1940

As the mining boom was fading, Colorado was already coming to realize the tremendous potential of farming and ranching, and for many years these would dominate the economy. On the western slope, vast tracts of land are ideal for raising both cattle and sheep, and countless acres awaited only the addition of water to change them into rich crop and orchard lands. On the eastern slope, general farming, both dry and irrigated, began very early but it was the introduction of the sugar beet that had the most profound effect on the agricultural economy. Chief respon-

The Mining Exchange Building, at 15th and Arapahoe Streets, was completed in 1891, and for many years was the financial center of the mining industry of the Rocky Mountain West. The miner on the top of the building was preserved when the building was razed in 1963, and is now displayed in front of Brooks Towers on the same site.—*State Historical Society Collection*

sibility for the growth of the sugar beet industry lies with Charles Boettcher who studied their use in Germany and then provided financial backing to launch the industry in the Platte Valley. Today, sugar beets are raised in many parts of the West and several large firms produce beet sugar to supply much of the western part of the nation.

The growth of farming and ranching brought a demand for facilities to process the raw materials into food products, and a wide variety of firms entered this business to eventually form the companies which today provide many major food brands on our grocery store shelves. The network of railroads reaching into all parts of the state helped to provide easy access for the rancher to bring his cattle and sheep to market. The Denver stockyards became one of the nation's largest with most of the famous brand name packers having plants along with many smaller local operators.

The food processing business remains of major importance, but the increase in other businesses has caused a drop in its relative standing in total employment.

The clouds of war on the nation's horizon brought many lasting changes to the economy and life style of the Mile High City. There already were several military bases in the Denver area and these were quickly enlarged to meet wartime requirements, bringing great numbers of military personnel to the city. Major defense plants, such as the Remington Arms in Lakewood, attracted much additional new population and the city found itself caught up in a boom. Denver, which had seen a steady but not too spectacular growth, suddenly saw its "cow town" image disappearing never to be regained, to the regret of many Denverites who fear today's very real problems of urban crowding and pollution.

After the war, the city never really saw the end of the boom. Many thousands of men who had been to Denver in military service decided to make this their home and the expansion which began in the early 1940's, simply continued through the decade.

MID-CENTURY AND BEYOND: 1950-1970's

Denver now holds an unquestioned position as the business center of the Intermountain West. No longer based on mining or agriculture, today it is broad based. The city is still, however, not what might be termed an industrial center. Long time industries such as Gates Rubber and Samsonite Luggage have greatly expanded, but the large part of new business is the light manufacturing type and many firms engaged in products for defense and aerospace.

A very important growth factor has been the great increase in the number of Federal Government offices located in the city. The Federal jobs, in addition to the countless positions at the state and local level, as well as in schools and colleges, combine to make government one of the major employers in the Denver area.

The growth of business and industry has been paralleled by continued expansion in the related fields of real estate, insurance, banking and finance. From the humble beginnings made by such pioneer banking firms as Clark, Gruber & Company, which eventually became the First National Bank of Denver, and Kountze Broth-

ers, which eventually became the Colorado National Bank, the city has become the region's financial headquarters.

Because of a lack of capital, buying or building a home was very difficult for the average citizen in pioneer Denver. To meet this need, a number of savings and loan associations were formed to provide investers the opportunity to lend their money for home mortgages. A number of such organizations sprung up and some have continued until the present. Oldest association to survive has been First Federal Savings and Loan Association which dates to 1885, when it opened as the Co-Operative Association, with Robert Collier as president.

Today, Denver is the headquarters for several insurance companies including the state's oldest, Capitol Life Insurance Company which dates to 1905, and the largest local company, the Security Life and Accident Company which recently built one of the city's highest skyscrapers.

Guiding the business progress of the city has always been one of the roles of the Chamber of Commerce. The first such organization can be traced to 1867, when the Denver Board of Trade was founded and did much to gain a railroad line to the city. The present chamber was formed in 1884, and has devoted itself to advancing the business prosperity of the area.

POWER FOR THE CITY

As the city continued to expand, there developed an urgent need for efficient lighting and this led to the organization of the Denver Gas Company, which in 1871 began to offer gas for lighting. This was, of course, not natural gas but rather was manufactured in a coal-burning retort house located at 18th and Wewatta Streets. The demand for gas increased rapidly even after the advent of electricity and to meet this need, a pipeline was laid by the Colorado Interstate Gas Company bringing an abundant supply to the city from Texas Panhandle gas fields. With the use of natural gas in June, 1928, the retort houses were closed, and in ensuing years additional pipelines were laid to assure an ample supply for both industrial uses and for home furnaces and appliances.

While by eastern standards Denver was still

a "cow town," it became a pioneer in the use of electric power. On April 21, 1880, the city was thrilled by a demonstration of electric lighting and shortly the clean, silent new power began to replace gas for lighting in the downtown area, making Denver the third city in the world to adopt electricity for street lighting. During this time, some of the first experiments were taking place with electric trolley cars, leading to Denver having one of the earliest electric street railway systems in the world, and according to some records, the second operating electric trolley line in America.

Today, all the gas and electric services for the city are provided under a franchise held by the Public Service Company of Colorado. This firm, resultant of numerous mergers and consolidations, is now ready to introduce Denver to nuclear electricity. The region's first nuclear powered generating plant, located at Fort St. Vrain, north of the city, was completed and placed in experimental operation in 1972. Eventually, such plants may provide a substantial proportion of our power, while the present coal fired steam generating plants will likely continue in service far into the future.

BINDING THE NATION WITH TELEGRAPH AND TELEPHONE LINES

It is difficult to envision the telephone not being a part of our everyday way of life, but to early Denverites the telegraph offered the hope for speedy communications. The first transcontinental line passed through Julesburg in the fall of 1861 and messages could then be taken by stage the 200 miles to Denver, vastly speeding communications between Denver and both east and west. The large volume of telegraphic business even with such a gap, made obvious the need to complete a line to the city and finally on October 1, 1863, the first through service was opened from an office at 15th and Market Streets connecting Denver to Julesburg.

Eventually, several competing firms merged, including the Postal Telegraph-Cable Company, to form Western Union Telegraph Company.

The telephone era opened in Denver just one year after the world's first commercial phone service began in New Haven, Connecticut. Opening on October 24, 1879, at 1514 Larimer Street,

the first switchboard served only 161 phones, mostly in business offices. Expansion from that day forth has continued at a dizzying pace with 1,619 phones in the Denver area by 1890, 4,560 at the turn of the century, 58,067 in 1920, 120,699 in 1940, 400,000 by 1960, and something over 760,000 by 1972.

For a time some competition existed but by 1880, one system was serving the entire area and eventually became the Mountain States Telephone and Telegraph Company, better known today as Mountain Bell.

WESTERN HOSPITALITY—THE HOTELS

In our age of freeways and motels, it is easy to lose sight of the role which the hotel played in the early days of the West. In pioneer times a hotel was literally a haven of rest for the weary traveler and provided not only the necessities of rest and food but also developed into a center of luxury dining and entertainment for the local citizenry as well.

On February 1, 1859, David Smoke opened his cabin at 10th and Larimer to the public and gave it the impressive name "El Dorado Hotel." With him in the venture was Count Henri Murat who with his wife provided both the first barber service and the first laundry business.

By spring, Charles Blake and Andrew Williams had opened their large cabin as a combination store and hotel on Blake Street between 14th and 15th Streets. It became the "Denver House" and during its brief history was a favorite of Denverites as well as travelers, including Horace Greeley who spoke to a gathering of local citizens there on his trip touring the West that summer. By 1861, the facility was expanded to include a large corral and became known as the "Elephant Corral," named after a similar establishment in Council Bluffs, Iowa. Blake and Williams advertised on the routes leading to Denver and soon the Elephant Corral was the center for freight wagon trains with a constant bustle of buying and selling in supplies and livestock. Destroyed in the fire of 1863, it was rebuilt of brick and stood for many years.

As the city prospered and gained an air of permanence, numerous fine hotels began to rise; the Windsor at 18th and Larimer opened in 1880 and for a time was widely hailed as the

The Windsor Hotel, opened in 1880, is portrayed here as artist Herndon Davis perceived it about 1940.—*Denver Public Library Western History Collection*

"Finest Hotel in the West," the Albany entered the competition in 1885 and the Metropole (now part of the Cosmopolitan) opened for business in 1891. Others came and are now long forgotten; Inter-ocean, Planters' House, Alvord House, the American, the Wentworth, and the tragic Gumry Hotel at 1725 Lawrence, which was destroyed by a boiler explosion and fire in August, 1895, resulting in 22 deaths.

Among the hostelries of the world, the Brown Palace continues today as one of the ranking members. Opened in August, 1892, it has never lost its position as the city's finest and its slogan "Where the World Registers" has been proven by the names on its register; royalty, presidents, and a long parade of those who want only the finest.

In 1903, both the Shirley and the Savoy, back to back at the corners of Broadway and 17th and Lincoln and 17th, opened in competition but were combined in 1919 as the Shirley-Savoy to survive until the early 1970's when finally razed to make way for a skyscraper.

After World War II, the auto oriented society realized the advantages of the motel; ample parking, fast service, swimming pool out back, and close access to the interstate highway. Across the nation and in the Denver area, hotel building was replaced by motel building or, as along the fringe of downtown, several hotel-motel facilities which combine the two concepts.

The most recent hotel construction, and perhaps the last in Denver of the traditional style, took place in the late 1950's when the Brown

Palace West was added across Tremont Place to give the facility additional guest rooms as well as a beautiful new ball room, and with the construction of the Denver Hilton on most of the block bounded by 15th and 16th Streets, Court Place and Cleveland Place. The Hilton, while of modern design, was designed to blend well with the area's architecture and has provided much needed space to lure large conventions and has gained a place as one of the fine hotels of the area.

THE LABOR MOVEMENT

As business has grown, so has the desire of working men and women to better their lot in life as employees. While Denver can not be termed an industrial city and has thus not been one of the stronger areas for organized labor unions, the city's union history began almost with the arrival of the first settlers.

On April 20, 1860, a group of workers at the Rocky Mountain News organized what continues today as Local No. 49 of the International Typographical Union; it was the first labor union in the Rocky Mountain West. Among the other early unions were Local No. 3 of the Journeymen Tailors of America, formed in 1871, and the Cigarmakers Local Union No. 129 which dates to 1884. Most of the earlier unions were organized among workers in the crafts and trade skills and by 1882, enough locals had been formed to permit the organization of the Denver Trades and Labor Assembly which today continues as the Denver Area Labor Federation.

In more recent times, the labor movement has found considerable success in organizing workers in various levels of government, including public school teachers, and thus today the labor movement includes a wide range of men and women from many trades and professions who have found it desirable to join together for mutual benefit.

Sam Mayer's "Diamond Palace" at 1638 Larimer Street, was typical of countless businesses in downtown Denver at the turn of the century. The firm continues in business in the 1970's.—*Denver Public Library Western History Collection*

Business Hub of the West

Typical of turn of the century businesses were the A. Jacobs & Co. clothing store (above) and the A. T. Lewis & Son Dry Goods Co. whose advertisement (above-right) appeared in 1904. The Lewis store opened in 1888, and moved to 16th and Stout Streets in 1901. It is visible at the left of the Symes Building in the photo below. After the Lewis store went bankrupt in 1933, the location was used by the W. T. Grant variety store until the early 1970's.

The original Symes Building was built at 16th and Champa Streets by George Symes in 1880, and for a short time housed the Federal District Court prior to opening of the Federal Building. The building burned in February, 1905, and was replaced that same year by the present Symes Building, seen below when it was new. In this scene, the Fontius Shoe Company occupies most of the first floor but today that space, along with the basement and the entire half block along Champa to 15th Street, is occupied by the F. W. Woolworth variety store.—*Above, State Historical Society Collection; right and below, Denver Public Library Western History Collection; advertisement, Gene C. McKeever Collection*

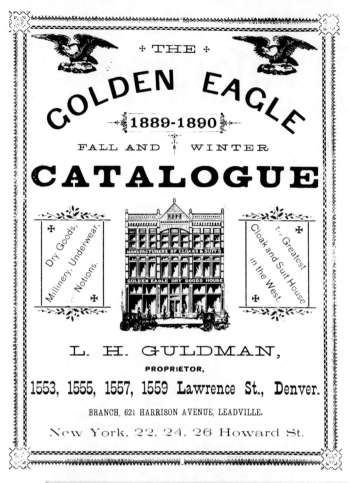

+ THE +
GOLDEN EAGLE
1889-1890
FALL AND WINTER
CATALOGUE

Dry Goods, Millinery, Underwear, Notions.

MANUFACTURERS OF CLOAKS & SUITS
GOLDEN EAGLE DRY GOODS HOUSE

The Greatest Cloak and Suit House in the West

L. H. GULDMAN,
PROPRIETOR,
1553, 1555, 1557, 1559 Lawrence St., Denver.

BRANCH, 621 HARRISON AVENUE, LEADVILLE.

New York, 22, 24, 26 Howard St.

To many older Denverites, the Golden Eagle is the city's best remembered department store. Over the years, the store occupied three different locations in the 1500 block of Lawrence Street, opening in 1879, in the Denver Times Building, a few years later moving to mid-block, and in the early 1890's moving to the large building seen below, at the corner of 16th Street. The store had a fleet of delivery trucks, and also developed a mail order business and operated a branch store for a time in Leadville. The company went out of business in the early 1940's, and its building was occupied by the Miller Western Wear Company until razed in 1971 as part of an urban renewal project.—*All, Denver Public Library, Western History Collection*

Business Hub of the West

John J. Joslin, a Vermont businessman, moved to Denver in 1872, and in May, 1873, purchased the "New York Store" at 15th and Larimer Streets which he opened as the Joslin Dry Goods Company. In 1880, he moved the business to 16th and Lawrence Streets and in 1889, moved to the store's present building (right) at 16th and Curtis Streets. For a short time, the late J. C. Penney was a clerk in Joslin's prior to beginning his own merchandising empire. In 1915, Joslin sold his interest in the store but remained as the company president until his death on January 1, 1926, at the age of 96.—*Both, State Historical Society of Colorado*

David May came to Leadville seeking a better climate for his health, and in 1877, he began selling dry goods and clothing from a tent store. Regaining his health and with a bustling business, he moved to Denver in 1888, and purchased a store at 15th and Larimer Streets which he operated until 1906, when he moved to the May Company Building on the corner of 16th and Champa Streets. This building, seen on the right, along with later additions on Champa and Curtis Streets, served the firm until July, 1958, when after purchasing the Daniels and Fisher Store, they moved to their new building at Court House Square (far right) and became known as the May-D&F Store.—*Far right, Tom Masamori, courtesy May-D&F Store; others, Denver Public Library, Western History Collection*

NEUSTETERS

In July, 1911, Meyer and Max Neusteter opened a new women's clothing store on 16th Street just beyond the Denver Dry Goods store, in mid-block between California and Stout Streets. In 1924, the present building, seen on the right, was constructed on the corner of 16th and Stout Streets and included the earlier building. Max Neusteter died in 1925, and in 1946, Meyer Neusteter's son, Myron, assumed control of the firm.—*Both, Denver Public Library, Western History Collection*

MAY-▱-D&F

McNamara Dry Goods Co.

**Best Material and Elegant Finish,
LADIES' MUSLIN UNDERWEAR,
Cor. Sixteenth and California Streets.**

The Denver Dry Goods Company had its start in 1886, as the McNamara Dry Goods Company at 15th and Larimer Streets in the Granite Building. By 1889, the firm had moved to a new building at 16th and California Streets, on the site of a once popular skating rink. The panic of 1893, forced the sale of the store and it was purchased by Dennis Sheedy and Charles Kountze. In 1894, they renamed the store the Denver Dry Goods Company and with business prospering, they added a fourth floor in 1900. In 1905, a six story building was constructed at 15th and California Streets, as seen in the 1910 photo above, giving the store the "longest department store isle in America." The building was completed in 1924, with the addition of a fifth floor on the 16th Street building. The "Denver" was a pioneer in the use of delivery trucks; one of their fleet of 1900 White Trucks is seen on the right.

A tradition among Denverites for three quarters of a century has been to eat lunch at the Denver Tea Room. Located in several different parts of the building in its early years, the Tea Room opened at its present fifth floor location (below) on November 28, 1924. While for a time the restaurant served three meals a day, in recent years it has confined its efforts to serving lunch to an average of 1,200 persons a day. With a seating of 600, it is one of the city's largest restaurants and is very unusual in its continued policy of preparing all food in its own kitchen and from scratch; this includes even salad dressings and ice cream.—*Below, Mrs. Virginia McMahon, Denver Dry Goods Company; others, Denver Public Library, Western History Collection*

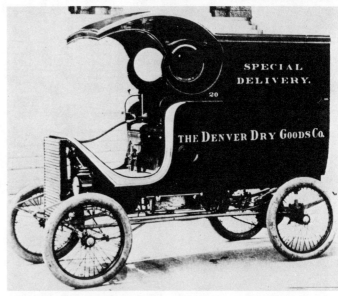

Montgomery Ward opened its first Denver store in 1926, at 1730 Champa Street, but in 1929, moved to a large new store and mail order warehouse (top photo) on South Broadway and Virginia Avenue. The firm marked its 100th Anniversary in 1972.

The stores whose advertisements appear below are but a few of the best remembered of the many that have helped to make Denver the business center of the Intermountain West.

The Cherry Creek Shopping Center, the area's first, is seen above soon after opening in 1953. It was soon followed by University Hills Center in 1955, and by Lakeside Center in 1956. The expansion of suburban neighborhoods has brought a combined growth of such shopping centers.—*Top. Univ. of Colo. Historical Colls.; above, D.P.L., Western History Coll.*

THE DANIELS AND FISHER STORES CO.

In 1864, William B. Daniels (below-center) and his partner, J. M. Eckart opened a small dry goods and general merchandise store at 15th and Larimer Streets. Within a few years they opened a second store at 390 Larimer Street but in 1872, Eckart sold his interest to William M. Fisher (below-left) and thus began the era of the Daniels and Fisher store. In 1875, the firm decided to move to a two story building at 16th and Lawrence Streets and also sold the store at 390 Larimer Street. As business continued to grow, it became necessary to rebuild the two story building and by 1894, a third and fourth floor had been added with a fifth following soon after, resulting in the store seen above, displaying what was said to be the largest U. S. flag ever made. With the death of William B. Daniels on December 25, 1891, his son,

Major William Cooke Daniels (below-right) became the partner to Fisher, but with Fisher's death on April 7, 1897, Major Daniels obtained full ownership of the business, and set out to build a larger and finer store which would also give Denver a landmark. During his travels, Daniels had come to admire the Campanile in Venice and this became the inspiration for the tower and store building at 16th and Arapahoe Streets, seen above while under construction in 1910, and completed in 1912. Following Major Daniels' death in 1918, the store had several owners until acquired by William Zeckendorf who sold it to Younker Brothers of Des Moines who in turn sold to the May Company, resulting in formation of the May-D&F Store.—*Below center, State Hist. Society of Colo.; others, D.P.L., Western History Coll.*

THE DANIELS AND FISHER TOWER

Inspired by the Campanile of Venice, has an observation balcony, the highest viewpoint in Denver, which affords a magnificent panoramic view of over 200 miles of the Rocky Mountain Range. It's 375 ft. from the street to the top of flagpole.

DENVER, the "QUEEN CITY of the PLAINS"...the "GATEWAY to the WEST"

CARL SANDELL

Carl Sandell, a giant of a man at 7 foot 3 inches tall, posed for his picture on March 26, 1948, with the tower in the background that was so closely associated with his life. Carl came to D & F's in 1910, and when the tower opened in 1912, he became the "Special Officer." Much more than a doorman, he was himself a landmark to half a century of Denverites. When the store moved to Court House Square in 1958, Carl went along but in 1961, he retired with 51 years of service. He died on May 8, 1965, at the age of 75.

Above is seen a souvenir ticket to the observation tower; below is an early D & F delivery wagon.—*Right, May-D&F Store; below, State Hist. Society of Colo.; above, Authors' Coll.*

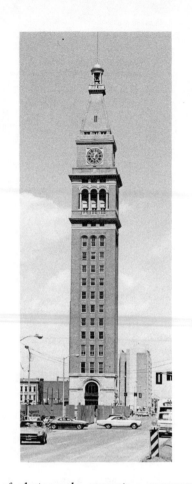

This series of photographs presents a panorama of the Daniels and Fisher Store in about 1910. From upper left to lower right: the main floor center shopping aisle; the crystal and chinaware department, displaying fine pieces from around the world; ladies wear, with the finest fashions of the era; the "tube room" which was connected to all parts of the store by means of the pneumatic tube system; the main dining room with fresh carnations on every table; and the gourmet grocery department, displaying everything from prize sides of beef to imported delicacies.—*All, Denver Public Library, Western History Collection*

THE FUTURE?

After the merger of the Daniels and Fisher Store into the new May-D&F store in the summer of 1958, the old building was renamed the Tower Merchandise Mart. By the fall of 1965, the number of tenants had dropped to a point that the decision was made to close the entire building on October 1, 1965. Pat Oliphant, Denver Post cartoonist, sensed the impending doom that overshadowed the future of Denver's beloved landmark, the D & F Tower. His cartoon (above) of September 20, 1965, shocked and enraged many Denverites and brought an immediate public outcry to save the tower. At almost the same time, William S. Pierson, owner of radio station KBPI-FM, announced that he would continue to maintain his radio antenna on the top of the tower and would also hand wind the tower clock. Pierson and his employees were forced to climb the tower stairs since the elevators no longer operated, but his determination helped to gain widespread support to save the tower. In 1971, the remainder of the D & F Building was torn down, and the tower stood alone (upper right, page 174) but with a bright new future. The Skyline National Bank and several other tenants hope to move into the tower by 1973, and the structure may well become the jewel of the newly revitalized lower downtown area.—*Photo, Ronald C. Hill; Editorial cartoon by Pat Oliphant, Copyright by the Denver Post and reprinted with permission of the Los Angeles Times Syndicate*

DENVER'S SMELTERS

Denver has had three major smelters, the first of which was the Argo Smelter of the Boston and Colorado Company. The plant, seen in these three photos, began in Blackhawk but moved to Denver in 1878, and located at a point just to the north of the interchange of Highways I-25 and I-70. The men on the left are posed with the first silver bars produced by the smelter. As the state's gold and silver mining boom waned, so did the smelter business and the Argo Smelter was closed prior to World War I.

The Globe Smelter (upper right) began as the Holden Smelter in 1885, but after purchase by a group of Denver businessmen headed by Dennis Sheedy, the plant was enlarged and renamed the Globe Smelter in 1889. Located at 51st Avenue and Pearl Street, the plant is now used to produce cadmium and is a part of the American Smelting and Refining Company which was formed in 1899 by a merger of several smelters including the Globe and the Omaha and Grant Smelter.

Both the towns of Argo and Globeville took their names from the smelters which attracted the workers to settle in the area.—*Upper right, First Federal Savings Collection; others, State Historical Society of Colorado*

"The Haunted House of North Washington." In 1873, John B. Hindry built a fine home at 5500 North Washington Street, a short distance from the smelters. The house was surrounded by fine trees and guarded by massive stone lions at the door. The gasses and vapors from the smelters are believed to have caused the trees to die and after Hindry left Denver the house had several owners including the Bomareto family which purchased it in 1921. By the mid-1950's, the house appeared as seen here, and on July 15, 1962, the "Haunted House" was destroyed by fire.

The office of the Herald Mines Company in Room 405 of the Mining Exchange Building, is seen below in 1909. It was typical of numerous offices of that era. —*Left, Denver Public Library, Western History Collection; below, State Historical Society of Colorado*

The Omaha & Grant Smelter was built in 1883, on the east bank of the Platte River, a short distance southwest of the present Denver Coliseum (Stockyards Stadium). The company resulted from a merger of the Grant Smelter which had operated in Leadville from 1878 until destroyed by fire in 1882, and the Omaha Smelter at Omaha, Nebraska. Between 1883 and 1900, the smelter produced approximately $130 million dollars worth of gold, silver, copper and lead. In 1892, the company built its towering stack which remained a Denver landmark for almost 60 years. Looming 352 feet high on the skyline, it contained over 10 million bricks, weighed 7000 tons and was built in 199 days at a cost of $5000. In 1899, the Omaha & Grant Smelter, along with the Globe Smelter and others around the nation, became part of the American Smelting and Refining Company which continued to operate the plant until 1902. In later years numerous suggestions were made for using or disposing of the stack, including creation of a park. However, the presence of cracks led to rumors about the unsafe structure of the stack and caused officials to order its removal and on February 25, 1950, the stack was toppled while a crowd of thousands watched the action. The plant is seen at left, in the mid-1890's, when in full operation. The two photos below catch the dramatic moment when the stack was ripped apart by massive explosions.—*All, Denver Public Library, Western History Collection*

Coal was the major fuel for home heating and industrial uses until the natural gas lines reached the city in 1928. Numerous companies supplied coal, much of which was mined north of Denver and elsewhere in Colorado. In recent years the coal business has been given new life with the demand for vast quantities for electric generating plants.

Colorado's first oil field was developed near Florence in 1862, but it was not until the 1920's, that the state's oil boom got under way. An early tanker of the Continental Oil Company (Conoco) is seen at the left, while the Oil Exchange and Board of Trade is shown below in the Albany Hotel in the mid-1920's.—*Photos, Denver Public Library, Western History Collection; advertisements, Authors' Collection*

OIL EXCHANGE AND BOARD OF TRADE
ALBANY HOTEL
Denver's first Oil Exchange that has made

Denver's first stockyard, known as the Bull's Head Corral, was located near the present Union Station in 1865. The stockyards were later briefly located along Cherry Creek near 2nd Avenue and Broadway, then for a time at 35th and Wazee Streets. In 1881, the Denver Union Stockyards were located at their present site to the northeast of downtown and in 1916, the Livestock Exchange Building, seen above in about 1920, was built at 47th Avenue and Lafayette Street.

Denver's first "City Market" opened in 1883, at 23rd and California Streets but was replaced in 1915, by the larger facility, seen below, which extended from Curtis to California Streets along the southwest bank of Cherry Creek. By 1938, however, it had deteriorated to the point that the city decided to replace the facility and two new markets were built by the railroads serving the city; the Wazee Market extending between 9th and 13th Streets along Wazee, and the Denargo Market at 29th Street and Broadway.—*Above, State Historical Society of Colo.; below, D.P.L., Western History Collection*

Long before the super market was even dreamed of, Denver was served by a host of small grocery stores. One of the most prominent of these was Birks Cornforth's Grocery Store which opened in 1863, and is seen on the left when located at 205 15th Street. The store later moved to much larger quarters at 1714-1720 Lawrence Street, where the interior view (below) was taken in the late 1880's. The advertisement above appeared in the 1889 Denver City Directory.—*Photos, State Historical Society of Colorado*

Typical of the city's many bakeries was the Old Homestead Company. One of its last horse drawn delivery wagons is seen above, shortly before being replaced by a modern truck. The 1911 advertisement for "Twin Scotch Bread" shows the plant located near West 27th Avenue and Clay Street where it continued to operate until the mid-1960's.

In 1923, Mr. and Mrs. Russell Stover began to sell hand-dipped chocolates which they made in their home at 960 Detroit Street. By 1929, their candy was being sold in this shop at No. 7 Broadway.—*All, Denver Public Library, Western History Collection*

THE
MILK
MAN

CARLSON-FRINK Denver's Finest DAIRY FOODS

Dairies are vital to the city's existence and two of Denver's dairies are seen here. The Windsor Dairy's motto was "Honest Milk from Clean Cows." Their bottling room is seen on the left while above is displayed a turn of the century milk truck. The dairy is still operated but under the Meadow Gold name. The Bredan Creamery, especially famous for their butter, is seen below at Broadway and Mississippi Avenue in "Little Holland." Another of the well remembered dairies was Carlson-Frink, located at 1200 13th Street, which is now operated as the Sinton Dairy.—*All, Denver Public Library, Western History Collection*

In December, 1859, James Endlich established a small brewery at 10th and Larimer Streets. The following year he sold it to John Good who enlarged and renamed the plant after the famous Tivoli Gardens in Copenhagen. In 1901, Tivoli merged with the Union Brewing Company to form Tivoli-Union Brewery and the plant, seen above in the 1890's, continued in operation until 1969, when its last product was the popular Denver Beer. The plant remains, but its future is uncertain as it sits in the midst of the Auraria Urban Renewal Project. The bottling room is seen below (left) in the 1930's, while below, an historic Tivoli beer wagon is displayed in recent years. For a time, Tivoli was operated under the name Milwaukee Brewery as seen in the advertisement from the 1900 Denver City Directory.

Philip Zang worked for the Tivoli Brewery, but went on to establish his own plant at 7th Street and the Platte River, as seen in this 1889 advertisement.—*Lower left, State Historical Society of Colorado; others, Denver Public Library Collection*

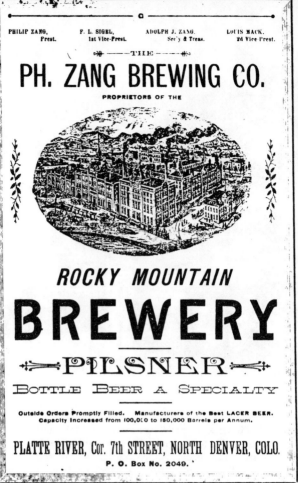

In 1873, Adolph Coors selected Golden as the location to establish his Coors Brewery. Now in its 99th year at the same site, the plant is among the nation's largest and in the midst of a continual expansion program. During prohibition the company produced "near beer" and malted milk, as advertised in the mid-1920's scene below; malted milk production was dropped in 1956, allowing full attention to be given to beer production. The plant is seen at lower left, in 1886, with Golden in the background to the north.—*All, Adolph Coors Company*

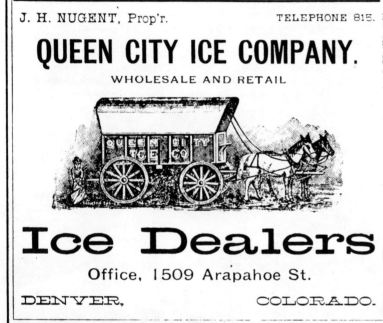
The Empire Bottling Company (above) at 17th and Platte Streets, is ready to quench the city's thirst with three wagons of birch beer, ginger ale, and assorted other beverages. The giant bottle on the roof is a surprising style of advertising for 1910.

Ice was a daily necessity and was supplied to homes and businesses by a number of firms including the Queen City Ice Company.

A popular product at the turn of the century was Cudahy's "Rex" Extract of Beef, being displayed in this photo at the Humphrey and Brinker grocery store at 1640 California Street, on May 8, 1902.

In 1886, Max Kuner started the Kuner Pickle Company which has grown into one of the areas major canning firms. This unusual display truck appeared on Denver streets in the mid-1920's.—*Lower left, State Historical Society of Colorado; others, Denver Public Library, Western History Collection*

The Barteldes Seed Company began in Kansas in the 1860's and entered the Denver market in 1885. Their store at 1521 15th Street is seen above, in 1895. The company is still in the seed business in Denver.

"Denver Mud" was a cosmetic preparation of great popularity in the area for many years, gradually fading from the market by World War II. First appearing in 1891, the company expanded into a new store at 425 Lincoln Street in 1928, when their "Lady Mud" beauty mask was at the peak of its sales appeal. In this photo, the company had just purchased a new truck from the Swenson Auto Company.

Typical of downtown shoe stores was this shop of the Edwin C. Burt Company. The photo probably dates to about 1900.—*Above, State Historical Society of Colorado; others, Denver Public Library, Western History Collection*

Denver's largest industrial plant, the Gates Rubber Company, traces its start to October, 1911, when Charles C. Gates purchased a small business, the Colorado Tire and Leather Company, at 1025 Broadway. Gates is seen here with his first employee, Paul Steel (right), in front of the shop which they shared with the Jonas Brothers Taxidermy business (Jonas Brothers remains in business in the same block as a furrier). Their first product, the "Durable Tread," was a band of steel studded leather designed to be placed around a tire to provide longer wear. The scrap pieces of leather were used to produce harness, but soon rubber was used and resulted in an improved product, the "Gates Half-Sole." In 1921, the company began to produce tires and later pioneered the V-Belt fan belt. Renamed the International Rubber Company, in 1914, it moved to 1320 Acoma Street and in 1919, became the Gates Rubber Company and moved to its present plant at 999 South Broadway, seen below in the mid-1930's. In 1913, the Ford Motor Company (bottom) built an assembly plant opposite where the Gates plant was later located. Ford closed its Denver operation and sold the plant to Gates in 1921, and it continues in use today.—*Bottom, University of Colo. Hist. Coll.; others, D.P.L. Coll.*

In 1910, Jesse Shwayder began a luggage manufacturing business which has grown into the Samsonite Corporation. An early plant of the Shwayder Trunk Company is seen above, at Platte Street, viewed from the 16th Street Viaduct in about 1919. The firm moved in 1923, to South Broadway (below) opposite the Gates plant and remained there until 1966, when a new facility was opened in Montbello. The trunk assembly line is seen in the bottom photo during the late 1920's. In 1916, the photo at the upper right was taken for an advertisement and proved so popular in displaying the strength of Shwayder luggage, that it was used as a trademark for many years. Standing on the trunk, from left to right, are Isaac Shwayder, the father, and Sol, Jesse, Ben and Maurice; a fifth brother Mark, joined the firm in 1923.—*Upper left, Authors' Coll.; upper right, Samsonite Corporation; others, D.P.L., Western History Coll.*

Three almost forgotten industrial plants are seen. The Overland Cotton Mill (top) was built at Evans Avenue and South Mariposa Street in 1890, but closed in the early 1900's. The building remains in use as a warehouse, although partially destroyed by fire in 1942. The Rocky Mountain Paper Company (center) was built at 1000 West Louisiana Avenue in 1883, continuing in operation for a number of years, and was later known as the Continental Paper Products Company. The Griffin Wheel Works, located at Evans Avenue and South Navajo Street, is seen below about World War I. The company, which continues to supply railroad wheels and brake shoes from other locations, closed its Denver plant in the late 1960's.—*Above, State Historical Society of Colo.; others, D.P.L., Western History Coll.*

The Denver Chamber of Commerce Building (right) was opened in 1885, at 14th and Lawrence Streets. In later years it served as a resident hotel until razed in September, 1967, to make way for a parking lot.

The Tabor Block, a project of Horace Tabor, was completed in late 1879, on the corner of 16th and Larimer Streets. Built at a cost of almost $300,000, it boasted the first elevator in the city, and was the first building over four stories in height. A later owner changed the name to the Nassau Building but Denverites knew it as the Tabor Block until its demise in mid-1972, as part of the lower downtown urban renewal project.—*Top, State Historical Society of Colorado; below, 1st Federal Savings Collection*

PIONEER BANKING

Clark, Gruber & Company opened their bank and mint (left) at McGaa and G Streets (16th and Market) in late July, 1860, with coinage starting in August and continuing for two years, eventually ending with the purchase of its equipment by the U.S. Treasury Department. In 1864, Gruber left the business and the firm continued as Clark & Company, as seen in the listing from the Rocky Mountain News of August 5, 1864, at the right. The Kountze Brothers Bankers eventually developed into the Colorado National Bank, and Warren Hussey & Company later became the City National Bank, which in 1894, became part of the American National Bank. Clark & Company received its national bank charter and established the First National Bank of Denver on May 10, 1865.—*Left, State Historical Society of Colorado; advertisement, Rocky Mountain News, courtesy First National Bank of Denver*

In 1865, the new First National Bank Building was nearing completion when the photo above was taken at 15th and Blake Streets. A hundred years later the building remained in use by the Stores Equipment Company and plans call for its continued preservation. The third floor was added by the early 1870's and was the site for holding the Colorado Constitutional Convention, from December 20, 1875 until March 15, 1876.

The International Trust Building (far lower right) at 17th and California Streets is seen as it appeared about 1920. In 1958, the International Trust merged with the First National Bank and the building was refinished to become part of the present banking complex between California and Welton Streets. A typical turn of the century banking office is seen on the lower right, in the First National Bank.—*All, State Historical Society of Colorado*

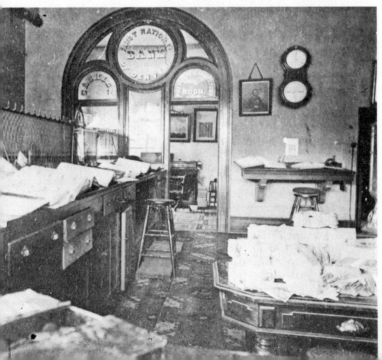

The Central Bank and Trust Company (center, above) is seen when its building at 15th and Arapahoe Streets was only a few years old. Opening in 1911, the bank continues at the same location. The firm traces its start to April 19, 1892, when it opened as the North Side Bank at Zuni Street and Dunkeld Place. In 1896, however, the bank moved downtown to 1032 Arapahoe Street, near its present building, and changed its name to the Central Savings Bank. A long time officer of the bank, Elwood Brooks, was honored by the naming of the Brooks Towers development, which was undertaken by the bank in the mid-1960's, on the former site of the Mining Exchange Building. The People's Bank Building (right, above) at 16th and Arapahoe Streets was opened in 1890, and served the dual operation of the People's Savings Bank and the People's National Bank, both of which closed soon after the panic of 1893. The structure was known in later years as the Interstate Trust Building and was demolished in the early 1970's.—Center, D.P.L., Western History Coll.; right, State Historical Society of Colo.

On January 1, 1959, the Denver National Bank (above) and the United States National Bank (above, left) merged and became the Denver United States National Bank.

For most of their years, the two banks were on opposite street corners or next to each other. The Denver National Bank opened on December 8, 1884, at 18th and Larimer Streets and in 1893, moved to the Cooper Building at 17th and Curtis Streets. In 1928 it moved to new quarters in the Ideal Cement Building at 17th and Champa Streets, where it remained until the merger. The United States National Bank opened in 1904, following the purchase of the Daniels Bank. The new bank was located in the Ernest & Cranmer Building at 17th and Curtis Streets for 4 years; it moved twice during the next 12 years, moving, finally, into the U.S. National Bank Building in 1921. It then constructed its own building at 17th and Stout Streets where it remained until 1956 when it moved to the new Mile High Center at 17th and Broadway. The old building is now occupied by the Guaranty Bank and Trust Company. Following the merger, additional space was constructed for the combined bank and in recent years the firm has become known as the United Bank of Denver.—*Both, United Bank of Denver*

The Colorado National Bank developed from the Kountze Brothers Bank which opened late in 1862, in the Cheesman Building at 15th and Blake Streets. In 1866, the Kountze Brothers received a charter to become the Colorado National Bank, and Charles Kountze remained active in the bank, as well as in other Denver businesses, until his death in 1911. The bank opened a new building at 17th and Larimer Streets in July, 1882, and moved to its present location at 17th and Champa Streets on September 1, 1915. The building, seen in the two photos on the left, was constructed of Colorado Yule marble. A third floor was added to the structure in the late 1960's.—*Both, State Historical Society of Colorado*

Until natural gas lines reached Denver in June, 1928, gas was manufactured in coal burning retort houses such as seen above, in the early 1920's. The building, now converted to other Public Service Company use, stands on 5th Street, with the Lawrence Street viaduct now at the left of the scene.

The interior view below, shows the ovens in the city's first gas plant, which opened at 18th and Wewatta Streets in 1871.

For three quarters of a century, from the late 1880's until 1964, huge gas storage tanks such as seen below, were familiar sights on the Denver skyline. The tanks were designed to store gas for peak periods of demand and were expandable, moving upward when filled, and dropping down as the gas was removed. A typical tank was 105 feet high, 112 feet in diameter, constructed of half inch steel plates, and could hold 750,000 cubic feet of gas. The tanks were no longer needed after the company developed underground storage at the abandoned Leyden coal mine, once used to supply coal for the Denver Tramway powerhouse.—*Lower left, Denver Public Library, Western History Collection; others, Public Service Company of Colorado*

GAS

&

ELECTRIC

Public Service Company of Colorado

The "electric era" spans 90 years, from the time of "Old Sally," (below) which when installed at 21st and Wewatta Streets in the spring of 1881, and was the first generating equipment west of the Missouri River, to the modern steam powered Arapahoe Generating Station (above), typical of several in the area. The Fort St. Vrain nuclear plant, north of Denver, is scheduled to open in 1973, and will be among the first such plants in the West. "Old Sally" is now preserved in front of the Valmont Generating Plant at Boulder. A scene that has been repeated since the first electric service began, is the job of pole installation, seen taking place in this photo of about 1920.—*All photos, Public Service Company of Colorado*

On November 10, 1910, the Gas and Electric Building opened with a dazzling display as 10,000 light bulbs illuminated the white finished structure. In 1962, the Public Service Company moved to a new building at 15th and Welton Streets but the old building at 15th and Champa Streets, renamed the Insurance Exchange Building, is still lit each evening. A wide array of appliances is displayed above in the 1920's scene in the Public Service's show room.—*Above, Public Service Company of Colorado; left, Denver Public Library, Western History Collection*

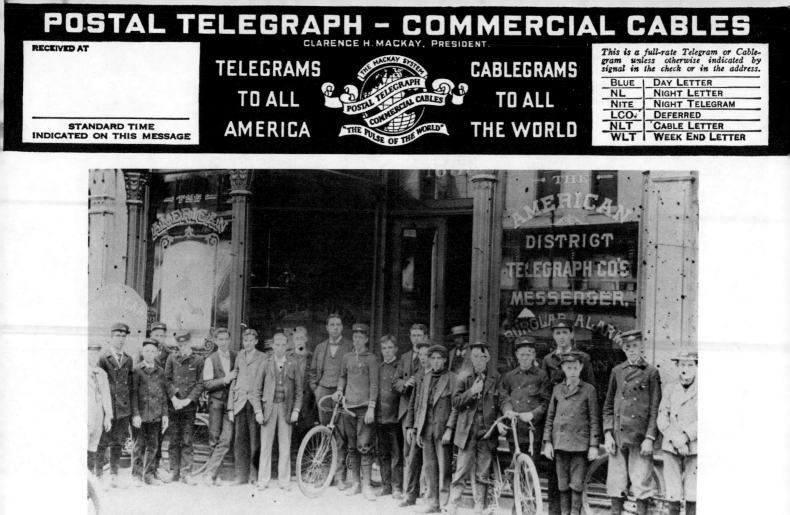

Prior to development of the telephone, the principal means of fast communication was by telegraph. Several companies competed for the business, including the Postal Telegraph and Cable Company, whose message blank is seen above, and the American District Telegraph Company, whose office force and delivery boys are posed in front of the firm's office at 1633 Lawrence Street in this mid-1890's photo. Eventually most of the nation's telegraph operations were merged into the still operating Western Union Company; however, American District continues to operate as the ADT Burglar Alarm Company, a service they were already advertising on their window in the photo.—*Photo, First Federal Savings Collection; message blank, Colorado Railroad Museum Collection*

Denver's first telephone system went into operation on February 26, 1879, but it was not until the turn of the century that telephones began to gain wide public acceptance. In 1903, the Colorado Telephone Company opened a new office building at 1421 Champa Street (right) and the site is still used by Mountain Bell, the successor company. On May 8, 1911, at 5:30 P.M., the first long distance call was placed between Denver and New York City. Company President E. B. Field is seen below, on the phone, while telegraphers simultaneously describe the activity over their lines. The 2,066 mile call cost $11.25 for three minutes but despite the high cost, the long distance operators were soon kept busy as in the 1914 photo on the lower left.—*Upper right and lower left, State Historical Society of Colorado; others, Denver Public Library, Western History Collection*

Prior to the development of dial equipment, every phone call was placed through an operator, requiring long rows of girls to work the switchboards, as seen in this 1926 photo on the right. It soon became necessary to construct a large building to house the rapidly expanding phone system and in May, 1927, machines (above) began work on the new Telephone Building at 14th and Curtis Streets. The building, still in use, was completed in 1929, and crowds turned out for guided tours (below) of the fine new facility, eager to learn something of the "miracle" of the telephone.—*All, State Historical Society of Colorado*

DENVER'S HOSTELRIES

The Palmer House, in the 1600 block of Larimer Street, is seen (right) in 1907. The U.S. Courts occupied the second floor between 1876 and 1884. By the early 1970's, every building in the block had been removed for urban renewal.

Within eighteen months, Denver experienced two hotel tragedies. On March 23, 1894, the St. James Hotel, on the south side of the 1500 block of Curtis Street, burned and took the lives of four firemen, including three from the Negro Company and their white captain. In the 1881 photo above, the tallest building is the St. James, while to the left is the Wentworth House, built in 1871, and by then combined with the St. James. On Sunday evening, August 18, 1895, disaster struck the Gumry Hotel at 1725 Lawrence Street. Engineer Helmuth Loescher, working a sixteen hour shift, left his boiler room for a quick trip to a nearby saloon. In his absence the boiler exploded and a fire quickly broke out in the wreckage, taking 22 lives, including owners Peter Gumry and Robert Greiner. It was later found that the city boiler inspector had passed the boiler without an inspection.—*All, State Historical Society of Colorado*

Business Hub of the West

Displayed here are three of Denver's well known hotels, only one of which is still extant. The Inter-Ocean (above), built by Barney L. Ford, a prominent Negro businessman, opened on October 29, 1873, at the corner of 16th and Blake Streets with accommodations for 132 guests. By the start of the 20th Century the hotel began to gradually deteriorate and for many years was a skid row flop house, prior to being razed in the early 1970's.

The Oxford Hotel, across from Union Station, at 17th and Wazee Streets, opened on October 3, 1891, and remains quite prosperous. The hotel's beautiful stained glass dining room windows have been preserved and new management is taking advantage of the Oxford's rich history by retaining its western aura. The advertisement on the right, appeared in the Railroad Red Book of April, 1907.—*Above, Denver Public Library, Western History Collection; below, State Historical Society of Colorado*

THE OXFORD HOTEL

European Plan $1 and $2 Per Day

Restaurant and Cafe in Connection

One Block From Union Depot. FIRE-PROOF DENVER, COLO.

The Grand Central Hotel opened at 17th and Lawrence Streets in 1872. The hotel was sold in 1882, and after being enlarged and remodeled, it was renamed the Markham Hotel, after co-owner V. D. Markham. For a number of years the building housed the offices of the Rocky Mountain News. In later years renamed the Miller Hotel, it was destroyed by fire on February 8, 1969.

THE WINDSOR HOTEL

The Windsor, at 18th and Larimer Streets, opened on June 23, 1880, and was without a doubt, the finest hotel in the Mountain West. Built by an English firm under the direction of James Duff, who was also involved in constructing the Duff Block and the Barclay Block, the exterior featured sandstone from the Fort Collins area and gray stone from near Castle Rock. Shortly before being completed, the hotel was sold to a firm which included Horace Tabor, William Bush and Charles Hall. The scene below dates to the mid-1880's, while above is a view of the dining room with the staff of waiters, impeccably dressed, ready to serve from the menu of gourmet delights. In the mid-1950's, the public began to find new interest in the fine old establishment and it once again had crowds in its dining room and at the Saturday evening melodramas; regardless, its owners closed the hotel early in 1958 and in November, 1959, it was sacrificed for a parking lot. —*Both, State Hist. Society of Colo.*

THE COSMOPOLITAN HOTEL

The Cosmopolitan, at 18th Avenue and Broadway, was built in 1926, and combined with the Metropole Hotel, on the right in the photo below; it continues as part of the Cosmopolitan although plans call for its removal by 1974. The Metropole was built in 1890, and included the Broadway Theater, which was removed in early 1955. The Broadway, as well as the Metropole, were projects of William Bush, noted Denver hotelman. —*McClure Photo, Denver Public Library, Western History Collection*

The Albany Hotel is seen above, at 17th and Stout Streets, soon after it opened in July, 1885. In 1893, the building was remodeled and in the late 1930's was given major rebuilding. The interior view, below, is of the main lobby and probably dates to the late 1890's. A large addition was built on Stout Street, providing almost double the space of the original hotel and is seen on the left, about 1925. The main building was hit by a large fire on September 2, 1962, and as a result was extensively remodeled and thus the Albany is one of Denver's major downtown hotels in the 1970's.—*All, State Historical Society of Colorado*

In 1888, Henry C. Brown, a prominent Denver real estate developer, decided to build a hotel on a triangle of land which he owned, between Broadway, Tremont and 17th Streets. He was joined in the project by Maxcy Tabor, son of Horace Tabor, and by Bill Bush who had gained fame as manager of the Windsor Hotel. The exterior was constructed of Colorado red granite and Arizona sandstone, while terra cotta blocks were used for much of the interior construction, and along with the steel framework, seen on the lower left from the cover of Scientific American magazine, the building was one of the first in America to be fireproof. The final cost of the hotel was two million dollars and it opened on August 12, 1892. The "Brown" has always been known for its fine dining facilities, and one of the restaurants is seen above, probably in the 1920's. The view on the lower right, includes the famed rotunda, as seen from the lobby. On April 25, 1959, the Brown Palace Tower was opened across Tremont Street, connected by a bridge, and added 300 rooms to the hotel, as well as a magnificent new ballroom. —*Lower left, State Hist. Society of Colo.; others, D.P.L., Western History Coll.*

A panorama of Denver hotel history is presented here, covering the first 70 years of the 20th Century. The Adams Hotel, at 18th and Welton Streets, was opened in 1901, and is especially remembered for its beautiful domed dining room. In 1969, the Adams closed and was razed soon after. The Hotel Kenmark, at 17th and Welton Streets, was originally known as the "Hotel Kaiserhof," but due to anti-German feeling in World War I, the name was changed in time for this 1917 advertisement. The Shirley Hotel opened in 1903, followed by the Savoy in 1904; both faced on 17th Avenue, the Shirley at Lincoln and the Savoy at Broadway. In 1919, the two merged and became the Shirley-Savoy Hotel, and while the Shirley building was removed in the early 1960's, the Savoy section continued as a fine hotel until January 30, 1970, being razed a short time later. When the Park Lane (right) opened in 1928, it was considered one of the finest hotels in the West. Its location away from downtown and from major freeways caused business to fade and early in 1966, the hotel closed and was removed to make way for the Park Lane Apartments.—*Right and center, State Historical Society of Colorado; top, Denver Public Library, Western History Collection*

THE DENVER HILTON

Denver's newest hotel, and perhaps the last to be built in the grand style of downtown hostelries, is the Denver Hilton. Located on most of the block bounded by 15th and 16th Streets, Court and Cleveland Places, it opened in the spring of 1960, and has proved especially popular with large conventions and tour groups because of its large size and extensive facilities.—*Art Bilsten, courtesy Denver Hilton Hotel*

DELMONICO OF THE WEST

When Fred Charpiot opened his hotel and restaurant, he decided to use the name of a famous eastern establishment and thus pioneer Denver received one of its first fine eating houses, Delmonico of the West, seen below near 16th and Larimer Streets in the late 1870's. Note the prices on the 1878 meal check.—*Both, State Historical Society of Colorado*

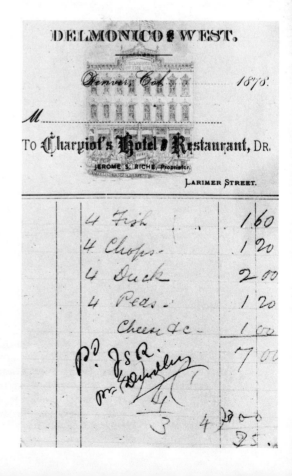

DELMONICO OF WEST,

Denver Col 1878:

M ....

To Charpiot's Hotel & Restaurant, DR.

JEROME S. RICHE, Proprietor.

LARIMER STREET.

4 Fish	1 60
4 Chops	1 20
4 Duck	2 00
4 Peas	1 20
Cheese &c	1 00
P? JSR	7 00

The Manhattan Restaurant, at 1635 Larimer Street, was opened in May, 1896, by Englishman Richard E. Pinhorn and was one of the city's most popular eating houses for the next forty years. Especially famous was the Manhattan's charcoal steak dinner with potatoes, combination salad and French fried onions. When Pinhorn died in 1922, he willed the business to his employees who operated it until it closed in 1938. The restaurant was re-opened in July, 1941, but closed forever in May, 1947, and is seen above, with a "For Rent" sign in the window shortly after closing. The fountain with a bronze statue of Cupid seen in front of the store, was designed by Artist Paul Gregg and paid for by the employees as a memorial to Pinhorn. The fountain is now preserved in Larimer Square. In the summer of 1972, the building which housed the Manhattan was demolished as part of urban renewal.

Three long popular restaurants are remembered by their menus (below) dating from the mid-1930's. On the left, the New Edelweiss, at 1644 Glenarm Place, in the center, the Blue Parrot, at 1716 Broadway, and on the right, McVittie's "Old Heidelberg Inn" in Arvada, one of several McVittie's restaurants, the others being downtown. By the early 1950's, all of them had served their last meal and had been relegated to history.—*Photo, D.P.L., Western History Coll.; menus, coll. of John B. Kunz.*

Otto Paul Baur opened a small bakery and confectionary shop in 1870, at 16th and Lawrence Streets and it was here that he is said to have invented the ice cream soda. His business prospered and after purchasing another shop, known as Schueler's, he moved to a large new building at 1512 Curtis Street in 1891. Baur died in 1904, but the firm is still in business and today operates the 1512 Curtis Street location as the Fisherman's Cove restaurant.—*Photo, Denver Public Library, Western History Collection*

One of Denver's most fondly remembered restaurants is Pell's Fish and Oyster House, seen here at 524 16th Street, near Glenarm Place, a few years before it closed in 1937. George Pell opened his first restaurant in the 1500 block of Arapahoe Street in 1881, but early in the century moved to the 16th Street location where it was a favorite spot for seafood, as seen in these two photos. —*Both, Denver Public Library, Western History Collection*

In 1880, Professor Joseph Brinker opened his Collegiate Institute for young ladies and gentlemen at 1727 Tremont Place. After the school closed in 1889, the building became the Richelieu Hotel and in 1902, was converted to the Navarre Restaurant as seen in this 1910 era photo (right). The Navarre remains as a fine Denver restaurant.—*Denver Public Library, Western History Collection*

FOR THE COMMON GOOD

EDUCATION: PROFESSOR GOLDRICK BEGINS!

In the late summer of 1859, a smartly dressed Irish gentleman arrived in Denver and announced his intention to open what would be the city's first school. Professor Owen J. Goldrick attended an Irish university, came to the United States to teach for a time in Ohio and Missouri, and then drifted west to Denver. He was successful in attempts to raise funds for his school and, with about $250, he established himself in a cabin between Market and Larimer Streets on 12th Avenue.

On October 3, 1859, Goldrick opened his school with thirteen students. A description of the first class casually notes the racial balance. "Two of them were Indian half-breeds, and of the remaining eleven, two were Mexicans; leaving only nine of what were then considered here as white children."—*Smiley, Jerome, History of Denver*

This pioneer educational effort continued and showed gradual growth in spite of competition from several other schools. All of the early schools were privately financed since there were no public funds yet appropriated for education. On December 1, 1862, however, two school districts were established in Denver, the boundary being Cherry Creek. The state legislature made faint attempts to raise funds for education but throughout the 1860's, public schools remained very poorly financed. For example, the entire 1870 budget for the Arapahoe County schools, which included Denver at that time, was only $17,347.37 and was expected to serve an enrollment of 1,200.

The situation began to show improvement in the early 1870's and there began a period of rapid expansion in public education leading to the establishment of twelve school districts in Denver. Several of these districts also served suburban areas; the situation was anything but satisfactory, because of the difficulty of management and wasteful duplication of facilities.

In 1902, the entire City of Denver was organized into one school district, and the state legislature provided that any areas annexed to the city were to become part of the Denver Public Schools system. This law has given rise in recent years to numerous problems and widespread concern among parents and school officials alike, for it now poses a threat to the suburbs that they will lose control of their local schools if they annex to Denver.

Following the formation of the single Denver school district, the school population began a steady rise to 27,000 in 1905 and 30,000 by the start of World War I. Following the war, Denver began one of the most active periods of school construction. Between 1920 and 1931, three new high schools were constructed—East, South, and West—while during the same era most of the junior high schools were also built, including Byers, Morey, Skinner, Cole, Lake, Smiley, and Horace Mann. Prior to World War II, the enrollment passed 50,000, and while the war caused a halt in construction, the late 1940's brought a new period of building as a result of the post-war baby-boom and the general growth in the Denver area. Today, the city's school population seems to be leveling off around 95,000, and there is little reason to expect any future large increases, except through annexation, since little room remains for housing expansion within the city limits. School construction continues, however, at a fast pace in the Denver suburbs.

OWEN J. GOLDRICK
—*Denver Public Library, Western History Collection*

Many of the schools built before the turn of the century are now coming due for replacement and it is expected that within the next several years most, if not all of these, will be razed.

PAROCHIAL SCHOOLS OFFER AN ALTERNATIVE IN EDUCATION

Parochial education got its start in 1863, when Rev. Joseph P. Machebeuf, later to become the city's first Catholic Bishop, opened a school in Denver. He purchased the large home of William Clayton, located between 14th and 15th Streets on California Street, converted it into a school, and placed the facility in the charge and care of the Sisters of Loretto. The Sisters arrived in Denver on July 8, 1864, from Kentucky, responding to a call from Father Machebeuf, and opened their school as St. Mary's Academy on August 1st. From a beginning enrollment of twenty, the school quickly expanded until it became necessary to divide; the Academy continued in the role of providing grade school education while Loretto Heights College provided higher education for young women.

The Catholic schools enjoyed a period of rapid expansion and by the 1960's, enrollment surpassed 20,000. In recent years, however, the rapidly rising costs of school operation have forced the closing of some of these institutions and there is now considerable question as to their future role.

Other private and parochial schools also served the city, the Lutheran Schools being the largest of these, tracing their history to April, 1882, when classes were begun in St. John's Church. Today, the Lutheran schools provide grade and high school facilities to several thousand students.

The Catholic, Lutheran, and other private schools all must face the challenge of increasing costs and they may well undergo marked changes when and if the question of government aid to such schools is finally settled.

HIGHER EDUCATION COMES TO MILE-HIGH DENVER

The start of higher education can be dated with the founding of the Colorado Seminary,

Emerson School, built in 1884-85, at 1420 Ogden Street, is one of the oldest schools still in use in Denver. Note the sundial on the wall to the left of the door.
—*State Historical Society of Colorado*

forerunner of the University of Denver. An act of the Colorado Legislature provided for the institution to confer degrees and also granted it tax free status on its property. Heading the list of names on the incorporation papers was Governor John Evans and twenty seven other prominent citizens such as William Byers, John Chaffee, and C. A. Cook.

After raising funds from both the trustees and local citizenry, a building was erected at the corner of 14th and Arapahoe Streets and the pioneer school opened on November 16, 1864. The early years were troubled by a continuing lack of funds and for a time during the late 1860's and into the 1870's, operations were suspended. In 1879, however, the Methodist Episcopal Conference, who operated the school, appointed a new board and undertook a reorganization, naming John Evans as President. Evans donated to the school the original building at 14th and Arapahoe Streets which he had purchased when the school had lacked funds to retain it, and he also provided a cash donation as did Vice President J. W. Bailey.

In 1880, it was decided to organize the University of Denver which would offer a wider range of studies and toward this end, land was acquired on the southeastern edge of the city for construction of the University Park campus which remains in use today.

Loretto Heights College, originally the Loretto Academy, began with the decision to split the operation of St. Mary's Academy. The location of the college, high on a hill overlooking the southwestern part of the city, is among the most scenic in the area and was a farsighted

For the Common Good

choice for the time. The first building was constructed in 1890, and the campus remains at the same site.

While Loretto Heights undertook the education of young women, the need for a Catholic school for young men was met in 1887, by establishment of the College of the Sacred Heart. Located in north Denver, it traced its history to a beginning some years earlier at Morrison, Colorado. Long known as "the Jesuit College" it continues today as Regis College. While most of the area's schools have seen fast-paced expansion, Regis has limited its growth and retains the charm of a small college even in the 1970's.

Denver's other major university, Temple Buell, originally was known as Colorado Woman's College. Although the cornerstone was laid in 1890, operations had to await funding until 1909. The present name was taken recently to honor Denver businessman Temple Buell who made very substantial contributions to the school in the late 1960's.

A number of other educational institutions have served our city. Some are only memories, such as the long active Episcopal girls school, Wolfe Hall, and both Jarvis Hall and Matthews Hall, the remains of which are now part of the State Industrial School for Boys at Golden. New institutions have grown to meet changing educational needs; among these are the Parks School of Business and Barnes School of Commerce, both of which opened their doors in 1904. One of the most unusual schools in the Denver Public School System is the Emily Griffith Opportunity School which provides vocational training to adults. From 1916 until 1933, the school was under the principalship of Emily Griffith, and has served the needs of adults in search of additional education to enable them to find a place in the work world. While vocational schools are finding wide acceptance today, Opportunity School was a pioneer in this field.

THE GOSPEL COMES TO DENVER

There is some basis for dispute as to who should receive credit as the first clergyman to serve Denver. In 1739, the French explorer Father Mallett passed through the area but being an explorer he was not here for missionary purposes. Arriving with the Russell party in June, 1858, was Rev. John Beck, the Cherokee Baptist preacher who had helped to interest the Indians in coming West from Georgia. As in the case of Father Mallet, Rev. Beck did not come here to preach but instead to explore, this time to find gold. The honor of being the first clergyman to serve the pioneer residents of Auraria and Denver City belongs to Rev. George W. Fisher. He arrived from a Methodist Episcopal Church in western Missouri and gave his first sermon outdoors, late in the fall of 1858, at the corner of 11th and Wewatta Streets. Remaining through Denver's first winter, he held services in private homes since there were no actual church buildings in the city until 1860.

The next religious activity came with the arrival of Rev. Lewis Hamilton, a Presbyterian, who arrived in June, 1859, and like Rev. Fisher, conducted services for a time in private homes. The following year Rev. Hamilton moved into the Central City mining region. Then, at the request of General William Larimer, the Presbyterian Board of Home Missions sent Rev. A. T. Rankin in the summer of 1860; he delivered his first sermon on August 5, 1860. On Sunday, September 2nd, an organizational meeting of the pioneer congregation led to the establishment of the present Central Presbyterian Church.

With the arrival of two more Methodist Episcopal preachers, Rev. Jacob Adriance and Rev. William H. Goode, a formal organization was set in August of 1859 and eventually led to Trinity Methodist Church of today.

The Rocky Mountain News of November 3, 1859, carried notice of the first Sunday School to hold meetings in the cabin of Rev. Adriance and Rev. Fisher with Professor Owen J. Goldrick assisting. The meetings proved so popular, that it became necessary to move the Sunday School to the city's first Masonic Temple which was located in the 1300 block of 11th Street.

Denver's first Episcopal church was organized in January, 1860, and established St. John's Church in the Wilderness in 1862. The church continues today as St. John's Cathedral.

The Roman Catholic Church had been active early in southern Colorado and had established Our Lady of Guadalupe Church at Conejos on June 10, 1858. It became the fourth of the Christian Churches to organize in the Denver area but was the second to erect its own church building, the first having been built by the Methodists. In the spring of 1860, Bishop J. B. Miege reached the city and established his church in the home of a Mr. Guiraud at 15th and Market Streets. Work on the first Catholic Church began that fall and was spurred by the arrival of Bishop Joseph Machebeuf from New Mexico, where he had been the Vicar General for ten years. Arriving on October 29, 1860, he issued an appeal for funds and with a good response the church building was rushed to completion in time to hold Christmas services. The church, St. Mary's, held its first regular Sunday Mass the following week on December 30th, thus permitting the record to show this pioneer church at 15th and Stout Streets open in the year 1860. In later years, the church obtained land at Colfax Avenue and Logan Street and on October 27, 1912, dedication services were held for the beautiful new Immaculate Conception Cathedral at that location. The dedication was highlighted by the presence of Cardinal John Farley of New York and the new church received the papal blessing of Pope Pius X.

The first organization undertaken by the Baptists came in December, 1863, through the leadership of Rev. Walter McDowell Potter. After meeting in several temporary locations, a small structure was partially completed at 16th and Curtis Streets and for several years served the congregation being locally known as "the Baptist dugout" due to its being a basement simply roofed over. Organized officially on May 2, 1864, this pioneer Baptist Church continues today as the First Baptist Church of Denver.

In 1860, a small group of followers of the Jewish faith organized and in 1873, became the Congregation Emanuel. The following year, they constructed the Temple Emanuel at 19th and Curtis Streets, under the leadership of Rabbi Fleischer.

Other pioneer religious groups, while not having arrived in the very first months or years of the city's existence, nevertheless were not too far behind. The First Congregational Church was organized in the autumn of 1864, building their first house of worship at 15th and Curtis Streets in 1870; the activities of the Lutheran Church—Missouri Synod, dates to 1872; the Christian Church (Disciples of Christ) organized in 1875; the Seventh-Day Adventist Church was established in 1883; and the Unitarians date their

beginning to 1871. An often overlooked religious movement was the organization of Negro Churches including Zion Baptist dating to November 7, 1865, and following shortly, in 1868, was the African Methodist Episcopal Church.

Late comers included the first Mormon Church (Church of Jesus Christ of Latter Day Saints) which was organized in 1897, and the first of the Christian Science faith who first organized to meet in 1885.

One of the unusual religious undertakings in this area has been that of the Pillar of Fire Church, a conservative Protestant denomination, which early in the century purchased the short-lived Westminster University's buildings. Located at the crest of Belleview Hill in suburban Westminster, it remains a landmark visible throughout the Denver area. As part of its ministry, the Pillar of Fire Church established radio station KPOF and became a pioneer broadcaster in the area.

Jerome Smiley, in writing of the status of churches in 1900, for his famed "History of Denver," described the religious scene thus:

"Almost every religious sect, from the most orthodox to the most liberal; from the ancient and historic Catholic to that of the doctrine promulgated but yesterday; may be found organized in the city and its immediate suburbs."

No better words could describe the wide range of religious groups serving the city today. There is change underway, however, for many of the historic religious buildings of our pioneer years are now giving way to progress, especially those in the center city, and few will remain very far into the future unless steps are taken for their preservation.

REST IN PEACE—THE CEMETERIES

A walk through the older of the city's cemeteries is in fact a walk in history, for here are to be found the names of those who laid the very foundations for the city we now know.

In the winter of 1858-59, General Larimer selected an area, on what later became East 11th Avenue, as the first burial ground. This later was known as the City Cemetery as well as Prospect Hill and during the first fifteen years of the city's existence served as final resting place for many pioneers. The City Cemetery was not well de-

Mt. Cavalry, a Catholic cemetery, is seen above in about 1900, shortly before it closed and the bodies were removed to other cemeteries. The location, just west of Congress Park, is now the site of the Botanical Gardens. The view is to the northwest across Cheesman Park (already converted from the City Cemetery) with the Capitol Building on the left.—*Denver Public Library, Western History Collection*

signed, lacked landscaping, and was in a poor location in the midst of the expanding city. Thus, as other locations developed, it was closed in 1890, and eventually most of the bodies were removed and the land became Cheesman Park. Adjoining the City Cemetery were also small Catholic, and Jewish Cemeteries, both of which closed by the turn of the century and whose land became part of Congress Park.

Several other small cemeteries served the city in its early years, including the "Masonic Cemetery" which was located in north Denver at W. 30th Avenue and Vallejo Street, and the Jewish Mt. Nebo Cemetery, which opened in Aurora in 1873, and remains open a century later. However, it was not until 1876, that the first large scale, well planned and landscaped cemetery was organized in the Denver area. This was done by the Riverside Cemetery Association which purchased 250 acres along the Platte River on the northern edge of the city and developed a facility which is still in use. Today, Riverside offers the visitor a glimpse of the past, for most of the pioneer graves in the old City Cemetery and other of the early graveyards were moved here around the turn of the century. Presently only a few burials are made at Riverside but the grounds remain a tribute to the early planners.

Fairmount Cemetery was incorporated in 1890, and situated on 560 acres in what was at the time the far southeastern suburbs. It continues to be one of the principle burial grounds in the Denver area.

At almost the same time as Fairmount was being organized, Mt. Olivet Cemetery was under development by an association of the Catholic Churches of Denver and was located on some 200 acres in Jefferson County, east of Golden. Also, in Jefferson County, in what is today Wheat Ridge, Crown Hill Cemetery was opened in 1906. Both Mount Olivet and Crown Hill can be expected to continue in operation for some years because of large areas yet to be developed.

An unusual aspect of burials at these four cemeteries was the transportation provided on the trolley lines of the Denver Tramway. A dignified "Funeral Car" pulled by a trolley car was often used to carry the funeral party to the cemetery entrance where they could be met by carriages, thus avoiding a long hard ride into the suburbs over dusty, unpaved roads.

Not to be overlooked, is the Fort Logan Military Cemetery, located on the southwestern edge of the city. Known for many years as the Denver National Cemetery, it gained its present status in 1952, and continues to provide for military burials. Recently, new cemeteries have opened in suburban areas but Mt. Olivet, Crown Hill, and Fairmount continue to provide the major service to the city.

FROM PIONEER DOCTORS TO MEDICAL CENTER OF THE MOUNTAIN WEST

The medical profession can trace its Denver history to the spring of 1859, and the arrival of Dr. Drake McDowell from St. Louis. Within less than a year he launched a drive for the establishment of a hospital and gained the willing assistance of the Denver Town Company who offered him town lots for that purpose. The City Hospital was organized the following spring and opened in a small building on Larimer between 19th and 20th Streets. Dr. Hamilton was soon appointed Surgeon of the First Regiment of Colorado Volunteers and with the start of the Civil War, he left his work in Denver, but not until he had also founded the Jefferson Medical Association, the first such group in Colorado.

Throughout the years of the Civil War a military hospital was operated at Camp Weld but for the most part private medical needs were handled in the home during the span of the city's first decade. It was not until 1873, that the first permanent buildings of the Arapahoe County Hospital were constructed in the vicinity of what is today West 6th Avenue and Cherokee Street. During ensuing years, several more buildings were added, including the nurses home in 1889, a surgical building in 1892, and a 200 bed wing completed in 1900. The Steele Memorial Hospital was founded in 1892, by Dr. H. K. Steele, the City Health Commissioner, to handle contagious diseases. Eventually this hospital, along with the County Hospital facilities, became the Denver General Hospital complex after the city gained home rule. Most of the early buildings in the complex along West 6th Avenue at Cherokee Street, have been replaced by the new Denver General Hospital which opened at the same location in 1971.

Several other hospitals share a long history of service to Denver residents. St. Joseph's Hospital finds its beginnings with the work of that most active Catholic leader, Bishop Machebeuf, who called upon several Sisters of Charity in Leavenworth, Kansas, to staff a hospital facility which opened in 1873, at 1421 Arapahoe Street. Five years later a three story brick building was completed at 18th and Humboldt Street with a much larger structure being added in 1890, for the costly sum of $60,000.

The efforts of the Episcopal Church brought about the founding of St. Luke's Hospital in 1881. It was first located in a frame building at West 17th Avenue and Federal Boulevard, once occupied by the Grand View Hotel. In 1891, the hospital moved to new quarters at 19th and Pearl Street, built at a cost of almost $100,000.

When St. Anthony's Hospital was opened in 1892, it was "out in the country" at its site across from Sloan's Lake at Quitman Street, just a block north of Colfax Avenue. Operated by the Sisters of St. Francis Seraph, it was for some years the largest hospital in the state and traces its medical care history even earlier than the establishment of the hospital. In 1884, seven sisters arrived in Denver led by Sister Huberta to serve in the Union Pacific Railroad Hospital located at 40th Avenue and Williams Street. The railroad had requested help in staffing their facility and Bishop Machebeuf had succeeded in bringing the sisters from Lafayette, Indiana. After six years with the railroad hospital, they determined it wise to construct their own facility and undertook a campaign which eventually gained wide public support and resulted in the founding of St. Anthony's Hospital.

Tuberculosis was a very serious health problem in the late 19th century and many doctors advised their patients to seek the dry, clean air that was in abundant supply in the West. Denver soon became a gathering point for these "consumptives," and many who "came West to die" instead found a new lease on life. A pioneer institution in dealing with this disease was the National Jewish Hospital for Consumptives. After founding in 1890, a lack of funds prevented completion of their new facility until 1899, but the hospital then gained a unique reputation for its policies of serving only consumptives and of making no charges for these services. Being nonsectarian, the hospital has drawn patients from far and wide and continues today as a leader in its field.

In the late 19th Century a system of medical treatment known as homeopathy became popular and resulted in the founding of the Denver Homeopathic Medical College and Hospital Association in 1894. First located at 2348 Champa Street, the facility soon moved to new quarters at Humboldt Street and Park Avenue. In later years, this medical system, whereby minute quantities of remedies were administered which if given in massive doses produced the effects similar to those of the disease, lost favor and gradually faded from the scene.

During the early years of the new century, several other hospitals were established and continue to serve today, including Colorado General Hospital, operated by the University of Colorado Medical School; Children's Hospital; Mercy Hospital; Presbyterian Hospital; the Jewish Consumptives Relief Society (J.C.R.S.), located in Spivak (now part of Lakewood) and operated today as the American Medical Center at Denver; and two military facilities, Fitzsimons General Hospital and Veterans Administration Hospital. Since World II, numerous other facilities have sprung up to serve medical needs, including General Rose Memorial Hospital, Valley View Hospital in Thornton, and Lutheran Hospital in Wheat Ridge.

Needy children found shelter at the House of the Good Shepherd, seen above, at West Cedar Avenue and Cherokee Street in about 1910. The home moved to Colorado Boulevard and Louisiana Avenue in 1913, and that building was destroyed by fire in 1969, shortly after the home had moved to newer quarters.
During the depression years of the 1930's, Denver Police (below) distributed food baskets to the poor.—*Both, Denver Public Library, Western History Collection*

DO UNTO OTHERS—THE POOR, THE AGED, THE ORPHANED

In a time long before our modern, often controversial, public welfare system was even imagined, a wide range of public and more often, private facilities were established to handle the needs of the less fortunate members of society.

As early as 1866, Arapahoe County established a forty acre "Poor House" farm to the southeast of the city. This was later moved to Globeville but in 1898, was finally moved to Henderson, north of Denver, and known as the Infirmary Farm. In later years it was widely called the Denver Poor Farm.

The very old and the very young have always created special problems for society and to meet their needs The Ladies Relief Society of Denver was organized in October, 1874. Their first undertaking was to establish a children's shelter but this soon expanded to help women in need, regardless of age. In 1897, the group sold their original site and built the landmark Ladies Relief Home at West 38th Avenue and Quitman Street which continues to serve in the 1970's.

A short time later, the Oakes Home opened on West 32nd Avenue at Decatur Street. Under the management of the Episcopal Church, it provides a home for aged men and women.

Across the city, several facilities were established to care for children including St. Clara's Orphan Asylum, Denver Orphans' Home, the Working Boys' Home, St. Vincent's Orphan Asylum and Colorado Christian Home. With the changing patterns of welfare most of these facilities have either closed or turned to different uses, several now serving as day-care centers for children of working mothers, and others converted to youth recreation centers.

Both the Y.M.C.A. and Y.W.C.A. have long served the city as have such groups as the Goodwill Industries, the Salvation Army and the Denver Rescue Mission, all three of which seem to find special fulfillment in the core city areas.

Along with the national organizations serving boys and girls, such as Boy Scouts, Girl Scouts, Camp Fire Girls, and 4-H Clubs, Denver has been fortunate in having an active local group—the Highlander Boys. Begun by George Olinger, a successful Denver mortician, the group has continued in its efforts to aid boys in growing up in the city.

DENVER PUBLIC SCHOOLS

Arapahoe School (upper left) was opened in 1873, on the north side of Arapahoe, between 17th and 18th Streets. As downtown businesses expanded, the building was no longer in a residential area and thus closed in 1888. Another pioneer school, the Broadway School (left) opened in 1875, on Broadway between East 13th and 14th Avenues, opposite the present main Public Library, and until recently the site of the American Legion Building. For a time the school included a branch of East High School and in 1908 became a junior high, while still later it housed school administrative offices, until sold and torn down in 1928.

In 1891, the eight room Cheltenham School opened at West Colfax and Irving Street. After an addition in 1905, it appeared as in the photo below. In 1921, an "open air" annex was added for use as a Tuberculars school. For a number of years the school also offered Americanization classes to immigrants, mostly Jewish, who had settled in the area.—*Below, Denver Public Schools; others, State Historical Society of Colorado*

The American schoolroom—circa 1900. This scene, typical of the era, is in Gilpin School at 29th and California Streets. Built in 1881, the building was torn down several years ago and replaced by a modern Gilpin Elementary School.—*John Henderson, Denver Public Library, Western History Collection*

AARON GOVE

In 1874, Aaron Gove came to Denver to become superintendent of School District No. 1, at an annual salary of $2,500. At that time the city was divided between several school districts and thus one of Gove's most important tasks was the smooth consolidation of all the city schools into a single Denver Public Schools system in 1902. After 30 years of service, Gove retired in 1904 and died on August 1, 1919.—*Denver Public Library, Western History Collection*

KENNETH E. OBERHOLTZER

After becoming superintendent in April, 1947, Kenneth Oberholtzer faced the difficult task of providing schoolrooms for a rapidly increasing population. Many new schools were built and only in the late 1960's, did the school enrollment finally level off. Oberholtzer retired in 1967, after 20 years of service.—*Denver Public Schools*

The history of East High School spans 90 years. The high school grades were included in the Arapahoe School until January, 1882, when the old East Side High School (below) was opened at 19th and Stout Streets. The school's main lobby is seen on the left, with three statues visible, all of which were later moved to the present East High building.

The new East High School opened in 1925, at 1545 Detroit Street and remains one of the city's most handsome school buildings. The old building continued in use for several years to house administrative offices but was razed in 1929, to make way for construction of the New Customs House.—*All, State Historical Society of Colorado*

THE ANGELS EAST SIDE HIGH

North High School traces its history to 1872, when a one room school was opened at 15th and Central Streets, accommodating all ages and grades. In 1873, the original Ashland School (right) was built at West 29th Avenue and Dunkeld Place but was torn down in 1888, to make way for the large new Ashland School (below) which is still in use as an elementary school. For several years the one building, which was enlarged in 1894, continued to offer all grades but eventually became the North Side High School. In September, 1911, the new North High School (bottom) opened at West Lake Place (Speer Blvd.) and Eliot Street, and remains in use, having received several additions since that time.—*Bottom, Denver Public Library, Western History Collection; others, State Historical Society of Colorado*

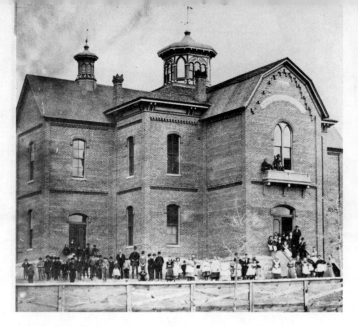

NORTH SIDE HIGH

THE VIKINGS

Grant School, seen above in 1927, was built at South Pearl Street and Colorado Avenue in 1890, and included all grades. Eventually, the lower grades went to other schools and Grant Junior High was established in the same building with South Side High School. The term "Side" was dropped from the Denver high schools in 1923, and thus when the new building, seen below, opened at 1700 East Louisiana Avenue on January 25, 1926, it was known as South High School. A boys cooking class is seen below, shortly after the new South High opened. The old Grant School was torn down and replaced by the new Grant Junior High, on the same site.—*Above, Denver Public Schools; others, State Historical Society of Colorado*

The first school in "West Denver" School District No. 2, was opened in 1865, in the old Federal Arsenal Building at 11th and Lawrence Streets. The two room school enrolled all ages and grades, but in 1871, two large rooms were added and the building renamed the Eleventh Avenue School. In 1873, the old Arsenal section was replaced by the building seen on the left, and this remained the district's only school until Central School (above) opened in 1880.—*State Historical Society of Colorado*

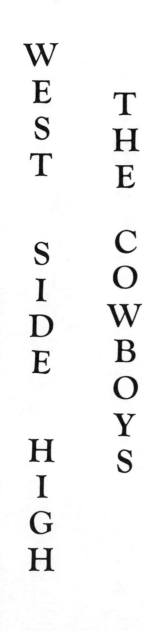

WEST SIDE HIGH

THE COWBOYS

When Central School (opposite-upper right) opened in 1880, it became the "West Denver" secondary school but was converted to an elementary school in 1883, when Franklin School (center-opposite) opened at West Colfax and Stout Street. Central remained an elementary school until 1949 when replaced by Greenlee School. Franklin was a secondary school until 1893, when it became an elementary school until razed in 1952. The first West Side High School (bottom-opposite) opened in 1893, at 5th Avenue and Fox Street and remained as such until the new West High School was built in 1925. The old building then became Baker Junior High and was replaced in 1957, by the present Baker building. The new West High, seen above, behind the Sunken Gardens, rivals the other senior high schools as one of the city's handsomest school buildings.

In 1947, the Westwood area was annexed to Denver and the Westwood School, built in 1912, at South Lowell Boulevard and West Kentucky Avenue, became an elementary school, as seen in the mid-1960's photo below. After 1947, Westwood area high school age students entered West High School.

One of the most beautiful of the city's junior high schools is Lake, opened in 1926, at the east end of Sloan's Lake. Students from Lake Junior High have advanced to both West High and North High School.—*Below, State Historical Society Coll.; bottom and opposite-center and bottom, D.P.L., Western History Coll.; others, Denver Public Schools*

Manual Training High School opened in 1894, at 27th Avenue and Franklin Street. The school is seen above, after receiving additions in 1899 and 1924. For many years the school specialized in training students for jobs in the manual arts and trades but in recent years the curriculum has been made similar to the other Denver high schools. In 1953, a new building was constructed in the same block and is now known as Manual High School, the term "training" having been dropped. The Manual Training High girls basketball team is posed below, and looks ready for action.—*Both, Denver Public Library, Western History Collection*

The Emily Griffith Opportunity School traces its history to 1914, when a few night classes were first offered at the Longfellow School (upper left-page 225), built in 1882, at 13th and Welton Streets. The program received wide public support and on May 11, 1916, Longfellow was officially designated as Opportunity School. As the program grew, new facilities were added, such as the addition at 12th and Welton Streets (upper right) which is still in use. Eventually, Longfellow School was torn down but today the school, along with educational televison station KRMA, occupies the entire block between 12th and 13th, Glenarm and Welton Streets. Two scenes, typical of classes in the school's early years, are seen opposite; a ladies automobile repair class and a naturalization class.

The school's success was due in great measure to the efforts of Miss Emily Griffith, who came to Denver to teach in Central School in 1895. In 1904, she joined the State Department of Education and was the Deputy State Superintendent of Schools during 1910-12. Returning to teaching, she went to the 24th Street School and also became involved in the night school program at Longfellow School. She became the first principal of Opportunity School and continued in that post until she resigned on December 12, 1933. Miss Griffith moved to Pinecliff and on June 19, 1947, was found, along with her sister, murdered in their cabin. The case remains unsolved.—*Upper right, State Historical Society of Colorado; others, Denver Public Library, Western History Collection*

O
P
P
O
R
T
U
N
I
T
Y

S
C
H
O
O
L

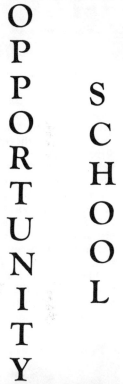

MISS EMILY GRIFFITH

Two of Denver's earliest private schools were Wolfe Hall and St. Mary's Academy. Wolfe Hall was begun in 1867, by Rev. George Randall, Denver's first Episcopal Bishop, as a seminary for young ladies. Named for its benefactor, John Wolfe of New York City, the school is seen above in the early 1880's, at 17th and Champa Streets (now the site of the Boston Building). In February, 1889, the school moved to 14th Avenue and Clarkson Street (right) and remained there until closed for a lack of funds in 1913. The school was torn down in 1920, and Morey Junior High School built on the site. St. Mary's Academy was begun by Roman Catholic Bishop Joseph Machebeuf in 1864, in a house on California, between 14th and 15th Streets (now the site of the Denver Post Building). Later, new school buildings (below) were constructed at the same location. In 1911, the Academy moved to 1370 Pennsylvania Street, and since 1952 has been located in Cherry Hills Village.—*State Historical Society of Colorado*

Denver boasts two historic Roman Catholic colleges, Loretto Heights and Regis. Loretto Heights College began as an off-shoot of St. Mary's Academy and was opened in 1890, in the landmark building seen in the photo above. The structure is still in use and is visible for many miles from its location near South Federal Boulevard and Cornell Street. Regis College began as a Jesuit school in Morrison in 1884, later became the College of the Sacred Heart and then was renamed Regis College. The Regis campus, at 50th Avenue and Lowell Boulevard, is seen below, in a 1930's aerial view. For most of their history, Loretto Heights enrolled only women while Regis served only men but recently both schools have begun a move to becoming co-educational.—*Above, State Historical Society of Colo.; below, D.P.L., Western History Collection*

In 1864, the Colorado Seminary was organized by the Methodist Episcopal Church and chartered by the Territorial Legislature on March 5, 1864, under the leadership of Governor John Evans. A fine building was constructed on the southwest corner of 14th and Arapahoe Streets (upper left) and the school opened on November 16, 1864. Due to a lack of funds the school suspended operations in 1867, and the building was used for a short time to house the Territorial Legislature. By 1880, the school was in full operation, had enlarged the building, as seen above, and had also established the University of Denver to offer an expanded academic program. To meet the demands of continued growth, the Haish Building (left) was opened in 1887, on the southeast corner of 14th and Arapahoe Streets. After D.U. left the building it was purchased by the Keith Safe Company and known as the Keith Building until razed in 1963.

In the late 1880's, the university moved out of downtown to the area now known as University Park. The land was donated by the farmer turned real estate promoter, Rufus "Potato" Clark. On April 3, 1890, a large crowd (above-opposite) gathered to observe the laying of the cornerstone of University Hall, which is seen on the right in 1891, soon after completion. The building, now known as "Old Main" remains in use and is little changed after 80 years.—*Left, D.P.L., Western History Coll.; others, State Historical Society of Colo.*

After moving to University Park, the school began a period of rapid expansion. In 1892, H. B. Chamberlin, a Denver real estate promoter and amateur astronomer, built the Chamberlin Observatory (lower left) as a gift to the university. Containing a 24 inch refraction telescope, it was once considered one of the outstanding observatories and was especially popular with astronomers because of the very clear air which Denver had at that time, providing for better observations. Professor Herbert A. Howe, a long time member of the science department, is seen at the telescope controls.

As football gained in popularity, it was obvious that the D.U. Ministers (later known as the Pioneers) needed a stadium and thus Hilltop Stadium was built and is shown below while under construction in July, 1925. In 1961, D.U. dropped football and as the stadium came to need expensive repairs, it was decided that its usefulness was past and it was removed in 1971.—*All, State Historical Society of Colorado*

THE PIONEERS

CWC TEMPLE BUELL

The cornerstone of Colorado Woman's College (above) was laid in 1890, but financial problems delayed the school's opening until 1909. On July 1, 1967, Mr. and Mrs. Temple Buell took part in ceremonies (left) to officially rename the school Temple Buell College. The action was in appreciation of financial assistance from the Buells, but on March 29, 1973, the school was renamed Colorado Women's College.—*Denver Public Library, Western History Collection*

BELLEVIEW COLLEGE—WESTMINSTER
The Pillar of Fire Church was organized in Denver in 1901, by Alma White, wife of a Methodist minister. It is now active across America and foreign lands. In January, 1920, the church purchased the former Presbyterian operated Westminster College property in suburban Westminster. Today it is operated as Belleview College and grade school. Located here also, is the non-commercial radio station KPOF which broadcasts religious programs and classical music.—*Pillar of Fire Church*

CHURCHES AND RELIGION

THE CONGREGATIONAL CHURCH

The first Congregational Church in Denver was organized on October 23, 1864, and the congregation met in various locations until construction of a frame building (above) at the corner of 15th and Curtis Streets in 1869. In January, 1881, the First Congregational Church moved to a large new building (above-right) between 16th and 17th Streets on Glenarm Place. In 1906, the building was sold and the church merged with the Plymouth Congregational Church.—*Both, Denver Public Library, Western History Collection*

THE METHODIST CHURCH

The Methodist (or Methodist-Episcopal) Church was among the city's first organized churches. On August 2, 1859, the Denver City Mission was formed and later became the Lawrence Street Methodist Church (below) which was opened in 1865 and served until 1887. With the completion of the Trinity Methodist Church (below left) at 18th Avenue and Broadway on December 23, 1887, the Lawrence Street building was used for a time by the Salvation Army and later torn down.—*Both, State Historical Society of Colorado*

THE ROMAN CATHOLIC CHURCH

The Roman Catholic Church did not organize in Denver until the spring of 1860, but was the second to actually erect a church building. Bishop J. B. Miege reached Denver from Leavenworth, Kansas, in the spring of 1860, and did preliminary work towards construction of St. Mary's Cathedral at 15th and Stout Streets. Bishop Joseph Machebeuf (below) arrived in the city from Santa Fe, New Mexico, in October, 1860, and gave a new impetuous to the project. The structure was completed to the point that it could be used for the Christmas services in 1860, and in the next several years the building was greatly enlarged as seen in the photo (right) taken in the 1880's. On May 13, 1900, the last service was held in St. Mary's and the church razed for a business structure. Work was soon started on the Immaculate Conception Cathedral (lower right) at East Colfax and Logan Street, and the church was dedicated on October 27, 1912.

Many of Denver's older Catholic Churches have been torn down in recent years, due to urban renewal and changing neighborhoods. One such church was St. Leo's, (far right) which is seen here shortly after its completion on January 25, 1891, at 10th Street and West Colfax Avenue. The church drew most of its members from the German and Polish communities but with the change in the neighborhood from residential to business, the church closed and was removed in March, 1965.—*Below and far right, Denver Public Library, Western History Collection; others, State Historical Society of Colorado*

BISHOP JOSEPH PROJECTUS MACHEBEUF

THE EASTERN ORTHODOX CHURCH

On September 18, 1938, the congregation of the Russian Serbian Orthodox Church gathered (below) to mark their church's 40th Anniversary. Located in Globeville, at 47th Avenue and Logan Street, the church continues today as the Eastern Orthodox Church of the Transfiguration.—*Denver Public Library, Western History Collection*

THE UNITARIAN CHURCH

The Unitarian Church was first organized in Denver in 1871, and on September 4, 1887, opened this building (below) at 19th and Broadway. The structure remained in use until 1959.—*State Historical Society of Colorado*

For the Common Good

THE BAPTISTS

The city's first Baptist Church was organized in December, 1863, and after several temporary meeting locations, work began on a church at 16th and Curtis Streets. When the basement was completed it was roofed over but no further work done above ground. This resulted in the building gaining the nickname of "the Baptist dug-out." The property was sold and a small church built at 18th and Curtis Streets in 1873; here the church remained for ten years. In the early 1880's, work began on a large new building on Stout between 17th and 18th Streets, and that church, seen in the photos above, was dedicated on May 8, 1883. The congregation moved in 1937, to 14th Avenue and Grant Street where it remains. The Stout Street building was torn down several years ago.—*Both, State Historical Society of Colorado*

AUNT CLARA BROWN

Denver's pioneer Negro population organized several churches. In November, 1865, Zion Baptist Church was begun and in 1868, the African Methodist-Episcopal Church was started. An unidentified Negro church is shown below, in the late 1870's. A pioneer in Denver's religious history was Clara Brown. Aunt Clara Brown, as she was often called, was a freed slave who came to Auraria in June, 1859, on one of the first wagon trains. She helped to organize the first Sunday School, working with two Methodist ministers and Professor Goldrick. She later moved to Central City where she ran a laundry, organized the town's first Sunday School, and very wisely invested her money in mining claims. Eventually, she saved enough money to bring many of her relatives to Colorado and later located her daughter who, many years earlier, had been sold as a slave. Clara Brown died in Denver at the age of 82 in 1882.

In September, 1860, Rev. A. T. Rankin helped to organize what is now Central Presbyterian Church. Its first church home was built near 15th and Lawrence Streets in 1863, but in January, 1878, it moved to a larger building at 18th and Champa Streets. Originally known as First Presbyterian Church, it was renamed Central Presbyterian in 1874, and moved to its present home at 17th Avenue and Sherman Street in December, 1892.

The church now known as First Presbyterian was founded in 1883 and in 1895 moved to 14th Avenue and Lincoln Streets. The building (center) was razed in 1964, and the congregation moved to Lakewood.

A pioneer north Denver church, the North Presbyterian Church was organized on January 5, 1882, and soon completed a small church at West 34th Avenue and Vallejo Street. A large new church (bottom) was built on the same corner in 1905, and both still stand, although North Presbyterian moved in 1922, to its present location at West 37th Avenue and Federal Boulevard.—*All, D.P.L., Western History Coll.*

THE PRESBYTERIAN CHURCH

THE EPISCOPAL CHURCH

On January 17, 1860, Rev. J. H. Kehler, of the Episcopal Diocese of Virginia, arrived in Denver and began to meet with a small group of Episcopalians in Professor Goldrick's school. A congregation was organized and regular services began on January 29th. By the spring of 1862, the congregation had grown enough to warrant the purchase of a church building. In the fall of 1860, the newly organized Methodist-Episcopal Church had built a small brick church at 14th and Arapahoe Streets (later the site of the Haish Building) which was the first building constructed for religious purposes in Denver. When the Methodists decided to move to larger quarters, the property was sold to the Episcopalian congregation. On June 20, 1862, the church was consecrated as St. John's Church in the Wilderness, and is seen on the right about 1865, after a frame addition was placed in front of the original brick building. In November, 1881, the original St. John's was replaced by St. John's Cathedral (center photos) at the corner of East 20th Avenue and Welton Street. On May 15, 1903, the cathedral was destroyed by fire and the congregation made the decision to build at a different location. The present St. John's Cathedral was begun in 1905, at 13th Avenue and Clarkson Street and is seen (lower right) soon after completion.

On September 17, 1877, the Emanuel Episcopal Church opened at 10th and Lawrence Streets. Seen at the upper left (opposite page) the church still stands and is now preserved as a landmark. For some years it also served as a Jewish synagogue; see text on page 237.—*Lower right, L. C. McClure, Denver Public Library, Western History Collection; others, State Historical Society of Colorado*

JUDAISM

In 1860, members of the Jewish community organized to provide burial services for the dead of their faith and also to observe the Passover and other important religious days. By 1873, their numbers had grown sufficiently to organize the Congregation Emanuel and the following year to build the Temple Emanuel at 19th and Curtis Streets. Under the leadership of Rabbi Friedman, the second Temple Emanuel (below) was constructed at 16th Avenue and Pearl Street in 1898, and dedicated on January 29, 1899. Rabbi Friedman and Rabbi Charles E. H. Kauvar were for many years the city's most notable leaders of their faith. The stone church seen in the photos above, was built at 10th and Lawrence Streets in 1877, as an Episcopal Church (left photo), and served in this capacity for many years. In 1903, however, it was sold and became the Schearith Israel Synagogue (right photo), continuing as such until 1957. Now unoccupied, it is to be preserved as a National Landmark.—*Lower right, Denver Public Library, Western History Collection; upper right, Authors' Collection; others, State Historical Society of Colorado*

RABBI WILLIAM STERNE FRIEDMAN

The Sunshine Mission (above and right) has long served the physical and spiritual needs of those who have "reached bottom" and roam the streets of lower downtown Denver. Known as the Denver Rescue Mission, it was located near the corner of 18th and Larimer Streets until recent urban renewal programs forced them to relocate in the former Dieter Building at 23rd and Lawrence Streets, where it continues to issue its call of "Whosoever Wilt May Come."—*Both, Denver Public Library, Western History Coll.*

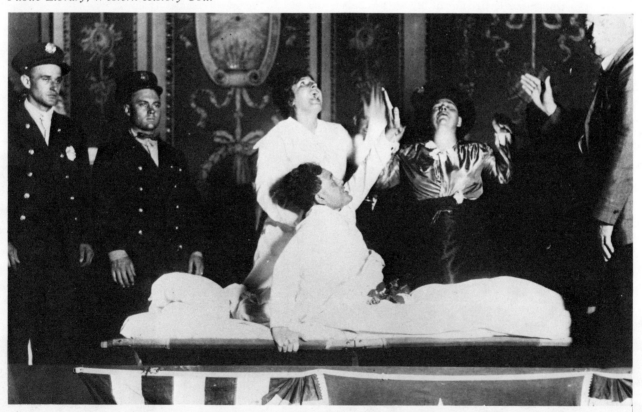

Aimee Semple McPherson, a Pentecostal evangelist and founder of the International Church of the Foursquare Gospel, came to Denver in January, 1927. Crowds packed the City Auditorium for her services which included faith healing as seen above, with Mrs. McPherson standing at the center of the photo.—*Denver Public Library, Western History Collection*

REST IN PEACE

By the 1890's, several new cemeteries were opened at locations which were far out in the suburbs. To avoid a hard trip over rough roads, the Denver Tramway began to serve the cemeteries with their funeral car, seen below (right) pulled by a regular trolley which carried the mourners. When Fairmount Cemetery opened in 1890, it built its own railroad to connect with the trolley line on East Colfax Avenue. The little steam powered train is seen below in 1893. Fairmount Cemetery's lovely Little Ivy Chapel (left) opened in 1890, and is seen here in more recent times.—*Left, D.P.L., Western History Coll.; below, Fairmount Cemetery Association; below-right, H. E. Jobes Coll.*

John W. Olinger and his wife Emma came to Denver in 1890, and opened a small undertaking business at 15th and Platte Streets. In 1900, the firm moved to larger quarters nearby at 2409 15th Street, and in 1910 constructed the well known building at 16th and Boulder Streets. Seen below when new, the building is still in use although the company has expanded to other locations. Following the death of John Olinger in 1901, the business was for many years operated by his son, George Olinger. One of the most famous persons to be interred by Olingers was William F. (Buffalo Bill) Cody who died in 1917.

A once prominent but now forgotten undertaking firm was the H. D. Martin Company. Its fine new hearse is parked in front of its funeral home at 10 West Colfax Avenue which was located in the old cable power house. The photo dates to about 1910.—*Both, Denver Public Library, Western History Collection*

HOSPITALS

Two of Denver's pioneer hospitals, St. Anthony's and St. Luke's, are seen in these historic photos. St. Anthonys Hospital (above) was founded by the Sisters of St. Francis Seraph and opened in May, 1892, at West 16th Avenue and Quitman Street, on the south side of Sloan's Lake. Additions were made to the original building in 1901 and 1920, and after major new construction between 1962 and 1965, the last segment of the 1892 structure was removed.

St. Luke's Hospital was founded by the Episcopal Church and opened in June, 1881, at West 17th Avenue and Federal Boulevard. The hospital's first building (left) had once been the Grand View Hotel and had also been used for a short time as a private insane asylum. The building held only sixty beds and thus, from both a desire for a larger building and also to avoid being separated from the rest of the city by the railroad yards to the east, the decision was made to construct a new building in east Denver. The new hospital, betwen 19th and 20th Avenues at Pearl Street, opened on St. Luke's Day, October 18, 1891, and has since been enlarged and the original building replaced during the late 1960's.—*Left, State Historical Society of Colorado; others, L. C. McClure, Denver Public Library, Western History Collection*

Three of the city's major hospitals are seen in these views. St. Joseph Hospital was among the first in Denver, tracing its history to 1873. After operating for short periods at three different downtown locations, including the St. James Hotel, a large new hospital building was opened in 1878, at 18th Avenue and Humboldt Street. The hospital is seen above, after receiving a major addition (on the left) in 1905. By the late 1960's, the 1878 structure had been replaced by additional new construction. Mercy Hospital (left) opened in 1901, at 16th Avenue and Milwaukee Street and was enlarged in 1903, and again in 1931. An entirely new facility was opened in 1964, and the old building removed soon after. Presbyterian Hospital is one of the city's newer hospitals. The building, seen below, at Franklin Street and 20th Avenue, opened in 1934, and has recently been greatly enlarged.—*Above, State Historical Society of Colorado; others, Denver Public Library, Western History Collection*

PRESBYTERIAN HOSPITAL

DENVER GENERAL HOSPITAL

In 1971, the city proudly opened its new Denver General Hospital; its history can be traced back more than a century to May, 1860, when the first City Hospital opened at 16th and Wazee Streets. Despite the fact that the hospital's first patient died, the facility remained in operation and was soon enlarged. The hospital moved to 9th and Champa Streets later in the 1860's, and in 1873, moved to West 6th Avenue and Cherokee Street, where it remains. The photo above dates to about 1903, and includes structures added in 1889, 1892 and 1900. The complex was enlarged again in 1910 and 1939, and with the opening of the new facility in 1971, it is expected that most of the older buildings will be removed by the mid-1970's. The interior of the surgical wing is seen on the right, while a typical ward of the 1890's, is seen at the upper right (page 243). The Steele Memorial Hospital (below) was housed in three small buildings on 7th Avenue, behind the main hospital and handled contagious diseases. Named for its founder, City Health Commissioner, Dr. H. K. Steele, it was eventually made part of Denver General Hospital.—*All, State Historical Society of Colorado*

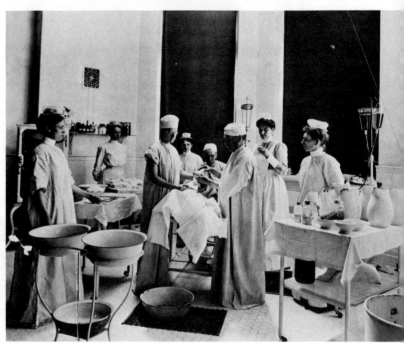

A medical emergency in 1890, could mean a ride to the hospital in a horse drawn ambulance such as this one at the Arapahoe County Hospital. By the 1920's, the trip to the hospital could be both faster and smoother in the substantial looking vehicle seen below. The front-mounted bell could be counted on to warn traffic and clear a route to the hospital.—*Both, Denver Public Library, Western History Collection*

DR. FLORENCE RENA SABIN

Dr. Sabin, seen above in her laboratory, became nationally known as a leader in the field of public health medicine. Born in Central City in 1871, she spent considerable time engaged in research at the Rockefeller Institute of Medical Research in New York City, working in both cancer and tuberculosis. In 1938, she returned to Denver and in 1941 was appointed the city's Manager of Health and Charities, a position she held until she retired in 1947. Dr. Sabin died on October 3, 1953, at the age of 81 and is especially remembered for her efforts to improve the city's public health programs.—*Denver Public Library, Western History Collection*

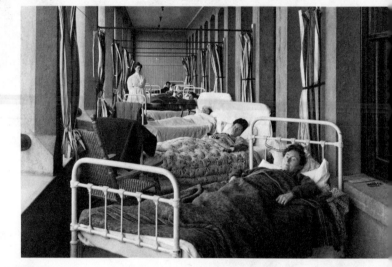

By the turn of the century, Denver's clean dry air was drawing many persons hopeful of being cured of consumption, better known today as tuberculosis. The Agnes Memorial Sanatorium (top) was built by Lawrence Phipps in memory of his mother, Agnes McCall Phipps, and opened in 1903. Eventually, the number of cases of tuberculosis decreased and on August 1, 1932, the sanatorium closed. The buildings and land later became part of Lowry Air Field and the main building (center of photo) remained in use until 1963. Summer cottages, such as those above (right) at Agnes Memorial, allowed patients to take full advantage of the fresh air. Bethesda Sanatarium, (above-left) built by the Dutch Reformed Church in 1910, allowed its patients to "take the air" from their balcony. In 1948, Bethesda converted its facilities to become a mental hospital. The Jewish Consumptives Relief Society (JCRS) (below) was founded by Dr. C. D. Spivak in 1904, at Colfax and Lamar Street and continues today as the American Medical Center.—*All, D.P.L., Western History Coll.*

THE CONSUMPTIVES' CURE

Lutheran Hospital, at West 38th Avenue and Brentwood Street, was begun by the Lutheran Church in the summer of 1905, as a TB sanatorium. During the first years, tents were used but soon the buildings, seen in this 1921 photo (right), were completed and remained in use when the facility was converted to a modern hospital in the mid-1960's.

The National Jewish Hospital for Consumptives was opened in December, 1899, at East Colfax and Jackson Street. The project had been started in 1890, but the panic of 1893 blocked completion for several years. One of the prime supporters of the hospital was Mrs. Abraham Jacobs, sometimes referred to as the "Mother of Charities," and who was the only woman included in the series of stained glass portrait-windows in the Colorado Capitol Building. The hospital eventually moved two blocks to its present building (below) at East Colfax and Colorado Boulevard, and maintains its policy of aiding only those in financial need.

"None may enter who can pay—
none may pay who enter."
—National Jewish Hospital

One of the city's most widely known institutions of healing is Children's Hospital. Opened in February, 1910, a modern building (right) was completed in 1917, and has since been expanded. The hospital was a favorite charity of Harry Tammen, co-owner of the Denver Post, and after his death the work was continued by his widow Agnes Tammen.—*Center, State Historical Society of Colorado; others, Denver Public Library, Western History Collection*

Fitzsimons General Hospital, one of the world's largest military medical installations, is named in honor of First Lieutenant William Thomas Fitzsimons, Medical Officers' Reserve Corps, who was killed on September 4, 1917, near Dannes-Camiers, France. A native of Kansas, he was the first American officer to die as a result of enemy action in World War I. In 1918, the Army decided to establish a hospital near Denver and on April 19, 1918, broke ground on a 600 acre tract of land at East Colfax and Peoria Street, which had originally been the A. B. Gutheil Nursery. On October 13, 1918, the facility was formally dedicated as U.S. Army General Hospital No. 21, but on July 1, 1920, by order of the War Department, it was renamed Fitzsimons General Hospital. The hospital is seen above, as it appears today, after being enlarged to serve in World War II, the Korean War and the Vietnam War. —*Both, U. S. Army Photographs*

LT. WILLIAM T. FITZSIMONS

Colorado General Hospital and the Colorado University Medical School trace their development to the Denver Municipal Dispensary (upper left) at 13th and Welton Streets, which had once been the home of Colonel John Archer. The C. U. Medical School began in Boulder in September, 1873, but moved to Denver in 1910, and used this house as well as the facilities of Denver General Hospital. In 1911, C. U. merged with the Gross College of Medicine which had itself been formed from the merger in 1902, of the University of Denver School of Medicine and the Gross Medical College. The C. U. Medical School moved to its present location in September, 1924, when the new Colorado General Hospital was opened at 12th Avenue and Colorado Boulevard. The facility is seen above (right) about the time of World War II.—*Left, Denver Public Library, Western History Collection; right, State Historical Society of Colorado*

General Rose Memorial Hospital, seen below (opposite) in 1971, was built in honor of General Maurice Rose and opened in January, 1949. Maurice Rose, the son of Rabbi Samuel Rose, grew up in Denver and went on to a fine military career. In March, 1945, while riding in a jeep at the head of his troops as they moved toward Berlin, he was confronted by several German tanks. Rose surrendered but for some unexplained reason was shot by a young German officer. Many Denverites, along with 10,000 of the officers and men in Rose's command, donated to the building of the hospital in his memory. Maurice Schwayder played a major role in the entire project and on September 1, 1948, General Eisenhower came for the laying of the cornerstone. A lobby plaque contains the names of 1500 Denverites lost in the war; arranged in alphabetical order and including the name of Maurice Rose.—*General Rose Memorial Hospital*

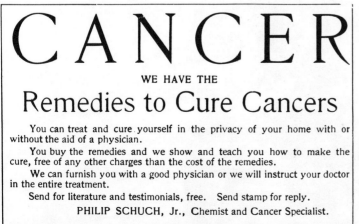
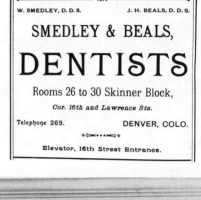

The Homeopathic Hospital served practitioners of the homeopathy system of medicine which flourished in the 1880's, but faded by the 1920's. The hospital was located at Park Avenue and Humboldt Street and is seen here in about 1900.—*State Historical Society of Colorado; advertisements, Denver City Directory of 1889 (above) and 1911 (below)*

SOCIAL SERVICES

Some of the earliest efforts in the area of social welfare were to provide homes for the elderly. Three such institutions, which are still serving this need, are seen on this page. Above—The Oakes Home was built at West 32nd Avenue and Decatur Street under the direction of Rev. Frederick W. Oakes and remains under the management of the Catholic Church. Opening on September 9, 1895, it was eventually enlarged to include men as well as women. Right—The J. K. Mullen Home for the Aged at West 30th Avenue and Meade Street was built in 1916, and is operaed by the "Little Sisters of the Poor," an Episcopalian order. The home was one of several charities of Mr. Mullen who had established the Hungarian Flour Mills. Below—The Ladies Relief Home (commonly known as the "Old Ladies Home") was built at West 38th Avenue and Quitman Street in 1897, and was enlarged in 1916 and again in 1929.
—*Above and below, L. C. McClure photos-all, Denver Public Library, Western History Collection*

Prior to the development of our modern welfare system, the poor were sometimes forced to resort to unusual means in an effort to earn a living. During the early 1930's, many unemployed persons were able to exist by panning for gold on the Platte, and scenes such as this one in South Denver became pitifully common.

The Women's Christian Temperance Union (WCTU) has long been active in Denver. One of its early efforts was the establishment of this dispensary at 1100 10th Street, before the turn of the century.—*Below, Joseph Collier photo-both, Denver Public Library, Western History Collection*

St. Vincent's Orphanage (above) at West 41st Avenue and Lowell Boulevard, was established by Sister Frances Xavier and is operated by the Catholic "Sisters of Charity." The original home opened in 1882, but was destroyed by fire twenty years later. By 1904, this large home was constructed and is still in use.

The Denver Orphans' Home dates to 1872, and operated in several different buildings including the small house seen in the two photos below. In 1880, a large home (right) was built at East 14th Avenue and Race Street and used until 1902, when the orphanage moved to 1501 Albion Street where it continues today as the Denver Children's Home.—*Above, L. C. Mc-Culre photo-all, Denver Public Library, Western History Collection*

The Byers Home for Boys was founded in 1901, by Mrs. William N. (Elizabeth) Byers, wife of the founder of the Rocky Mountain News. First located at 1129 15th Street, the home moved in 1903, to a new building (right) at 64 West Alameda Avenue where the boys are seen (above) gathered in the reading room. The building was torn down in 1966.

George W. Clayton, a pioneer merchant, died on August 15, 1899, but provided in his will for the establishment of the Clayton College (below) at East 32nd Avenue and Colorado Boulevard. Built in 1911, the home, as stipulated in Clayton's will, was to accommodate "poor white orphans ages six to ten years old of reputable Colorado parents." There were to be none whose fathers were alive. In recent years, following a long court battle, the will was broken on the basis that it was unlawful to limit the school's facilities to white boys alone. Still operating, it now draws from a wide racial background.—Below, L. C. McClure photo-all, Denver Public Library, Western History Collection

Denver has been fortunate in having several groups dedicated to helping boys to become fine young men. The most famous such local organization has been the Highlander Boys. The group was begun by George Olinger, a prominent Denver mortician, and derived its name from the Highlands area of north Denver where Olinger operated his business and first formed the group. Formally organized on January 1, 1916, as the Olinger Highlanders, the group gained considerable fame after standing inspection for General John Pershing in 1920. The boys are seen above, posed with their White bus in Berkeley Park in the mid-1920's, while below they are on parade in Cheesman Park. In later years the group's name was changed to the Highlander Boys.

The Denver Boys' Club (lower left) at 1329 15th Street, advertised itself as "an evening home for boys—open from 5:45 to 8:45 P.M." The club provided a much needed place for boys to spend the evening and be off the streets.

The Boy Scouts have long been active in Denver, and are seen below, preparing to deliver Christmas baskets to the poor in about 1920.—*All, Denver Public Library, Western History Collection*

The Young Men's Christian Association (YMCA) opened in Denver in 1875, and during the next thirty years was located in several different buildings. A small space was once used in the Daniels and Fisher store, the Junior Department (center) was located for a time at 1747 Arapahoe Street, and for several years the "Y" was located in the Keith Building. It was in the latter that the first basketball games were played in the mid-1890's, as interest in the new sport spread west after its invention by Dr. James Naismith at Springfield, Massachusetts, in 1891. In 1906, the building at East 16th Avenue and Lincoln Street (left) was built and remains in use, having been enlarged in 1961.

The Young Women's Christian Association (YWCA) began in 1887, as the Woman's Home Club but with the formation of YWCA's across the nation, the Denver group changed its name in 1893. In 1899, the building seen below was built at East 18th Avenue and Sherman Street and was torn down in 1972.—*Left and bottom, L. C. McClure photos-all, Denver Public Library, Western History Collection*

T
H
E

Y.
M.
C.
A.

&

Y.
W.
C.
A.

THE SOCIAL ORDER

In any community the social order is a reflection of the divergent life styles of its people. Metropolitan Denver has the full range of social and economic strata and all of the institutions, good and bad, which accompany them.

A CITY OF HOMES

Denver has always been known across the nation as a city of homes. Unlike most large cities, Denver has historically had the majority of its citizens living in private homes as opposed to the usual preponderance of apartment and tenement dwellers. It is difficult to determine reasons for this, but it may be partially because of two factors: the abundance of wide open space which meant that land prices were low enough to permit the average family to own or rent a home; and the city's economy was developed along the lines of banking, transportation, commerce, and the tourist business, as opposed to the heavy industry which sustains most cities and the uncertainty of which often helps to develop econominally depressed areas. Whatever the reasons, the city has gradually expanded from the downtown area, moving in a rather orderly pattern in all directions. Today, the older city is ringed by suburban areas including Westminster, Thornton and Northglenn on the north; Adams City, Derby, Aurora (originally Fletcher), Montbello, and Cherry Creek from the northeast to southeast; Englewood and Littleton on the south; and Lakewood, Edgewater, Golden, Wheat Ridge and Arvada from the southwest to northwest. As the city expands, its housing pattern is changing in its second century and many residents are finding it desirable to live in stylish new town houses, condominiums and high rise apartments.

Originally, many homes were located in what is now the center of downtown Denver but it soon became evident that the growth of business would require the development of new residential neighborhoods. The arrival of immigrants brought the development of ethnic neighborhoods as people sought to live with those who spoke their language and shared their customs and life style. The smelters and stockyards brought the development of Globeville, Argo, Swansea and Elyria, to the north and northeast of downtown. These areas at first included large settlements of Welsh, Cornish, Irish and Scots, while later there came sizeable numbers of Poles, Russians, Germans and Slovaks. Many Dutch settled in the town of South Denver, and for many years the area between Broadway and Downing Street, from Evans to Louisiana Avenues was known as "Little Holland." The Italians congregated in "Little Italy" of North Denver, while the Jews were heavily settled along West Colfax Avenue.

East Colfax Avenue is now a heavily trafficked thoroughfare but in 1905, when the photo above was taken, it was a pleasant street lined with stately homes such as that of Lawrence C. Phipps which is on the right at the corner of Marion Street. Typical of the city's fine middle class homes was the residence of Joseph Cornforth, a local grocer, seen below (opposite) about 1880.—*Above, Author's Collection; opposite, State Historical Society of Colorado*

Many railroad workers, regardless of ethnic background, chose the neighborhood closest to their job; for instance, West Denver was close to the Rio Grande's Burnham Shops, while the west side of the Platte River in North Denver was close for men working at the Burlington Yard. Southeast Denver contained a heavy concentration of teachers and professors in the University Park area, and in more recent times many military personnel have chosen to live near Lowry Air Force Base, Buckley Field and Fitzsimons General Hospital.

Many of Denver's pioneer Negro families settled in what is today the "five-points" area at the northeast edge of downtown. They chose this location because it was close to the railroad passenger yards from which many worked as Pullman porters and dining car cooks and waiters. In later years, the Negro community continued to expand in this area, although not always out of choice but rather because of the pressures on them to stay out of other residential areas.

The wealthy chose Capitol Hill as their favorite spot. It was close to the downtown businesses in which most were involved and also provided a fine view of the Rockies. Some of these fine homes retain their grandeur, but many are being razed and the land going to commercial uses. As the electric trolley system developed, it became possible to live further from the downtown area and still conveniently travel to and from work each day. Improved transportation thus made possible the opening of new middle class "subdivisions", including Highlands and Berkeley to the northwest, Park Hill to the northeast, Montclair beyond Park Hill, Harman in the area which today includes the Cherry Creek Shopping Center, Barnum, Valverde and Westwood to the southwest of downtown, Manchester to the south of Overland Park, and Villa Park in

The Social Order

the area southeast of West Colfax Avenue and Sheridan Boulevard.

The development of the Denver Country Club, Cheesman Park and more recently the Cherry Hills-Cherry Creek district, caused many of the wealthy to leave Capitol Hill and move into these areas which are now some of the city's most beautiful neighborhoods.

One of the city's strangest neighborhoods was Hop Alley—Denver's China Town. With the building of the transcontinental railroad, thousands of Chinese were employed as laborers, especially on the Central Pacific Railroad which built eastward from California to Utah. Many Chinese drifted to Colorado and settled in a small community between 20th and 21st Streets and from Blake to Market Streets. At one time there may have been more than 500 men, women and children crowded into this tiny area but today it has completely disappeared. The buildings have been removed or converted to other uses and the city's Chinese are scattered to all parts of Denver.

The Chinese were suspected of all manner of crimes, including gambling and operating opium dens. Much of this was quite likely exaggerated, but led to violence on October 31, 1880, when a mob gathered and drove the Chinese from their homes and shops, causing considerable property damage to Hop Alley. The police restored order and the city eventually paid for much of the damage. The people returned, rebuilt and the neighborhood continued until early in the 20th Century. On February 2, 1910, the Chinese celebrated their New Year 4607, with the colorful festival attracting many Denverites; this was the last important event in the history of Hop Alley, for already the population was leaving the area.

For a time a sizable community of Japanese developed just beyond Hop Alley, extending from 21st to 28th Streets. With the start of World War II, the Federal Government placed many thousands of West Coast American citizens of Japanese ancestry in "relocation" prison camps to protect the nation from acts of sabotage they might try to commit. However, the government allowed many to remain free if they moved east and could support themselves. Denver's Japanese community quickly swelled to around 5,000 as many settled in the area. Like the Chinese, the Japanese have gradually drifted to all parts of the city, but a number still farm on truck gardens to the north along the Platte River, producing fine crops of fresh vegetables for the Denver market.

One other neighborhood traditionally determined by profession is the red-light district. Denver's was long in the lower downtown area, originally along Cherry Creek's south bank in Auraria, just west of Larimer Street. Eventually the area moved to a three block stretch of Market Street between 18th and 20th Streets. Today's Market Street was first known as McGaa Street in honor of pioneer William McGaa. As Mr. McGaa became connected with various questionable activities the city government decided it would be desirable to change the street's name. It was decided to honor Ben Holladay, of stagecoach fame, and thus maps began to show Holladay Street as the center of the red-light district. The Holladay family soon complained that it was hardly an honor to have their name on the main street of that particular section of town and to avoid any more such problems, the unoffensive name of Market Street was selected. Over the years the "district" moved to Lawrence and Arapahoe Streets, later uptown and today is confined to no particular area. For many years the Queen of Denver's red-light district was Mattie Silks. She came to Denver in the mid-1870's, and until almost World War I, was a prominent businesswoman along Market Street. While she eventually married Corteze D. Thomson, a foot racer and gambler, she most often went by her maiden name, Mattie Silks.

BUSINESS—ON THE SHADY SIDE!

Like most western frontier towns, Denver was wide open for gambling and all manner of confidence games. The law was stern in dealing with many crimes; murder, horse theft, claim jumping and bank robbery, but many westerners were willing to tolerate gambling and confidence operations if not openly vicious or cheating. It was almost considered proper for eastern dudes to be "taken" and because of this attitude, these businesses became firmly entrenched. Denver's most famous and colorful underworld figure was Lou Blonger. He came to the area in the late 1880's, and began operating a saloon and mining office as fronts for his other businesses which included everything from pickpockets, con artists and gambling, to fixing horse races and other sporting events. For many years Blonger purchased protection from within the police ranks and so was allowed to operate successfully until the early 1920's. His downfall came at the hands of Philip S. Van Cise. Elected as district attorney during a reform movement, Van Cise began by cleaning the corruption from the Police Department and then started to do legal battle against Blonger and his associates, eventually gaining convictions for Blonger and nineteen others.

THE RIGHT TO READ—LIBRARIES

Books, or for that matter, any reading material, were scarce on the frontier. Many families brought a Bible west and there were pioneer newspapers, but little else. In 1859, Arthur Pierce made the first move to bring books to Denver when he sent to St. Joseph, Missouri, for an order of books and magazines which he began selling, eventually building a successful business. It was in 1873, however, that a group of citizens began to work for the establishment of a real library. For a few years the Denver Library Association operated a small library but by 1878, had gone broke. It was then that creditors, Walter Cheesman and William Todd offered to accept the loss and turn the books over to the public schools on the condition that they would be used to establish a free public library. The books became the basis for the old East High School Library and were placed under the direction of John Cotton Dana, well known during this era as a progressive librarian. He placed the books on shelves open to the public (most libraries use closed book shelves) and also began one of the first library collections of children's books.

The Denver Chamber of Commerce began a free library in 1885, and received some tax support for its operation as the Mercantile Library. In 1898, the two collections were combined and formed the basis for the present Denver Public Library. A grant of $200,000 was received from the Carnegie Foundation in 1902, and with this the library was built in Civic Center. That building remains in use today as head-

quarters for the Denver Water Board. Denver's beautiful main library in Civic Center was opened in 1956, and plans are being made for a major addition within this decade. A number of branch libraries have been opened in all sections of the city and these handle much of the public's reading needs. The main library, however, serves many special needs through its specialized facilities which include an audiovisual resource center, an extensive genealogy collection, and the Western History Collection which ranks as one of the nation's most extensive collections of western Americana.

TO PRESERVE OUR CULTURE

Every society has had those persons who sense the need to preserve and protect the tangible evidence of their civilization, that it might be passed along to future generation. It is thus that we have museums, and Denver is rich in this respect.

During the pioneer era, several significant contributions were made to preserving the record of the changing West. The work of S. Seymour in sketching many scenes while with Major Stephen Long's expedition in 1820, was of great use in recording the landscape before photography. Later, J. E. Willingham, J. Y. Glendenen and A. E. Mathews sketched Denver during its pioneer years. One of the single greatest contributions toward preserving a record of the early West, was the work of William Henry Jackson. Living for many years in Denver, Jackson took hundreds of photographs of scenery, buildings and important events, most of which have been preserved and a number of which appear in this book.

The Academy of Fine Arts was formed in 1877, the Denver Art League began in 1892, and by the 1890's, Denver University had a fine art school under the direction of Preston Powers, who also painted a number of works on display in the State Capitol. The present Denver Art Museum traces its history to the founding of the Denver Artists Club in 1893. In 1922, the group received Chappell House as a gift from Mrs. George Cranmer and her brother, Delos Chappell. In later years the museum expanded its collection into the new City and County Building and finally in 1971, opened a beautiful new building in Civic Center.

In 1879, the state legislature created the Historical and Natural History Society which continues today as the State Historical Society of Colorado. For a time the Society's rapidly growing collection was housed in the newly completed Capitol Building, but in 1909, the legislature appropriated $100,000 for the purchase of a site for a museum building. The present Museum, on the corner of Sherman Street and 14th Avenue, was opened on September 2, 1915, having cost a total of $550,000 including the land and furnishing. One of the moving forces behind the establishment of the Historical Society was Dr. F. J. Bancroft, who served as its first president. In later years another Denver pioneer, William Byers, of the Rocky Mountain News, served as president. The Society continues to make a herculean effort to preserve the state's historical resources, and does so on a very limited budget.

Denver's world renowned Museum of Natural History traces its founding to 1899, when Professor Edwin Carter, of Breckenridge, offered to convey his extensive collection of Colorado fauna, preserved by taxidermy, to either the State of Colorado or the City of Denver, the terms being such that it would be almost a gift. Arrangements were made with Professor Carter but before the transfer took place he died in January 1900. The collection was later purchased from the heirs and shipped to Denver for storage in the Capitol Building. An organization was soon formed to erect a museum building in City Park using both private funds and $35,000 from the City of Denver. From this start, the present museum has developed and displays life-like scenes of Colorado wildlife in beautifully detailed settings.

The growing interest in railroad history led to the establishment of the Colorado Railroad Museum at Golden in 1959. A large museum building preserves an extensive collection of photographs, documents and small items of railroad interest. The spacious grounds display one of the finest collections of railroad equipment, both narrow and standard gauge.

Several suburban communities have established small museums and each is playing a role in preserving the evidence of our culture.

Men and women have long sought to join ranks to further the more admirable goals of humanity. This desire has led to a wide range of fraternal and social clubs and organizations.

Freemasonry arrived with the first settlers, and the first recorded lodge meeting was held on November 3, 1858, with seven Masons meeting in the home of Henry Allen. The men received authority from the Grand Lodge of Kansas to organize Auraria Lodge and did so in August, 1859. Less than six months later, on January 21, 1860, Golden City Lodge No. 34 was also chartered from the same Grand Lodge. On August 2, 1861, the Grand Lodge of Colorado was formed and Golden City became Colorado Lodge No. 1. Freemasonry experienced rapid growth in early Colorado as did many of the associated bodies. The ladies soon became active in helping to organize several chapters of the Order of the Eastern Star and on June 6, 1892, eleven chapters formed the Grand Chapter of Colorado.

The Odd Fellows, while not as well known today, were a strong organization in pioneer Denver. After meeting sporadically for several years, the Union Lodge No. 1 was formed on July 6, 1864, and by 1867, three more lodges had been formed.

One of the most spectacular fraternal gatherings the city has seen was the 32nd Triennial Conclave of the Knights Templar held in mid-August, 1913. This gigantic figure of a Knight on horseback was constructed near 18th and Champa Streets.—*D.P.L., Western History Coll.*

Among Denver's first settlers were members of the Jewish community and thus interest soon grew in the formation of a local chapter of B'nai B'rith. Denver Lodge No. 171 was formed on April 6, 1872, with a gathering of twenty men; a century later it is among the largest chapters of B'nai B'rith.

The Benevolent and Protective Order of Elks organized in Denver on April 16, 1862, meeting in the Odd Fellows Hall at 369 Lawrence Street. At that time it was the only Elks Lodge between St. Louis and the Pacific Coast.

The Knights of Columbus formally established themselves in Denver in November, 1900, meeting in the Elks Hall on Lawrence Street. The Knights soon moved to a house at 14th and Glenarm Streets, and in 1920, settled in their present building at E. 16th Avenue and Grant Street.

Women have by no means been outdone in the formation of clubs. In 1860, the Denver Ladies Union Aid Society was organized at the home of Mrs. William Byers and the group set out to help unfortunate families. They later changed their goal and turned to preserving history and in 1943, merged with a men's group which had been doing the same work; combined they became the Pioneer Men and Women of Colorado.

The Territorial Daughters of Colorado formed in 1910, and have been responsible for placing historical markers at many locations around Colorado. From more than a dozen small groups, the Woman's Club of Denver was formed in 1894, and then branched out into various fields of endeavor, including the operation of a free library, work for women's suffrage, help to the Home for Newsboys, operation of one of the city's first day-nursery schools, and a fund raising drive for Belgian relief during World War I.

The influx of immigrants to Denver brought the establishment of numerous ethnic clubs; the Polish Club of Denver, the Alliance Francaise, and similar organizations to meet the interests of Italians, Irish, Germans, Japanese, and Hungarians, to name only some of the more active groups.

Purely social clubs have been equally popular, especially in catering to the interests of the wealthy. In 1863, the Denver Social Club was formed, later to be followed by many other such groups, including the Denver Country Club, the Denver Athletic Club, and in more recent times, a number of newer golf and country clubs. Many of the functions of these organizations, while for the pleasure of the members, are undertaken as charity events and the profits go to sustain very worthwhile causes and projects.

THE KU KLUX KLAN

Across America after World War I, the Ku Klux Klan gained considerable strength and surprisingly widespread support. The Klan reached the zenith of its power in Colorado in the mid-1920's, and in the 1924 election, Klan members won control of a number of seats in the state legislature. Governor Clarence J. Morley bowed to clan pressures and allowed Grand Dragon, Dr. John G. Locke to hold tight control over his administration. Throughout this period and especially during 1924-25, Klan parades and rallys were held on downtown Denver streets, in suburban communities and, as is well remembered to many residents of that era, on Table Mountain, overlooking Golden. The Klan even provided auxiliaries in order that the ladies could also take part. The failure of Governor Morley to push through legislation that Locke and the Klan needed in order to increase their control, brought an end to the Klan's strong position but it continued much in evidence for some time.

THE MAGIC OF SOUND AND PICTURE— RADIO AND T.V.

On March 10, 1922, W. D. (Doc) Reynolds, a radio pioneer in Colorado, was issued one of the first ten commercial radio station licenses, and KLZ was born. Others followed quickly: Captain W. L. Winner and Gene O'Fallon established KFEL in 1923; General Electric built KOA in 1924; in 1928, KPOF came on the air for the Pillar of Fire Church, being one of the pioneers in the field of non-commercial broadcasting; and in 1934, KDZQ became KVOD and joined the old Blue Network. The "Golden Days" of radio were the 1930's and 1940's, when in addition to the local programs, the networks provided top name stars in a full range of programs from variety and comedy to serious drama and the ever popular "soap opera."

The Social Order

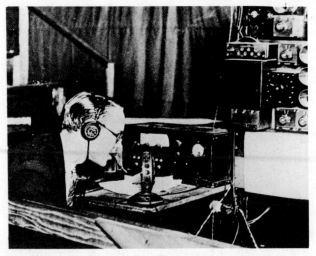

In this mid-1920's photo, Station KLZ is broadcasting the opera "Martha" from City Auditorium.—*D.P.L., West. Hist. Coll.*

Radio pioneer Gene O'Fallon became a pioneer again, when on July 18, 1952, KFEL-TV sent its first picture out to an anxiously waiting Denver audience. The test pattern of that first day turned to regular programing at 5:00 P.M. on July 20th and Channel 2 has remained on the air since. In quick order, Denver gained more stations with KBTV (Channel 9) coming on the air on October 6, 1952, KLZ-TV (Channel 7) appearing on November 1, 1953, and KOA-TV (Channel 4) offering its first broadcast on Christmas Eve, 1953. Later Denver gained educational television on Channel 6, owned by the Denver Public Schools and continues today with these five channels.

The programs have changed, but the magic of radio and television seems to show no sign of fading and the future appears to hold promise of continued expansion in both fields.

EXTRA! EXTRA! READ ALL ABOUT IT!

Today and for some years, Denver has had two major daily newspapers, the Rocky Mountain News, issued each morning, and the Denver Post, issued every afternoon except Sunday when it publishes a morning edition. The long series of events leading to the peaceful co-existence of the two great papers is an involved story of mergers and keen competition.

The Rocky Mountain News began publishing on April 23, 1859, as a weekly paper, but went to a daily schedule on August 27, 1860. During the period 1860-1880's, several papers appeared but soon faded into memory. By the turn of the century, however, the city had four major dailies: the Rocky Mountain News (morning); the Denver Times (evening), which was purchased by the News in 1902, as an evening companion; The Denver Post (evening); and the Denver Republican (morning).

Early in the new century a keen rivalry developed among the Denver papers and a series of events sharpened the battle. In 1902, the News purchased the Denver Times and in October, 1913, purchased the Denver Republican and combined it with the News. In 1906, the Denver Express had begun publication and was owned by the Scripps-Howard newspaper chain. On November 22, 1926, Scripps-Howard purchased the Rocky Mountain News and Denver Times and promptly combined the evening Denver Times and the evening Denver Express into the Evening News, with the first issue dated November 23, 1926. The Denver Post, under the ownership of H. H. Tammen and F. G. Bonfils, made plans at once to begin a morning newspaper and on January 3, 1927, began issuing the Denver Morning Post. A crazy but colorful battle was carried on between the rivals but with neither clearly winning, an agreement was reached to settle and on November 5, 1928, it was agreed that the Post would drop its morning paper and the News would drop its evening paper. NOTE— A detailed record of the publication dates of the various Denver newspapers is contained in the bibliography at the back of the book.

AUGUSTA TABOR

HORACE AUSTIN WARNER TABOR

ELIZABETH MCCOURT TABOR "BABY DOE"

THE
TABORS

Horace Tabor and Augusta L. Pierce were married on January 31, 1857, and began to work a 160-acre farm in Riley County, Kansas. News of the Colorado gold strikes lured them West and while Augusta earned a living doing laundry, taking boarders, and later running their general store, Tabor gradually saved enough to grubstake two miners from his now booming business in Leadville. They struck it rich in May, 1878, at the Little Pittsburgh Mine. Tabor's fortune seemed to know no limits and early in 1879, he purchased the Henry C. Brown home, built in 1875, at 17th and Broadway (above), for $40,000. As Tabor's wealth increased, so did his interest in other women. In the spring of 1880, on a trip to Leadville, he met "Baby Doe" who had just been divorced from Harvey Doe. The affair became the talk of the town and finally, on January 2, 1883, Augusta gave Horace a divorce in exchange for their home and $300,000 in mining stock. At the divorce trial she passionately proclaimed, "Not willingly, Oh God, not willingly!" Augusta died in Pasadena, California on February 1, 1895, and is buried in Riverside Cemetery. The United Bank of Denver now occupies the site of her home at East 17th Avenue and Broadway.—*State Historical Society of Colorado*

Tabor's political career, which included a term as Lieutenant Governor (1879-83), was damaged by the scandal of his divorce, but he did gain an appointment as U.S. Senator to fill the vacancy when Henry Teller was appointed to President Arthur's cabinet. He was sworn in on February 3, 1883, and on March 1st, the day before his appointment ended, he married Baby Doe in Washington. In December, 1886, Tabor purchased a fine home (left) at East 13th Avenue and Sherman Street, at a cost of $54,000. The silver panic of 1893, wiped out the Tabor fortune but in 1898, his appointment to be Postmaster of Denver gave Horace and Baby Doe some hope to make a new start. In April, 1899, however, Tabor became ill with appendicitis and died on April 10th. Baby Doe followed his advice to "Hang on to the Matchless" and she was found frozen to death in her cabin at the mine on March 7, 1935. She is seen about 1930, (above) on a downtown Denver street. Her older daughter, Lillie Tabor, died in Chicago in 1946, and her younger daughter, Rose Mary Echo Silver Dollar Tabor died in Chicago under mysterious circumstances in September, 1925.—*Left and far right—opposite page, State Historical Society of Colorado; others, Denver Public Library, Western History Collection*

THE BOETTCHERS

The home of Charles Boettcher I, at 1201 Grant Street, is seen above, about 1890. Like so many of the fine old homes of that era, it was gone by the mid-1950's.

A home of striking and unusual design, was that of Charles Boetcher II, seen below at 777 Washington Street. The home was torn down in 1963.

The home of Claude K. Boettcher (opposite page—top) is today one of the state's most famous houses, for in 1960, it was donated to Colorado for use as the Governor's Mansion. Located at 400 East 8th Avenue, only seven blocks from the Colorado Capitol Building, the house was built in 1906, for Walter Cheesman who died prior to its completion. Mrs. Cheesman and their daughter Gladys remained in the home for a number of years and in 1926, it was purchased by Mr. Boettcher. The house is now open to visitor tours and provides an opportunity to enjoy the splendor of an historic Denver house.—*Opposite-top, Colorado Division of Commerce and Development; others, Denver Public Library, Western History Collection*

Three generations of the Boettcher family are seen in this photo, taken in about 1925. Charles Boettcher I (1852-1948) is in the center; his son, Claude K. Boettcher (1875-1957) is on the left; and his son, Charles Boettcher II (1901-1963) is on the right.

Charles Boettcher I, a German immigrant, returned to Germany to study its sugar beet industry. Returning to Colorado, he encouraged farmers in northern Colorado to plant sugar beets and the success of this venture led to his establishment of the Great Western Sugar Company. At the turn of the century, during construction of facilities for his sugar business, Boettcher noted the lack of cement plants in the West. He purchased a small cement plant at Portland, Colorado, and from this built the Ideal Cement Company.—*Denver Post photo from Denver Public Library, Western History Collection*

The home of Lawrence C. Phipps, at 3400 Belcaro Drive, was built in 1932, and in the mid-1960's, was given to the University of Denver for use as a conference center. Phipps was a U.S. Senator from Colorado between 1919 and 1930, and is well remembered to Denverites both for Phipps Auditorium and the former Phipps Sanatorium, now the site of Lowry Air Force Base.—*Right, Denver Post photo—both, Denver Public Library, Western History Collection*

LAWRENCE COWLES PHIPPS

The Social Order

GOVERNOR JOHN EVANS

WILLIAM GRAY EVANS

JOHN EVANS II

Three generations of the Evans family are seen opposite, along with their homes. John Evans, a Chicago area physician, teacher and one of the founders of Northwestern University, was appointed by President Lincoln to be the second Territorial Governor of Colorado (1862-1865). He became deeply involved in Denver business circles. His first Denver home is seen at 14th and Arapahoe Streets in the late 1860's. William Evans, son of John Evans, rose to become President of the Denver Tramway and succeeded David Moffat as President of the Denver & Salt Lake Railway. His home, at West 13th Avenue and Bannock Street, was built by William Byers and sold to Evans in the 1880's and is still occupied by members of the Evans family. John Evans II, became President of the First National Bank of Denver and is seen at his desk in 1968. His home, built in 1932, at East Alameda Avenue and Race Street is still standing.—*Top row, State Historical Society Collection; center-right, Denver Post photo; others, Denver Public Library, Western History Collection*

David Moffat, seen at his desk, devoted much of his life and fortune to building the Denver & Salt Lake Railway. His beautiful home, (below) at East 8th Avenue and Grant Street was built in 1910, just a year before his death. Mrs. Moffat sold the home and for many years it was occupied by the American Hellenic Education and Progressive Association. Many attempts were made to preserve the home but the lack of interest by city officials in a plan to use it as the Mayor's Residence and the Association's determination to sell the property, led to its being razed in 1972.—*Both, Denver Public Library, Western History Collection*

DAVID HOLLIDAY MOFFAT

The Social Order

MOLLY

BROWN

Margaret Tobin, born and raised in Hannibal, Missouri, heard tales of the fortunes being made in Colorado's mines and determined to move to the West. In 1883, her brother Daniel moved to Leadville and she followed him the next year. At the age of nineteen Molly met J. J. Brown, manager of the Little Jonny Mine and they were married on September 1, 1886. Brown owned a one-eighth interest in the mine and its rich ore deposits soon made the Browns wealthy. Upon moving to Denver, they purchased a home at 1340 Pennsylvania Street (above) and Molly, seen in her dining room (left), planned to become part of Denver society. Her problems in being accepted into social circles have been subject for both a book and the stage and screen production of "The Unsinkable Molly Brown." Molly died on October 25, 1932, but her home, long known as the House of Lions for the carved lions which guard the property, stills stands and is now the headquarters for Historic Denver, Incorporated, which is working to preserve other unique buildings of the city's past.—*Both, State Historical Society of Colorado*

After spending the winter of 1911-12 in Europe, Molly decided to return to America on the maiden voyage of the R.M.S. *Titanic*. During the fateful night of April 14, 1912, as the great ship hit an iceberg and sank, Molly did much to help load lifeboats and to calm other passengers. Her efforts continued while on board the rescue ship *Carpathia* and upon returning to Denver she found herself a heroine. More important to Molly, however, was her immediate acceptance into Denver society, signaled by a luncheon invitation from Mrs. Crawford Hill. Molly is seen at the right, on June 1, 1912, presenting a gift to Captain A. H. Rostron of the *Carpathia*, commemorating that ship's rescue efforts. —*Denver Public Library, Western History Collection*

BARON WALTER
VON RICHTHOFEN

Baron Von Richthofen, a native of Prussia, came to Denver in the late 1870's and became involved in real estate development. After living for a few years in North Denver, he constructed a massive stone castle (above) at 7012 East 12th Avenue and surrounded it with two square blocks of landscaped gardens. The area he promoted as the Montclair subdivision. Richthofen also became active in the Denver Circle Railroad which served South Denver, and later built an art gallery and a beer garden.—*Above right, Edward Delder photo, Denver Public Library, Western History Collection; above, State Historical Society of Colorado*

One of Denver's well remembered houses was the castle-like home (above-right) of William Church. Church, who was active in both the cattle business and copper mining, built his home at 1000 Corona Street at the turn of the century and it stood until the mid-1960's. Unlike so many fine old homes which have been torn down in recent years, the home of Denver Tramway President Rodney Curtis still stands at the corner of East Colfax and Pennsylvania Street. Today, the Cathedral of the Immaculate Conception stands immediately to the west of the house (at the left in the photo).—*Both, State Historical Society of Colorado*

The mansion (right) of Mr. and Mrs. Crawford Hill (son and daughter-in-law of Senator Nathaniel Hill) was a center of Denver social life. From early in the century until the early 1940's, Mrs. Hill was the unofficial ruler of the city's highest social circle.

The Woodbury home built in 1885, at West 25th Avenue and Alcott Street was a North Denver landmark until razed in the early 1970's. Woodbury became a General in the Civil War and later had a long career in Denver newspapers and banking. He helped organize the Chamber of Commerce and the Denver Public Library.

A typical West Denver neighborhood is captured in this 1905 photo taken at West 2nd Avenue and Bannock Street.—*Below, H. E. Jobes Collection; others, Denver Public Library, Western History Collection*

ROGER WILLIAMS WOODBURY

HOP ALLEY

Almost forgotten today is Denver's once famous "Hop Alley". The Chinese neighborhood, bounded roughly by Blake, Market, 20th and 21st Streets, once had a population of over 500, but by World War I the population had begun to drift to other parts of the city and today almost no trace of the community is to be found. Hop Alley is seen in these three rare photos. On the left (above) is the Chinese Masonic Lodge #185 as it appeared in the mid-1920's, while on the right is a scene in the alley between Blake and Market Streets, when the Chinese influence was waning. Below, a Chinese funeral procession is seen on Market Street. There were several parlor houses in the area and two "ladies" can be seen leaning from an upstairs window of the building at the center of the photo.—*All, Denver Public Library, Western History Collection*

THE RED LIGHT DISTRICT

For many years Denver's red-light district was centered along Market Street, between 18th and 20th Streets. One of the district's most famous madams was Jennie Rogers whose real name was Leeah J. Fries. Jennie came to Denver in 1879 and opened a parlor house at 2009 Market Street (then known as Holladay Street) and soon expanded to a larger house at 1950 Market Street. In 1884, she built the famous House of Mirrors, named for a parlor completely lined with mirrors. The exterior featured carved heads including one of Jennie (left) which was five feet wide and four feet high. The house is seen above, as painted by Herndon Davis in the mid-1930's. From 1929 until 1948, the building housed the Bhuddist Church of Denver and served its last years as a warehouse.

After Jennie's death on October 17, 1909, the house was operated for a time by Mattie Silks, perhaps most noted of all Denver madams. Mattie came to Denver in 1877 and continued in business until 1919. She is seen below, at her place on West 44th Avenue where she maintained a small horse racing stable, a favorite pastime of her first husband, Corteze Thomson.

MATTIE SILKS (left in photo)

GAMBLING

EDWARD CHASE

Edward Chase reigned as Denver's gambling king for half a century. He came to Denver in June, 1860, and maintained an air of respectability that included a term as alderman (1865-1869) and service with Chivington's forces at the Sand Creek massacre. After operating the Progressive Club, he opened the Palace Theater (see page 291) on Blake, between 14th and 15th Streets, and organized his own theatrical troup to provide entertainment along with the gambling. Chase eventually became part owner of the Navarre, but his most famous establishment was the Inter Ocean Club, on Curtis between 14th and 15th Streets. At the turn of the century the Denver Times led a campaign against Chase as part of an effort to control gambling and in April, 1903, the paper ran the cartoon seen above. Chase continued his activities for several more years and died in 1921, at the age of 83.

Bella Bernard's parlor house at 1952 Market Street, is seen (left) about 1885. A part of the red-light district is seen (above) in this scene at 1840-48 Market Street. —*All photos on both pages, Denver Public Library, Western History Collection*

Denver's present library system is resultant from the merger in 1898, of the Mercantile Library, which was begun by the Chamber of Commerce in 1885, and the Denver High School Library, housed in a wing of the old East High School. The East High facility is seen in these two photos (above and left) with Librarian John Cotton Dana visible on the left, standing at the counter. In 1889, the new Public Library moved to a rented building at 15th Street and Court Place (below) where it remained until 1903. In 1902, the Carnegie Foundation made a grant of $200,000 to Denver for use in building a new public library. The city purchased the La Veta Place apartment building (top-opposite page) at West Colfax Avenue and Bannock Street, once owned by David Moffat and later by Horace Tabor, and temporarily used the building to house the library after it moved from the 15th Street and Court Place facility. The La Veta Place building was eventually razed and the new library (center and bottom-opposite) built in its place. After completion of the present Main Library in 1956, the old library was made the headquarters of the Denver Water Department.—*Above and top (opposite), State Historical Society of Colorado; others, Denver Public Library, Western History Collection*

Serving Man's Need
for Knowledge

Denver's fine new main Public Library building (above) was constructed at a cost of $3 million and opened on October 14, 1956. The facility has become one of the major research centers in the western United States and the largest public library between Kansas City and the West Coast. In sharp contrast to the Main Library is the system's smallest library, the Eugene Field Branch, seen at the right. The building once stood at 307 West Colfax Avenue and was the home of Field during the two years that he was Managing Editor of the Denver Tribune. When the home was about to be torn down in the late 1920's, it was purchased by Molly Brown and donated to the city. In 1930, it was moved to Washington Park and made a branch library. In 1972 a new Field Branch was built and the old building then became headquarters for the Parks and Recreation Department. Typical of the other branch libraries is the Warren Branch at East 34th Avenue and High Street, seen in the two lower photos.—*Above, Denver Public Library; right, University of Colorado Historical Collection; others, State Historical Society of Colorado*

DENVER LIBRARIANS

JOHN COTTON DANA   CHALMERS HADLEY   MALCOLM GLENN WYER

Three noted Denver librarians are seen in these photos. John Dana became librarian when the new free library was opened in the old East High School in the early 1880's. He initiated the first open shelf system in America, created the first children's room and did much to bring the library to the attention of the people of Denver. Chalmers Hadley served as City Librarian from 1910 until 1924 and under his direction the first six branch libraries were established and the Science and Engineering Department was begun. Dr. Malcolm Wyer headed the Denver Public Library from 1924 until 1951 and is best remembered for organizing the Western History Department. Under John Eastlick, who began serving in 1951, the new main library was designed and built and the library system continues to grow today, under the leadership of Henry G. Shearouse, Jr.—*All photos this page, Denver Public Library, Western History Coll.*

DENVER'S FAMOUS AUTHORS

WILLIAM EDMUND BARRETT

Author William Barrett, who came to Denver in 1942, is best remembered for his "Lilies of the Field" which eventually became a highly successful motion picture.

MARY COYLE CHASE

Mrs. Robert L. (Mary) Chase, wife of retired Rocky Mountain News Editorial Chief Robert Chase, won the Pulitzer Prize in 1945, for her story about an invisible rabbit named "Harvey." The play became one of the all-time comedy hits.

The Social Order

MUSEUMS

Three Denver museums are seen in this collection of photos. Below, is the new Denver Art Museum at West 14th Avenue Parkway and Acoma Street in Civic Center. Opened on October 3, 1971, the six million dollar, six story structure has a facade of almost a million glass tiles and houses a collection of world art that is valued in excess of ten million dollars.

In contrast to the new art museum, the city's first museum is seen on the left. Hamilton's Rocky Mountain Museum housed a collection of minerals and fossils, many of which were for sale as well as for display. Located on 16th between Market and Larimer Streets, next to the Denver Tribune Building, it is seen here in the mid 1880's. By the turn of the century this pioneer museum had gone out of business.

The Colorado State Historical Society was created by the Colorado Legislature in 1879 and its collection was housed for several years in the Capitol Building. The new State Museum is seen above, while under construction at East 14th Avenue and Sherman Street in 1912. The completed building appears on the upper right about 1920 and appears unchanged today.—*Bottom, Rush McCoy photo, Denver Art Museum; others, State Historical Society of Colorado*

THE DENVER MUSEUM OF NATURAL HISTORY

The Denver Museum of Natural History is widely known for its very lifelike wildlife displays such as in the scene below. The museum was organized at the turn of the century to house the collection of Professor Edwin Carter, a pioneer naturalist. The museum building is seen (right) in 1936; the center section opened in 1908, the left wing was completed in 1918, the right in 1929, and in recent years the building was further enlarged.—*Both, Denver Public Library, Western History Collection*

Adjoining the Natural History museum is Phipps Auditorium (below-left) which was built as a gift from Senator Lawrence C. Phipps. Opened on January 11, 1940, the auditorium seats 950, and is used for a wide variety of musical and cultural events.

The Colorado Railroad Museum (below-right) was opened in 1958, on a spacious site at the foot of North Table Mountain, just east of Golden. The museum has an outstanding collection of railroad equipment from Colorado and the West. Extensive displays of photos and small railroadiana are contained in the depot style museum building.
—*Left, D.P.L., Western History Coll.; right, Colorado Railroad Museum*

FREEMASONRY

On November 3, 1858, seven Masons met in the home of Henry Allen in Auraria, and from this meeting grew the organization of the first Masonic Lodge in Colorado. After receiving authority from the Grand Lodge of Kansas, the Auraria Lodge was organized in August of 1859 and on October 1, 1859, held their first meeting in the two story building, at the center of the photo above, located at 1361 11th Street. The building stood until 1939.

A downtown landmark, the Masonic Temple at 16th and Welton Streets was dedicated on June 24, 1890, and still serves various Masonic bodies.

The El Jebel Shrine is well known to most Denverites for its yearly sponsorship of the Shrine Circus. A group of El Jebel members are seen posed (center photo) about 1920, in front of the Capitol Building.

The Scottish Rite Temple (bottom) at East 18th Avenue and Sherman Street was built in 1907 as the El Jebel Temple, and continued as such until 1924, when El Jebel moved to its new temple at West 50th Avenue and Vrain Street.—*Center and bottom, L. C. McClure photos; center, Denver Public Library, Western History Collection; others, State Historical Society of Colorado*

In the years after the Civil War, many Denverites joined the Grand Army of the Republic, an organization of veterans of the Union Army. By the turn of the century there were eight GAR posts in Denver and a group of members posed for this photo (above) about 1905. On the far left is Major Shadrach K. Hooper, the long time General Passenger and Ticket Agent of the Rio Grande Railroad, who pioneered efforts to promote the state's tourist trade. As Civil War veterans died the GAR began to fade and held its last encampment in 1949, in Indianapolis.

The Knights of Columbus held their first Denver meeting in 1900 and in 1909 moved to this large building (below) at 14th Street and Glenarm Place. In later years they moved to East 16th Avenue and Grant Street and sold this building to the Knights of Pythias. The building was razed in 1962.—*L. C. McClure photo, Denver Public Library, Western History Collection*

The Denver Club was organized on July 28, 1880, and included among its founders, David Moffat, Walter Cheesman and Henry Wolcott. The Club's building (above) was opened in October, 1888, at 17th Street and Glenarm Place and remained in use until 1953. The modern Denver Club Building now occupies the same location.

In 1891, Baron Von Richthofen built an art gallery at 8th Avenue and Monaco Street. In 1901, the building was converted into the Montclair Casino (above), but in 1906, the building was destroyed by fire and the club faded into history.

The Denver Athletic Club organized in 1884, ". . . to maintain and operate a gymnasium." Its building, at 1325 Glenarm Place (below), was opened in December, 1890, and was enlarged in 1926. A fire caused widespread damage on February 18, 1951, but the building was rebuilt and remains in use.—*Top, D.P.L., Western History Coll.; bottom, State Historical Society of Colo.*

The Denver Country Club was begun in the 1890's, and for several years leased the golf course at Overland Park. In 1902, the club purchased the Reithmann estate along Cherry Creek and built its clubhouse (right) near East 1st Avenue and Gilpin Street. In the photo above the "Sacred 36," the upper echelon of Denver society, are enjoying the Crepe Paper Ball at the Denver Country Club in about 1910.—*Both, Denver Public Library, Western History Collection*

The Wellshire Country Club (left), at South Colorado Boulevard and East Hampden Avenue, is seen in the early 1920's, when new and far out in the country. In 1936 the club was purchased by the City of Denver and is now the Wellshire Municipal Golf Course.

When the Cherry Hills Country Club opened on September 8, 1923, it too, was out in the country. The clubhouse, at South University Boulevard and Oxford Avenue, is seen below, soon after completion.—*Both, Denver Public Library, Western History Collection*

KKK

After World War I, the Ku Klux Klan began gaining strength throughout America. Klan activity intensified in the Denver area during the early 1920's, and reached its peak about 1925. On the right, the Denver Ladies Auxiliary is gathered for a night meeting in 1925, while in the center scene, 2,500 Denver Klansmen have gathered in a canyon near Boulder to present a charter to the new Boulder Klan. Such events took on a social air, as in this case, with everyone enjoying an old-fashioned western barbecue. On May 31, 1926, Klansmen from throughout Colorado paraded in downtown Denver (bottom) prior to holding meetings at the cotton mill in South Denver. The Klan's influence began to fade by the late 1920's and has never gained wide support since.—*All, Denver Public Library, Western History Collection*

DENVER POST Radio Log

FRIDAY, NOV. 15.

	KOA NBC Net. 850 kc.	KVOD ABC Net. 630 kc.	KLZ CBS Net. 560 kc.	KFEL MBS Net. 950 kc.
4:00P	Road of Life	Ladies Be Seated	Budget Brigade	Newscast
4:15P	Joyce Jordan	Ladies Be Seated	My Serenade	Afternoon Melodies
4:30P	Aunt Mary	Teatime Tempos	Open House	Newscast
4:45P	Dr. Paul	Concert Time	Robert Trout	Buck Rogers
5:00P	This Woman's Secret	Terry and Pirates	Voice of the News	Hop Harrigan
5:15P	World News	Sky King	Shorty, Sue, Sally	Superman
5:30P	Headlines	Jack Armstrong	Traffikwiz	Captain Midnight
5:45P	News; Yelland	News	Here Comes Harmon	Tom Mix
6:00P	Hiways in Melody	The Lone Ranger	Baby Snooks	Burl Ives
6:15P	Hiways in Melody	The Lone Ranger	Baby Snooks	Henry J. Taylor
6:30P	Alan Young	This Is Your FBI	Thin Man	Love Story Theater
6:45P	Alan Young	This Is Your FBI	Thin Man	Love Story Theater
7:00P	People Are Funny	Break the Bank	Ginny Simms	Gabriel Heatter
7:15P	People Are Funny	Break the Bank	Ginny Simms	Education Program
7:30P	Waltz Time	The Sheriff	Durante-Moore	Spotlight Band
7:45P	Waltz Time	The Sheriff	Durante-Moore	Spotlight Band
8:00P	Mystery Theater	Fights	Pays Be Ignorant	Spotlight America
8:15P	Mystery Theater	Fights	Pays Be Ignorant	Spotlight America
8:30P	Bill Stern	Am. Sports Page	"Maisie"	Sweet Music
8:45P	Men of the West	Am. Sports Page	"Maisie"	Chuck Bennett
9:00P	Supper Club	Missing Heirs	Lowell Thomas	Newscast
9:15P	Bob Young; News	Missing Heirs	Jack Smith Show	Feature News
9:30P	Rabbi Berkowitz	News	Sparkle Time	Fulton Lewis Jr.
9:45P	Furs on Parade	Comic Opera	Sparkle Time	Bill Brandt
10:00P	News	Newscast	Voice of the News	The Symphonette
10:15P	Singin' Sam	Easy Rhythms	Henry Outland	The Symphonette
10:30P	News Roundup	Rhythm Spree	Red Barber	Willie Hartzell
10:45P	General Vandergrift	Dance Music	Dr. B. Cherrington	Muzak
11:00P	DENVER POST News	Rendezvous	Chet Huntley	Newscast
11:15P	Palmer Hoyt	Dance Music	American Legion	Winnie the Wave
11:30P	Palmer Hoyt	Freddie Martin	CBS Orchestra	Dance Band
11:45P	Midnight Dance	Freddie Martin	CBS Orchestra	Smile Time
12:00P	News Summary	Sign Off	Midnight Roundup	News Summary

On November 15, 1946, these were the radio programs (left) to which Denverites were listening. By the spring of 1953, Denver had enjoyed television for eight months and the March 21st issue of *Denver TV Weekly* was listing a wide array of programs from two stations. Above, a live program is seen being broadcast from the KLZ studio, probably about 1940.—*Above, Denver Public Library, Western History Collection*

SATURDAY, March 21

KFEL-TV, Channel 2 . KBTV, Channel 9

Symbols: L—Live, Local; LM—Live, via Micro-Wave; F—Film; K—Kinescope

10:00 2 TEST PATTERN

10:15 2 MULTISCOPE NEWS

11:30 2 SKY KING
Kirby Grant as a pilot-rancher always pursuing adventure. ABC (F)

12:00 2 T-BAR-V SHOW
Shorty Thompson with western songs and stories. (L)

12:30 2 NEWS
With Dick McDaniel. (L)

12:35 2 T-BAR-V SHOW (Part 2)

1:00 2 INDUSTRY ON PARADE
A visit to interesting industries of the U. S. (F)

1:15 2 YOUR OWN HOME
Decorating, remodeling in the home. (F)

1:30 2 JOBS FOR GI'S
State employment service interviews job-seeking G. I.'s. (L)

1:45 2 MULTISCOPE NEWS

2:45 2 SUN PONY STORY LODGE
Stories of Indian Folk Lore. (L)

3:00 2 MR. WIZARD
Bruce Lindgren and Don Herbent in science demonstrations. NBC (K)

3:30 2 THE BIG PICTURE
Documentary army films. (F)

3:45 9 TEST PATTERN

4:00 2 KFEL TV NEWS
With Jack Fitzpatrick. (L)
9 AIR FORCE TALENT PATROL
Entertainment from military bases emceed by Steve Allen. CBS (K)

4:10 2 WEATHERCAST

4:15 2 BETTER BUSINESS
Dan Bell in talks and interviews. (L)

4:30 2 VICTORY AT SEA
"Two If By Sea," depicting the capture of Palwa Islands, part of the plan to recapture the Philippines. Eighteenth in the series. NBC (F)
9 WESTERN PLAYHOUSE
Captain Ozie Waters introduces a western movie. (L & F)

5:00 2 THE CHRISTOPHERS
Catholic drama series. (F)

5:15 2 VARIETY TIME
Musical Shorts. (F)

5:30 2 THE RUGGLES
Comedy with Charlie Ruggles. (F)
9 BEAT THE CLOCK
Bud Collyer leads contestants thru stunts and prize quiz. CBS (K).

6:00 2 ALL-STAR REVUE
Sonja Henie and her troupe of 32 skaters present production numbers and individual dances, from Los Angeles. Harpo Marx is a special guest. NBC (LM)
9 TO BE ANNOUNCED

6:30 9 STORK CLUB
Sherman Billingsley, your host at the swank New York bistro. Interviews with celebrities and cafe society. Guests: Leslie Caron, Dave Atkinson, Les Paul and Mary Ford. CBS (K)

7:00 2 SHOW OF SHOWS
Sid Caesar and Imogene Coca, with star supporting cast including Hamilton Trio, Billy Williams Quartette, Jack Russell, and Kukla, Fran and Ollie, hosts. NBC (LM)
9 TO BE ANNOUNCED

7:30 9 GODFREY TALENT SCOUTS
Soprano Mary Lou Boyd, The Four Bards, and cellist Leslie Parnas provide the talent. CBS (K)

8:00 9 QUIZ KIDS
Joe Kelly with panel of erudite moppets. CBS (K)

8:30 2 YOUR HIT PARADE
Snooky Lanson, Dorothy Collins, June Valli, Hit Parade Dancers and Raymond Scott Band in Top Tunes of the Week. NBC (LM)
9 TV TEEN CLUB
Paul Whiteman presents youthful talent in music and variety. ABC (K)

9:00 2 GREATEST FIGHTS
Filmed highlights of outstanding matches in recent years. Bob Murphy vs. Dan Bucceroni March 16, 1951.
9 JACKIE GLEASON SHOW
Comedy and variety with Gleason, and June Taylor dancers. Guest: Sunny Gale. CBS (K)

9:15 2 WEEKLY NEWS REVIEW
Rundown of principal events of the week. (L)

9:30 2 FAMOUS PLAYHOUSE
Hollywood cast in drama. (F)

10:00 2 TWO FOR THE MONEY
Herb Shriner and audience participation quiz show. NBC (K)
9 WRESTLING
From Chicago; Russ Davis, Commentator. (F)

10:30 2 EMBASSY CLUB
Mindy Carson and Florian Zabach with songs and dances. NBC (K)

10:45 2 PULSE OF THE CITY
Drama set in New York City. (F)

11:00 2 ROLLER DERBY
Films of eastern matches.
2 GIRL WRESTLERS
Film Matches.
9 MOVIES TILL MIDNIGHT
"Melody club." English comedy with Terry Thomas, Gwyneth Vaughn.

11:30 2 WRESTLING
Filmed matches from California.

12:30 2 SIGN OFF

Radio station KOA began broadcasting on December 15, 1924, and was Denver's third station, following KFEL which began in 1923 and KLZ which became the city's first radio station on March 10, 1922. The KOA studio and broadcasting towers are seen (above-right) at East 14th Avenue and Krameria Street about 1930. On December 15, 1934, the new KOA studio opened at 1625 California Street and attracted crowds (bottom) eager to inspect the new facilities. As radio equipment was refined, it became possible to do remote broadcasts and most stations began to use trucks such as KOA's Mobile Unit No. 4, seen in the center photo while parked in front of the California Street studio.

To Denverites, it was big news when each new television station came on the air and thus the advertisement below, which appeared in December, 1953, was a sort of Christmas present for the city.—*Photos, Denver Public Library Western Collection; upper advertisement, Denver City Directory; lower advertisement, Denver TV Weekly*

TED MACK

Ted Mack, famed for his many years with Major Edward Bowes and "The Original Amateur Hour," was raised in Denver, was graduated from Sacred Heart High School and attended the University of Denver. Mr. Mack, whose real name is William Edward Maguiness, is seen above, in a photo taken on September 3, 1930.—*Denver Public Library, Western History Collection*

DON WILSON

Don Wilson, best remembered for his many years as announcer for the Jack Benny radio show, was raised in North Denver. His father, Lincoln Wilson, for many years operated the Wilson's Drug Store (later known as Alcott Drug Store) at West 41st Avenue and Tennyson Street.—*Denver Public Library, Western History Collection*

On March 9, 1927, radio station KPOF came on the air as one of America's pioneer non-commercial broadcasters, and continues to specialize in religious and musical programs. Bishop Alma White, founder of the Pillar of Fire Church which operates the station, is seen here during one of the station's first broadcasts. The station still has the microphone which appears in this photo.—*Radio Station KPOF*

The Social Order

Rocky Mountain News

A Scripps-Howard Newspaper

100TH YEAR: NO. 362 Published every morning by Denver Publishing Co. Entered as second class matter, postoffice, Denver.

Colorado's First Newspaper—Founded in 1859

DENVER 1, COLO., SUNDAY, APRIL 19, 1959

CENTENNIAL EDITION
★ FORECAST: Partly Cloudy
PRICE **15** CENTS
11 SECTIONS

532 Pages Celebrate Our 100th Birthday

HORACE GREELEY

WILLIAM NEWTON BYERS

Denver: A Pictorial History

286

Complete Wire Reports of UNITED PRESS, the Greatest World-Wide News Service

The Denver Evening News

NIGHT EXTRA

VOL. II: NO. 299.　　　　　DENVER, COLORADO, MONDAY EVENING, NOVEMBER 5, 1928. —18 Pages　　　　　PRICE: ⅔ Cents In Denver ½ Cents Outside Denver

EVENING NEWS, MORNING POST, SUSPEND TODAY

Denver Newspaper Field Reduced to Two Publications as Move for Fewer and Better Newspapers; Statement Is Issued by Roy W. Howard

Denver's pioneer newspaper, the Rocky Mountain News, was founded by William Byers and was first issued weekly, starting on April 23, 1859. One of the paper's first big stories was the reporting of the visit of Horace Greeley to the area in June, 1859. Greeley, the Editor of the New York Tribune, toured the West and sent back reports to his eastern readers. In one of these he advised "Go west, young man!" The Greeley reports did much to hasten the opening of the western lands.

The News was first located in the attic over "Uncle" Dick Wooton's store at what is now 1413 11th Street, but after two more temporary locations the paper moved into a new building (top-opposite) which was built in the dry bed of Cherry Creek near present day 13th and Welton Streets. Following this move the News began publishing on a daily basis on August 27, 1860. During the night of May 19, 1864, Cherry Creek flooded and swept the News building away. The paper occupied rented quarters for the next two years but moved to the News Block (bottom-opposite) located on Larimer between 15th and 16th Streets, on October 6, 1866. It remained at that location until 1887.

Byers eventually sold his interest in the paper but continued active in Denver business circles, serving as a vice-presidnt of the Denver Tramway and several times as head of the Festival of Mountain and Plain. In 1878, General William Austin Hamilton Loveland purchased control of the News and soon took John Arkins as a partner. The paper began a period of rapid growth and in 1887 moved to the ground floor of the Patterson & Quincy Building at 17th and Curtis Streets. In 1890, Thomas Patterson who was elected a senator from Colorado in 1901, began to purchase control in the paper and soon had major ownership. Patterson moved the paper to the ground floor of the Markham Hotel (above-right) at 17th and Lawrence Streets in 1897 and, as the paper's circulation continued to grow, he began work on a new home for the News. In 1901, the News Building at 1720 Welton Street (above-left) was completed at a cost of $75,000, and the paper remained there until moving to its present building at 400 West Colfax Avenue in 1952.

Patterson owned both the News and the evening Denver Times and a keen rivalry soon developed between them and the owners of the Denver Post, Fred Bonfils and Harry Tammen. In 1907, this actually led to Patterson becoming involved in a street fight with the much younger Bonfils. In 1913, Patterson sold both papers to John Schaffer of Chicago who combined the Denver Times with the Denver Republican which he had also recently purchased. The rivalry between Denver newspapers reached its climax after the News and Times were purchased by Roy Howard and Robert Scripps of the Scripps-Howard newspaper chain in 1926. They promptly merged their own Denver Express with the Times and changed the name to the Evening News. The Post then began publishing the Denver Morning Post and both papers began a battle for advertising and readers but with neither gaining the upper hand. The struggle came to a draw on November 5, 1928, when both the Denver Evening News and the Morning Denver Post announced they were ceasing publication that day; the next day Denver had only two daily papers.

On Sunday, April 19, 1959, the Rocky Mountain News celebrated its 100th anniversary with a Sunday Paper of 532 papers, of which the masthead is seen above (opposite).—*Above and lower left (opposite), Denver Public Library; others, State Historical Society of Colo.*

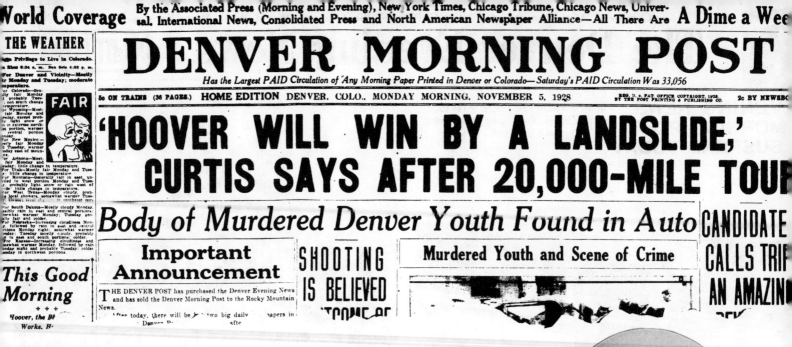

THE WEATHER

FAIR

This Good Morning

DENVER MORNING POST

Has the Largest PAID Circulation of Any Morning Paper Printed in Denver or Colorado—Saturday's PAID Circulation Was 33,056

5c ON TRAINS (36 PAGES.) HOME EDITION DENVER, COLO., MONDAY MORNING, NOVEMBER 5, 1928

'HOOVER WILL WIN BY A LANDSLIDE,' CURTIS SAYS AFTER 20,000-MILE TOUR

Body of Murdered Denver Youth Found in Auto

Important Announcement

THE DENVER POST has purchased the Denver Evening News and has sold the Denver Morning Post to the Rocky Mountain News.

SHOOTING IS BELIEVED

Murdered Youth and Scene of Crime

CANDIDATE CALLS TRIP AN AMAZING

The Denver Post was founded by F. G. Bonfils and H. H. Tammen on October 28, 1895. During the next thirty years the colorful, often flamboyant partners built their paper into one of the city's finest. Over the years, numerous newpapers were either closed or consolidated and by 1926, the three daily papers included the Evening Denver Post, and two companion papers, the Rocky Mountain News (morning) and the Evening News. To meet this evening competition, the Post began publishing the Morning Post on January 3, 1927, and the long brewing competition grew even keener. Finally, the two firms agreed to end the money losing battle and on November 5, 1928, the last Morning Post (above) was published. The Post's office on Champa between 15th and 16th Streets is seen below, in the 1930's. The statue of the "Blind Lady of Justice" was moved from the rooftop when the building was razed and is now on the new Post Building at 15th and California Streets. The Post's motto appears at the right.—*Below and lower right, D.P.L., Western History Coll.; others, State Historical Society of Colo.*

HARRY HEYE TAMMEN

FREDERICK GILMER BONFILS

"Dedicated in perpetuity to the service of the people, that no good cause shall lack a champion and that evil shall not thrive unopposed."

Denver Tribune.

L. XVIII---NO. 141.   DENVER, COLORADO, TUESDAY, MAY 20, 1884.   PRICE---FIVE CENT

EUGENE B. FIELD

The Denver Tribune was begun on February 6, 1867, as the Denver Daily. It was soon renamed the Daily Colorado Tribune and this was later changed to the Denver Tribune. The paper was first located on Lawrence, near 16th Street (above) but as the paper increased its business, it moved to larger quarters on the southeast corner of 16th and Market Streets as seen below about 1875. The Tribune's zenith came under Managing Editor Eugene Field who headed the paper between 1881 and 1883. Field became popular for his colorful writing and often included poetry as a means to comment on political and business affairs. After leaving Denver, Field wrote for the Chicago Daily Times and became widely known for his children's poems, including "Little Boy Blue" and "The Dutch Lullaby," better known by its opening lines:

> "Wynken, Blynken and Nod one night
>   Sailed off in a wooden shoe . . . ."

After Field died, Mayor Speer noticed a small statue depicting this poem and commissioned its maker, Mabel Landrum Torrey, of Sterling, Colorado, to produce a life-size statue in marble. The mayor died before the work was finished but Mr. and Mrs. Frank Woodward paid the $10,000 cost and it was placed in Washington Park as seen below.

On August 12, 1884, the Tribune was sold to the Denver Republican, controlled by Senator Crawford Hill and Kemp G. Cooper, and in 1913, the Republican was purchased by the Rocky Mountain News.—*Right, above and below, Denver Public Library, Western History Collection; others, State Historical Society of Colorado*

THE CITY AT PLAY

Life on the western frontier did not provide very much variety in entertainment. Social and recreational life centered around the activities of the church, school and fraternal orders and, of course, for some citizens a good variety of saloons provided the necessary respite from the day's work. As pioneer Denver began to settle down and gain some indications of real permanence, there began the first stirrings of activity in the entertainment arts.

THE THEATER COMES WEST

It was on the autumn evening of October 3, 1859, that the city had its first theatrical performance. The theater was located on the second floor of Apollo Hall, over a saloon and billiard parlor. Completed that previous summer by the Barney brothers, the hall was later known as the "People's Theater." Located between 14th and 15th Streets, on the north side of Larimer Street, it could hardly be termed a luxurious setting, yet it was the forerunner of a golden age of theatrics which would bring a degree of culture and enjoyment to the West. Apollo Hall was an immediate success and soon had competition from across Cherry Creek with the opening of Cibola Hall on October 24th, playing with the "Cibola Minstrels."

The arrival of Jack Langrishe and his subsequent purchase of the recently erected Platte Valley Theater at 16th and Lawrence Streets in 1861, was a milestone in Denver theatrical history. Langrishe reopened the theater as the Denver Theater and began a local stock company, while at the same time he purchased the Apollo Hall Theater and undertook some remodeling in order to permit offering an improved caliber of entertainment.

Among other pioneer theaters two are noteworthy, the Guards Hall at 15th and Curtis Streets, and Walhalla Hall at 16th and Curtis Streets. As its name implies, the Guards Hall was originally built to serve the Governor's Guards but in later years it was converted to a business block and included the theater which at a still later date was also operated as the Denver Opera House. While somewhat crowded in its seating arrangement and lacking in ventilation, the Guards Hall was a far better facility than had previously been available in Denver. The Walhalla Hall was the finest theater in the city during the late 1870's and until the opening of the Tabor Theater just across the street. The Walhalla may be considered the last of the pioneer era theaters soon to be overshadowed by the newer show places of the 1880's and 1890's.

The golden age of theater in Denver can be dated to September 5, 1881, and the opening of the Tabor Grand Opera House. Built at a cost of three quarters of a million dollars by silver king Horace Tabor, it was without question the finest theater in the West and ranked among the great theaters of America. The Tabor, seating 1,500, was constructed of red Ohio pressed brick and the interior was of cherry wood from Japan and mahogany from Honduras. Tabor selected fine art pieces from Europe to decorate the walls. Altogether it was a magnificent show place. The Tabor opened with "Maritana," sung by the Emma Abbott troup and began a decade during which the Tabor reigned supreme in Denver theatrics, under the management of W. H. Bush until 1883, and then under the direction of Horace Tabor's brother-in-law, Peter McCourt, whose career lasted almost 40 years.

The theatrical event of the 1890's was the opening of the Broadway Theater. Located in the Hotel Metropole Building on Broadway at 18th Avenue, the building still stands as a part of the Cosmopolitan Hotel but is slated to be razed by 1973. Seating 1,620 and constructed of pressed brick and sandstone, it was perhaps less spectacular than the Tabor on the outside but was certainly its equal within, making extensive use of fine woods for trim and decoration. The Broadway's grand opening was on August 28, 1890, under the management of W. H. Bush, formerly of the Tabor, and Denver then had two fine theaters in keen competition.

The Palace Theater, on the north side of Blake Street between 14th and 15th Streets, was built by Denver gambler Edward Chase and is seen here in the early 1870's. The Palace was more popular for its gambling than for its theatrical offerings.—*State Historical Society of Colorado*

In the same era, the lesser remembered Metropolitan Theater was built on the corner of 15th and Cleveland Place in 1889. Eventually coming under the ownership of Horace Tabor, the theater's name was changed to the People's Theater (not related to the earlier theater by that name) but when only three years old, the 1,000 seat house burned to the ground on June 10, 1892; it was said at the time that the spectacular blaze was a better show than ever was presented on the stage of the Metropolitan.

In 1890, Elitch's Gardens opened a summer stock theater, and the following year Manhattan Beach opened a theater in competition. While Manhattan Beach is now only a fond and distant memory, the Elitch Theater continues today and is the oldest continuous summer stock theater in America.

With the crash of the silver market, Horace Tabor lost his vast fortune including the Tabor Theater. Peter McCourt was fired as manager but quickly hired by W. H. Bush to manage the Broadway Theater. Together, Bush and McCourt leased the Tabor Theater from its new owners and effectively held a virtual monopoly on first class theater in the city.

THE SILVER SCREEN

Late in the 1890's, the inventions of Thomas Edison and George Eastman were about to bring a dramatic change to the entertainment world. The motion picture, while at first a novelty, fast became a definite part of theater operation. For a time movies were presented as an added attraction for the live stage show; a pioneer in this use was the Elitch Theater which included movies on the program in the summer of 1896. By 1910, the movies were pushing the "legitimate" theater into a back seat and by World War I, the movies were king. The golden era of the motion picture brought the movie palaces and with a string of them along Curtis Street, "Theater Row" was known as the best lit street in the world. On a visit to Denver, Thomas Edison called Curtis Street "Denver's Great White Way," so bright was the lighting.

The Tabor and Broadway, among others, soon remodeled and became leading movie theaters while keen competition came their way from several newly opened show places: the State (previously the Strand), the America, the Rialto, the Plaza, the Colonial, the Isis, the Paris, all on "Theater Row" and today all confined to memory.

One of the moving figures in Denver theater history was Harry Huffman. A Denver druggist, he opened two neighborhood theaters, the Bide-a-Wee on West Colfax Avenue and the Bluebird on East Colfax. With the coming of sound to the movies, Huffman determined to design and build a dream theater especially for showing the new talkies. Experiments with sound had been tried as early as 1913, by using the Edison Kinetoscope system in the old Orpheum, and the Tabor later briefly used the Cameraphone system; neither proved overly successful. Huffman's new theater, the Aladdin, opened in 1927, just when sound was catching the public imagination and signaled the real opening of the talkie era for Denver.

Sound ushered in a final burst of theater construction, bringing the Denver Theater in 1928 and, opposite it on 16th Street, the Paramount opened the following year. The old Orpheum was razed in 1930 and two years later the new Orpheum opened on the same spot. A long hold-out against the movies, the Denham Theater, finally converted to the silver screen in the face of cold facts of economics and public tastes.

After World War II the movies underwent marked changes. Television, while late in reaching the Denver market, kept many ticket buyers at home. Changing tastes sent many customers to the new drive-in theaters that were springing up around the nation; Denver's first, the East Drive-In, opened on July 4, 1947 and was an instant success. Many neighborhood theaters closed, their shells becoming furniture stores, warehouses, even churches. The downtown movie palaces were less fortunate, since their locations made their real estate values high, and by 1970, not a single theater structure remained on Curtis Street.

For Denver, the greatest losses were in the demolition of those two long-time rivals, the Broadway and the Tabor, and the Orpheum which had undergone major remodeling as late as 1963. By the late 1960's, only three of the classic downtown theaters remained, the Denham, Denver, and Paramount.

The City Auditorium Theater is Denver's only facility capable of seating the large audiences required to economically justify major stage productions. Conflicts in scheduling have caused Denver to miss numerous fine shows and more than once the wish has been expressed that the Tabor Theater had been preserved and remodeled to handle these productions.

While too small to accommodate road show productions, one of the finest theaters both mechanically and acoustically is the Bonfils Theater. Built by the late Helen Bonfils, when opened in October, 1953, it gained instant popularity and has provided the city with a full schedule of quality stage productions.

At the same time that many of the older movie houses were putting "CLOSED" on the marquee, a new generation of movie palaces was being constructed; the Centre opened at 16th

The America Theater, at 16th and Curtis Streets, boasted one of Denver's most spectacular signs. Built during World War I, the theater closed in the early 1930's. The Scholtz Drug Store occupied the first floor and by the mid-1930's, was replaced by Neisner Brother's 5 & 10 Cent Store. The building was razed in October, 1969.—*Denver Public Library, Western History Collection*

and Cleveland Place in the late 1950's; the Cooper Cinerama Theater opened early in the 1960's, to present a three dimensional effect on a giant curved screen; and a resurgence in the popularity of neighborhood theaters has seen compact, efficiently operated movie houses opened in several suburban shopping centers.

Despite dire predictions of a complete demise of the movie industry, the motion picture has established itself as a part of the entertainment business. However, the industry may well have forever lost the glamour of the era of the great movie palaces.

LET THERE BE MUSIC

In the frontier West one of the first forms of entertainment was that supplied by the fiddle and guitar that came west on a wagon train. Music continued to be an important aspect of the entertainment scene, ranging from opera on the stage of the Tabor Grand to musical comedies and vaudeville at the Denham, the Broadway, or any of the Curtis Street theaters.

Vaudeville was often included on the bill with other entertainment in the hope of pleasing a wide range of audiences and with the coming of the silent movies, vaudeville was an added attraction in the keen competition to keep the lines growing at the box office window. Perhaps best remembered of the vaudeville theaters was the Orpheum, a member of the Keith-Orpheum Vaudeville Circuit. Many of the nation's top entertainers played to happy audiences at the Orpheum, including Will Rogers, the Marx Brothers, Al Jolson and Sophie Tucker. Even after the New Orpheum was built in 1932, at the same location, 1537 Welton Street, the theater continued to feature vaudeville along with top feature films.

Brass bands became popular in the 1880's and many clubs, fraternal orders, and volunteer firemen sponsored bands which proudly paraded on holidays or on any good excuse. The great and near great came to Denver; John Phillip Sousa brought his band, Paderewski played at the Broadway, Caruso thrilled the city, and jazz king Paul Whiteman began his career playing in the Manhattan Beach orchestra, while a few years later Glen Miller brought out the crowds for his music in Elitch's Trocadero.

In 1912, the Philharmonic Orchestra Association was formed. It broke up during World War I, to reorganize later as the Denver Civic Symphony, and in 1934, it became the Denver Symphony Orchestra, now providing a full season of concerts.

To more than half a century of Denverites, summertime has meant concerts in City Park. Presented by the Denver Municipal Band in the band shell in front of City Park Lake, the music is enhanced by the vari-colored sprays of the fountain in mid-lake. For a large part of its existence, the band was under the baton of the late Henry Everett Sachs and hopefully the concerts will continue in the same tradition for future generations.

HOST TO THE NATION

Denver is one of America's favorite convention cities. While the conventions themselves have undergone marked changes and are now housed in a fine new convention center, the pattern is not new.

In 1881, a movement developed to organize an annual mining and industrial exposition and to this end the Exposition Building was erected just east of Broadway between Virginia and Exposition Avenues. Succeeding exhibitions were held in 1882, 1883 and 1884. Although substantial crowds were attracted and the expositions

The Festival of Mountain and Plain was held for several years, beginning in 1895, and featured elaborate parade floats such as seen here.—*State Historical Society of Colorado*

293

The City at Play

were generally successful, profits did not justify continuance and thus the building was sold and eventually torn down. In spite of this ending, the mining and industrial exposition helped to develop Denver's reputation as a host city and other groups began to select the Queen City as a meeting place. The most notable convention during this era was the convention of the National Encampment of the Grand Army of the Republic, which attracted 5,000 veterans in July, 1883.

One convention which came closest to capturing the city's attention was the Conclave of the Knights Templar, held in August, 1913. All of downtown was decorated for the occasion and grandstands were erected in the empty Civic Center area. An estimated 150,000 Denverites witnessed over 12,000 Knights parade through downtown in a procession lasting hours. More than 50,000 Knights attended the convention, making it one of the largest gatherings the city would host for many years.

In the mid-1890's, an idea began to catch the public's fancy that the city hold a yearly celebration, the result was the Festival of the Mountain and Plain. Held for the first time during the second week of October, 1895, the celebrations included a grand parade with elaborate floats, exhibits and social events in what might be termed a Mardi-Gras atmosphere. The festival was held early each fall for several years and attracted visitors from across the state and nation.

Denver's most enduring yearly event has been the National Western Stock Show. In 1899, a meeting of the National Stockgrowers Association in the Denver stockyard included an exhibition of range cattle. The event attracted such wide interest that by 1906, a group of stockmen and local businessmen organized what was actually the first of the yearly stock shows. Opening as the Western Livestock Show on January 20, 1906, in the stockyards auction arena, the event was such a success that a large circus tent was erected for the 1907 show and on that spot later stock shows and rodeos were held in the Stockyard Stadium but since 1952, have been at the 8,000 seat Denver Coliseum.

In 1908, the Democratic National Convention was held in Denver, using the just completed City Auditorium. Over the years almost every large national convention has followed this tradition by coming to the Mile-High city and, in fact, it is an unusual week in Denver when some convention is not in session.

THE OL' HOME TEAM

Pioneer Denver, having little in the way of sports equipment, turned to the horse, in plentiful supply in any western town, and began horse racing. At first, crude dirt tracks were used but soon small racing parks began to appear. In 1887, Overland Park opened to racing and continued as a popular track for almost 30 years. Early in the century greyhound racing was held at Adams City and once in Lakeside Park. In 1908, a state law was passed to make horse and dog racing illegal; however, weak enforcement allowed races to be held for several more years. In 1948, racing was made legal and today both dog and horse racing is growing in popularity.

Baseball was already a popular American game by the time of the "Rush to the Rockies" and doubtless many families moving West found space to bring along a bat and ball. It is known that the boys and "tomboys" of pioneer Denver played their own versions of the game and teams also developed among the men. Denver joined the Western League as the "Mountaineers" in 1886, playing for a time at 31st and Larimer Streets, then at River Front Park and finally in 1922, moved to the new Merchants Park stadium at South Broadway and Exposition Avenue. The team became the "Grizzlies" for a few years and then the "Denver Bears." The new Bears Stadium was opened on August 14, 1948, and greatly expanded, continues in use as Mile High Stadium, accommodating both baseball and the Broncos Football games.

According to one story, the first football came to Denver in 1867, purchased by six youths who each contributed a dollar to order the ball from back east. It was not until the late 1880's, that the game began to gain wide popularity. The Denver Athletic Club's team remained strong through the 1890's and until 1906, when it disbanded as the colleges moved into the sport. A rivalry during the 1890's between the Denver Wheel Club's team, and the area high schools was also drawing considerable public interest. Denver University fielded a team starting in 1885, while both Colorado University and Colorado School of Mines took up football in 1890.

The game has increased in popularity far beyond the expectations of the pioneer Denver teams.

The game of basketball was invented in Springfield, Massachusetts, but it was in Denver that Dr. James A. Naismith perfected his game while at the Y.M.C.A. during the year 1898. Dr. Naismith moved on to a position at Kansas University the following year, but already basketball was soaring in popularity. The Y.M.C.A. sponsored several teams and it was not long until high schools and colleges organized and entered the competition, leading to the popularity the game enjoys at present, with Denver now supporting its own professional team, the Rockets, which began some years ago as the Ringsby Rockets.

Golf, highly popular today, is by no means a new sport. The game first appeared in the Denver area in the early 1890's, but waited widespread interest until golf courses became more numerous. Several country clubs built choice greens, and Denver began to develop several golf courses around the city. A major boost for the sport came in 1931, when the old Overland Park race track and camp ground were closed and the Overland Park Golf Course developed on the site.

Boxing flourished in the West from the arrival of the first men willing to make a match. During frontier days, fisticuffs lacked the amenities later provided by strict rules, timed rounds, and trained referees; nevertheless, the bouts attracted the crowds. The sport soon came under some degree of supervision and a number of colorful promoters became active, including Bat Masterson, Professor P. R. (Reddy) Gallagher, Johnny Corbett, Abe Pollock, Otto Floto, and Jack McKenna. These men brought a steady stream of fighters to the city and trained and promoted local talent as well, holding matches at the old Stockyards Stadium, City Auditorium, or the Olympic Club at 26th and Curtis Streets. Boxing interest received a big boost when Heavyweight Champion John L. Sullivan visited Denver on December 28, 1886, for a four round exhibition bout against Duncan MacDonald. Denver had its own champion in 1901, when Young Corbett (William Rothwell) won the Featherweight title in a fight against Terrible Terry McGovern in a match held on Thanksgiving Day in Hartford, Connecticut. In later years, Colorado had another world champion, Jack Dempsey. From the small town of Manassa,

Dempsey brought new life to the fight scene and was hero to countless boys and men in Denver who considered the Manassa Mauler to be a local boy. Recent years have seen a decline of public interest in boxing and it remains to be seen if its popularity will ever return.

Hockey, relatively a new sport to Colorado, was first introduced in 1939, at Colorado College in Colorado Springs. Denver University moved into the game in 1949, and during the past decade the sport has undergone marked growth, leading to establishment of the Denver Spurs professional team.

Hardly to be considered in the same sense as the spectator sports, skiing has captured the nation's interest. With a host of the best ski areas within a few hours drive of Denver, the city has become a hub of ski interest, and has found that the sport brings millions of dollars into the local economy. For Denverites, one of the most popular close-in ski areas is at Winter Park. Located at the west portal of the Moffat Tunnel, the facility is owned by the city and was the result of farsighted planning before World War II when the sport was in its infancy. Denver was selected as the site for the 1976 Winter Olympics, however, the high cost and ecological factors caused voters to reject the plans in November, 1972.

Wheels, wheels, wheels—man seems fascinated with speed and the wheel; together they mean racing. In the 1880's, the bicycle was in vogue, while the turn of the century brought the automobile to the race track. The Denver Wheel Club was the city's most popular and famous bicycle club, but both the Ramble Wheel Club and the Arapahoe Club vied for popularity. These clubs attracted not only racers, but large numbers of members interested in the varied activities they offered, including weekend excursions, leisurely rides into the country for a picnic, and the fellowship the club offered in the era before the automobile.

As the primitive "gas buggies" and "steamers" began to become a bit sturdier and less of a plaything, serious minded car buffs began to race, first on dirt tracks in the country, but soon at Overland Park and later at Lakeside Park. Cross country racing was popular early in the century and Denver was a stop on several of the grueling transcontinental runs which tested men and machines. Overland Park's raceway was considered one of the nation's finest and attracted top name racers to Denver, including Barney Oldfield who raced as early as 1903.

Today racing, while no longer held at Overland Park, continues high in popularity in the Denver area; the cars have changed dramatically but the thrills have only grown more intense. By contrast, the bicycle is experiencing a renaissance, not for racing, but as a pleasant way in which to travel in the crowded city, and the prospects of special "bike paths" may guarantee their revival.

A CITY OF PARKS

Denver's many beautiful parks are a tribute to the planning of years past. It is not surprising, that in the vast wilderness of frontier Colorado, the earliest town planners saw little reason to create public parks. In 1868, however, the city park system began with the donation of 2.44 acres at 31st and Curtis Streets to the city by Francis Case and Frederick Ebert. The area continues as a park today, named after Samuel Curtis, an early settler. In 1872, through the efforts of Jerome B. Chaffee, territorial delegate to Congress, 160 acres of Federal land were turned over to the city for $250; the city had already paid $500 to John Walley to settle his questionable claim on the land. The area was named Congress Park and while a small piece of the land continues under that name, a larger part was renamed Cheesman Park in 1907, being combined with land that had included early burial grounds.

Late in the 19th Century, the city made additional land purchases for parks, including City Park in 1887, Washington Park in 1898, and several small parks scattered about the city. It was during the administration of Mayor Robert Speer (1904-1912 and 1916-1918) that the greatest thrust was given to park construction and similar civic beautification projects. These projects included: the embankment of Cherry Creek and construction of the Speer Boulevard parkway along the stream; purchase of Inspiration Point in the extreme northwest corner of the city for $8,000; planning and much of the work on Civic Center; installation of the still operating City Park fountain; addition of Berkeley Lake,

Rocky Mountain Lake and the Sloan's-Cooper Lake park area to the city through annexation of suburban areas; construction of the first city golf course to the north of Berkeley Lake, known then as Rocky Mountain Golf Course, it is now the Case Municipal Golf Course; construction of the Sunken Gardens at 11th Avenue and Elati Street; and opening of the swimming pool in Lincoln Park.

In more recent times, the planning of George E. Cranmer, Manager of Improvements and Parks during the administration of Mayor Benjamin F. Stapleton (1935-1947), resulted in numerous improvements including construction of Red Rocks Amphitheater, development of Winter Park, and continuation of work in the Denver Mountain Parks System, begun under Mayor Speer. The public parks of the City of Denver are among the finest to be found and do much to make life in the city pleasant and attractive for both residents and tourists.

SELLS—FLOTO, DENVER'S OWN CIRCUS

Denver has twice been selected as home for a circus. In the late 1880's the famous showman, P. T. Barnum, purchased land in southwest Denver and planned to build winter quarters for his world famous circus. These plans never materialized and the land was sold to housing developers, continuing to be known today as the Barnum area of southwest Denver.

Another circus did become a reality in Denver. Shortly after the turn of the century, Harry Tammen, co-owner of the Denver Post with F. G. Bonfils, became interested in circuses and determined to build one. Starting with the Floto Dog and Pony Show, named for Denver Post sports editor Otto C. Floto, and by later adding the name of the famous Sells Circus through the maneuver of hiring a minor member of the Sells family, there resulted the Sells-Floto Circus. Tammen and Bonfils decided to rival the other major circuses and invested in numerous top grade acts. Eventually, they were able to add Buffalo Bill to the show after his own Wild West Show went into bankruptcy and his name was an important attraction until his death in 1917. The circus wintered in Denver allowing Tammen to exercise his personal control and he became

This circus poster dates to about 1907, prior to use of the Sells-Floto name.—*Denver Public Library, Western History Collection*

very fond of the elephants, especially Princess Alice. It was a great event when Alice had a baby, since this is unusual in captivity, but sadly none of her four babies lived more than a few months. The second, named Tambon (from the names Tammen and Bonfils), was stuffed and displayed in Tammen's office until destroyed by rioters during the 1921 Tramway strike.

In 1920, with Tammen's health starting to fail, the Sells-Floto Circus was sold to a circus syndicate and a colorful era was closed.

SUMMERTIME AT THE AMUSEMENT PARK

Late in the 19th Century, amusement parks began to spring up across America, usually along a trolley line and often near the edge of the city by a lake or in pleasant countryside. Changing life styles have seen most of these parks fade away as the city aged around them, but Denver has been fortunate that two amusement parks, Elitch's Gardens and Lakeside Park have retained much of their past charm into the present.

The first amusement park venture in pioneer Denver was begun in 1866 as Ford Park. Located between East 35th and 37th Avenues and Downing and Race Streets, the park contained a small horse race track and a variety of other con-

cessions but was closed by the early 1870's. Our present "Race Street" takes its name from this early park.

In 1882, Baron Von Richthofen opened Sans Souci Gardens on South Broadway across from the new Exposition Hall. Successful for a few years, the park gradually faded after the late Exposition Hall closed.

Arlington Park opened in the 1880's, along Cherry Creek at Corona Street and East 4th Avenue and during the 1890's, was famous for its trained animal acts and for a high chute down which boats plunged into a small lake. It was this attraction which caused the name to be changed to Chutes Park in 1892. Two fires in 1901 and 1902, brought heavy damage to the park and led to its closing.

In 1883, there began a series of events leading to the establishment of the Overland Golf Course. The Denver Circle Railroad, an early attempt at public transit, purchased a tract of land south of the city along the Platte River from Rufus H. (Potato) Clark and laid out a park to attract riders to its railroad. It should be noted that Clark got his strange nickname from the fact that he made considerable wealth from potato farming near Denver. The new park was named Jewell Park in honor of Charles A. Jewell, an ex-governor and stockholder in the company, who had just died. A racetrack, bandstand, and

The City at Play

picnic grounds were soon added and the park became quite popular. In 1887, the railroad sold the park to a group of businessmen planning to use it as a country club. Renaming it Overland Park Club, perhaps because of the long overland distance from the city, the club gained fame for its early efforts to establish the game of golf in the West. Henry Wolcott, who eventually purchased major interest in the club, laid out a golf course in 1896, and soon it became popular with Denver businessmen who organized the Denver Country Club to lease the club from Wolcott. In 1902, however, the Denver Country Club moved to its present site along Cherry Creek west of University Boulevard, and Wolcott continued to use Overland Park for various activities including horse, motorcycle and automobile racing. The city eventually purchased the park and during the 1920's used it as a tourist campground; finally, in 1931 the race track was closed and today the park is a fine golf course.

In the late 1890's, Orchard Place, a beer garden style amusement park opened on South Broadway at Hampden Avenue and was especially popular because of the wide variety of gambling activities it provided. In 1906, the park was acquired by Jacob Jones of Englewood and renamed La Tuileries Gardens. For a time big name acts were brought to the park including high wire acts and balloonists, but with another change of management the park turned to bicycle and motorcycle racing and by the First World War was starting to fade and soon closed. The Cinderella City Shopping Center now occupies the site.

John Brisben Walker made his fortune by building the circulation of the faltering Cosmopolitan Magazine and then selling it to William Hearst in 1905, for a price in excess of one million dollars. Previous to this, however, he undertook several ventures in Colorado including farming in what is now northwest Denver and purchase of the rock area that later became the Red Rocks Theater. He is best remembered, however, for his River Front Park. Built along the east bank of the Platte River between 16th and 19th Streets, it included a gray stone building which Walker named the Castle of Culture and Commerce. The building was used for all types of displays from an art gallery to exhibits of farm products and minerals from Colorado mines. The park also included a race track, band-stand and ball field. During the summer, fireworks displays and plays were put on along the river. During the winter, a toboggan slide kept the park busy and while Walker sold the park in 1891, it remained the scene of various activities for many years, with everything from circuses to revivals using this ideal location. Early in the century the park was sold to the Northwestern Terminal Company and served various freight and storage uses until the castle burned in 1951.

River Front Park served one other function that was far removed from its original role of providing amusement. The silver panic of 1893 placed thousands of men from the state's mining towns in search of work and they poured into Denver, heedless of any mention that jobs were not available. The City of Denver decided to provide the men with a refugee camp and received Walker's permission to use the park. The National Guard provided the men with tents and the city starting feeding as many as 1,000 men each day beginning late in July, 1893. The railroads lowered the fare to the mid-west and hundreds left on special trains at almost no charge. One group, however, decided the best way to go east in search of work was by the river. The city provided lumber and the men built boats on which several hundred started down the Platte late in the summer of 1893. Numerous boats were wrecked and a few men drowned but most made the trip successfully and went their ways in search of a job. One group, after meeting with no employment success, joined up with Coxey's Army on that great march on Washington in 1894.

Among older Denverites, the name Manhattan Beach still stirs fond memories. The park was built along the northwestern shore of Sloan's Lake at what today would be West 25th Avenue and Sheridan Boulevard, and opened in 1891. The park featured a fine summer stock theater which was for some time managed by Mary Elitch along with her own theater. Finding good public support, the park continued to grow, built a large roller coaster, and seemed headed for a bright future. Sadly, on December 26, 1906, a fire destroyed the theater and about the same time the park's steamboat, *City of Denver*, sunk in a storm. In 1909, the park reopened under new ownership as Luna Park with a fine new boat, the *Frolic*, but from that time on, the park, again called Manhattan Beach in its last years, was losing in the competition with the newly opened White City, or Lakeside, and Elitch's Gardens. By World War I, the park was forever closed.

Just beyond the city limits of Denver's northwest corner is Lakeside Amusement Park. Opened on May 30, 1908, the park was long known as White City, because its landmark tower and main buildings were painted white. In later years the park name was changed to Lakeside, named for the picturesque lake that lies within the park, just west of the amusement area. White City soon added a theater and a dining and dancing pavilion and became a favorite summertime spot for Denverites. Usually, they rode out to the park on the trolley and on summer evenings extra cars were operated to handle the fun-seeking crowds. Both Lakeside and Elitch's were well located with not only the city cars but also the interurban trolleys to Golden, Arvada and Leyden passing their front gates. Among Lakeside's many rides, one of the most unusual and enduring has been the miniature railroad which runs completely around Lake Rhoda, a distance of over a mile. The line's two steam locomotives were originally built for use at the Louisiana Purchase Exposition (World's Fair) held in St. Louis in 1904. A handsome streamlined train was added to the line in the early 1950's, but the steam train remains the favorite of park visitors. It is interesting to note that the park lake is named for the daughter of the long time park manager, the late Ben Krasner. Miss Rhoda Krasner assumed management of Lakeside after the death of her father.

Denver has had two other amusement parks in recent years, but both of these, Magic Mountain and East Tincup, were short lived. Magic Mountain, like East Tincup was located west of the city along the old U. S. Route 40 (prior to construction of I-70) and was heralded as being patterned after Disney Land. The park attracted investment from many Denverites and construction at first moved along well to a point that the park opened briefly in 1959. The financial structure was insecure and the park soon closed, having never fully opened. After standing as a modern ghost town for a full decade, the facilities were taken over and reopened in 1971 as Heritage Square, a community of small shops and businesses featuring handicraft and art, accompanied by restaurants and a theater.

East Tincup opened at almost the same time as Magic Mountain and only a short distance to the east. The buildings simulated an early western mining town and contained an interesting array of shops, displays and amusements. Operated in part by the popular radio personality Pete Smythe, who had long used the name East Tincup as the setting for his daily radio program, the park was popular during its brief years in operation but was closed due to problems within the ownership of the firm. The site was converted to use today as a trailer park.

"NOT TO SEE ELITCH'S IS NOT TO SEE DENVER"

In the 1880's, John and Mary Elitch were operating a successful restaurant business in downtown Denver. Their Palace Restaurant at 1541 Arapahoe Street was making money and popular with Denverites. The Elitches began to think about opening an amusement park and started hunting a suitable location to the west of the city. Just beyond the town of Highlands they found what they sought; the Chilcott Farm. Already richly planted with apple and cottonwood trees, John and Mary began adding extensive flower gardens, more trees, and a large vegetable garden to supply their restaurant. Soon, becoming absorbed in planning their park, they sold the Palace in 1888 and turned full time to preparing the park, organizing a vaudeville company and collecting animals for the park's zoo.

On May 1, 1890, Elitch's Gardens opened, and as seems to be the custom on Elitch's opening days, it rained. Despite the weather, a fine crowd turned out, most of them taking the steam powered transit line, the same line which would serve the park for the next sixty years with electric streetcars. Opening day was considered a grand success.

John Elitch died in 1891, but Mary determined to maintain the park. In 1916 she married her assistant, Thomas D. Long, and while they were never divorced, they lived apart the rest of their lives, Mary being known as Mrs. Mary Elitch Long.

In 1897, the park's summer stock theater opened and has presented summer programs each year since, now holding the record as the oldest continuous summer stock theater in America.

The theater lobby is lined with the photographs of those who have appeared on its stage and is a virtual gallery of the greats of stage and screen.

Mary gradually became too deeply in debt with her park and in 1916 was forced to sell it to meet her obligations. J. K. Mullen purchased the park and soon sold it to J. M. Mulvihill who invited Mrs. Elitch to continue to live in her home in the park, which she did until just before her death in 1936. The grandsons of Mr. Mulvihill, Budd and Jack Gurtler, now own and operate the park and while making numerous changes to meet modern tastes, they have generally been able to maintain the atmosphere of Elitch's as Denverites like to remember it. The theater, the Trocadero ball room, and Orchard Cafe have continued virtually unchanged in taste or quality.

Many Denverites who rode the big yellow trolleys of the Denver Tramway out to Elitch's as youngsters, now return with their children to visit the park that truly justifies the slogan, "Not to See Elitch's is Not to See Denver."

For more than sixty years the Orpheum Theater was known as one of the city's finest showplaces. The first Orpheum (above) was opened at 1537 Welton Street in October, 1903, and featured top entertainers from the Keith-Orpheum Vaudeville Circuit. George Jessel, Will Rogers, the Marx Brothers and countless others played at the old Orpheum. With the growing popularity of movies, the new RKO Orpheum (RKO stands for Radio-Keith-Orpheum) was built on the same site and opened on February 11, 1932, featuring both films and vaudeville. The photo on the left was taken a few days before the theater's grand opening. In 1963, it was remodeled and renamed the RKO International 70, but only four years later it closed and was torn down in 1967.

Below, is a rare photo of Denver's round cyclorama exhibit arena. Known as the Gettysburg Building, it was constructed in the early 1880's, to house a huge cyclorama of the Battle of Gettysburg. In later years the building was used by the post office and for court rooms, and during the administration of Governor Waite (1893-95) was used to house troops called up to keep order after his controversial rulings. The building was destroyed by fire on February 26, 1905.—*Below, State Historical Society of Colorado; others, Denver Public Library, Western History Collection*

THE TABOR

"So fleet the works of men, back to the earth again,
Ancient and holy things fade like a dream."—Kingsley
(Quote appeared on the Tabor curtain.)

TABOR GRAND OPERA HOUSE

The most memorable of all Denver theaters is the Tabor Grand Opera House. Built by Horace Tabor, it opened on September 5, 1881, and while its glory faded with the years, it was a magnificent showplace even in its last years. The theater is seen at the upper left in the 1890's, while on the right is a view of the interior when new. At the lower left is a rare interior photo of the Tabor during a performance; the occasion was the 1000th Night Performance. By the late 1950's, lower downtown was fading and with it the Tabor. In a final burst of glory, the Tabor was selected in the late 1950's, to exhibit the epic film "Around the World in 80 Days." Once again crowds filled the theater, but the reprieve was brief. When urban renewal began to close in on the Tabor, efforts were made to save the historic theater, but to no avail. At the lower right, the Tabor is seen in one of its last photos, taken in 1964, during demolition.—*Lower right, D.P.L., Western History Coll.; others, State Historical Society of Colo.*

TABOR GRAND — LAST TIME TONIGHT
25c, 50c and 75c
ROSE MELVILLE
IN THE
Rural Comedy — SIS HOPKINS
TOMORROW and WEEK
Owen Wister's Remarkable Drama
THE VIRGINIAN
With One of the Strongest Casts This
Play Has Ever Had.

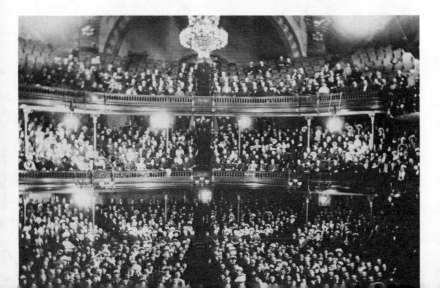

THE BROADWAY

The Broadway Theater opened on August 19, 1890, and for many years was a rival of the Tabor for the distinction of being the city's top showplace. Located in the Metropole Hotel (now part of the Cosmopolitan Hotel) at 18th Avenue and Broadway, the theater is pictured in the top photos when new, while below it is seen in its last days.

On February 21, 1955, the wreckers are seen at work (below) in what was probably the Broadway's last photo.—*Left, State Historical Society Collection; lower left, Authors' Coll.; others, D.P.L., Western History Coll.*

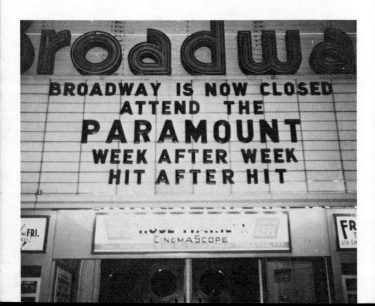

THE DENVER

The Denver Theater, at 16th Street and Glenarm Place, was built in 1927, and is seen in the two photos above on opening night, November 19, 1927. The Denver was one of the most lavish of the city's movie palaces and while remodeled in 1972, much of the original splendor remains.

Across 16th Street from the Denver Theater, stands the Paramount, pictured below, just prior to opening on August 30, 1930. The Paramount Theater is the last of Denver's grand old movie palaces which continues basically unchanged in the 1970's.

One of the most attractive of the theaters built outside of the downtown area is the Mayan (left) at 112 Broadway. This photo was taken shortly after the theater opened on November 13, 1930.—*All, Denver Public Library, Western History Collection*

C U R T I S   S T R E E T

Curtis Street, Denver's "Great White Way," is seen in this pair of photos taken about 1920, from the intersection of 17th and Curtis Streets. On the above right (opposite) the view is towards 18th Street and on the above left towards 16th Street.

The Empress and America theaters are visible in these photos. The America, at 16th and Curtis Streets, was built during World War I, and closed by 1933. For many years the building was occupied by the Neisner Brothers variety store and was torn down by 1970. The Empress opened on December 23, 1907, next to the future sight of the America. For a short time, when new, the theater was known as the Majestic; then, after being known for a number of years as the Empress, it was renamed the Victory. After World War II it gained a special fame for its showing of films which were considered quite risque.—*Above, State Historical Society of Colorado; top and left, Denver Public Library, Western History Collection*

Both the Paris and the Isis are visible in the Curtis Street scene above, and are shown below soon after opening. The Paris, at 1751 Curtis Street, was built in 1912 and is pictured in 1913. The car in the foreground is a 1911 Hupmobile. The Isis, almost opposite at 1722 Curtis Street, opened in 1913 and stood until 1953, far outlasting the Paris which closed in the mid-1930's.—*Above, State Historical Society of Colorado; below, Denver Public Library, Western History Collection*

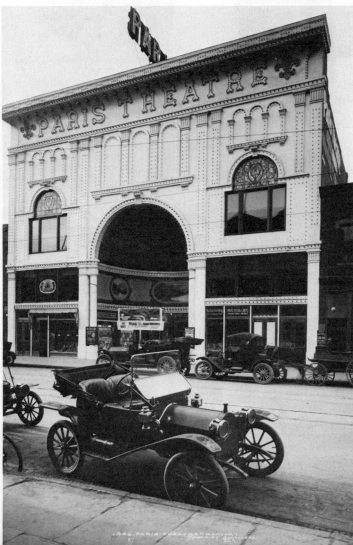

The Aladdin Theater (upper right) at East Colfax and Race Street, opened on October 28, 1926. It was one of the first theaters especially designed for showing sound pictures, and is still one of Denver's most popular theaters. The Denham Theater (above) at 18th and California Streets, was a popular vaudeville house and did not completely convert to being a movie theater until the 1930's.

Four Denverites who rose to show business fame are seen here. Spring Byington grew up in north Denver and became popular in both films and television. Douglas Fairbanks graduated from East High School and went to Hollywood to become one of the top actors of his era. Paul Whiteman was raised in Denver and gained his musical experience from his father, Wilberforce J. Whiteman, who was for many years the Director of Music for the Denver Public Schools. Paul Whiteman began his career by playing with local groups but eventually rose to become one of America's top jazz musicians. George Morrison became interested in the violin as a small child and began working as a shoeshine boy near his home in Boulder to pay for lessons. As a young man he organized his own orchestra and by the 1920's was known as one of the nation's finest violinists. —Center (middle row) and lower right, Denver Post; all, D.P.L., Western History Coll.

SPRING BYINGTON

DOUGLAS FAIRBANKS

GEORGE MORRISON

MR. & MRS. PAUL WHITEMAN (center), MR. & MRS. WILBERFORCE J. WHITEMAN

Denver: A Pictorial History

MUSIC

Today's Denver Symphony Orchestra is descended from several earlier orchestras, beginning with the old Denver Symphony which first performed on November 30, 1900, at the Broadway Theater, under the baton of Henry Houseley. The Denver Philharmonic Orchestra was founded in 1919 and conducted by Horace Tureman. Like the earlier Denver Symphony, it was short lived, but was replaced in 1922, by the Denver Civic Symphony which was also under the direction of Tureman. The present Denver Symphony was organized in 1934 and performed its first concert on November 30, 1934, under Horace Tureman, who continued in this position until retired in 1945. The Denver Symphony (above) was conducted by Saul Caston between 1945 and 1963, followed by Vladimir Golschmann until 1968. The orchestra is now led by Brian Priestman.

The Sans Souci Concert Gardens (right) were built in 1881, at South Broadway and West Virginia Avenue and offered Denverites programs of fine music. Located across the street from the National Mining and Industrial Exposition building, it flourished for a few years but soon passed from the scene.

The Denver City Band is pictured below, ready to present one of their popular park concerts at the turn of the century. The band was later known as the Denver Municipal Band and for almost half a century it was directed by the late Henry Sachs (lower right), and is best known for its summer concerts in City Park.

—*Above and right, Denver Public Library, Western History Collection; upper right, John Pulliam; below, State Historical Society of Colorado; lower right, Mrs. Henry Sachs*

HENRY EVERETT SACHS

THE MINING & INDUSTRIAL EXPOSITION

On August 1, 1892, the National Mining and Industrial Exposition opened in the newly completed Exposition Building (above), at South Broadway and Exposition Avenue. The event attracted large crowds to view the extensive displays (below) and an added attraction, especially for Easterners, were the Ute Indians, who posed for this photo (left) on September 21, 1882. The show was successful enough to be repeated in 1883 and 1884, but after closing on October 4, 1884, it was decided that the financial results would not warrant it being continued and the buildings were removed a short time later.—*All, State Historical Society of Colorado*

THE NATIONAL WESTERN STOCK SHOW

During the third week of January each year, Denver is caught up in the spirit of the West as the annual National Western Stock Show opens. The show was first organized by a group of stockmen and local businessmen and opened on January 20, 1906, as the Western Livestock Show. In 1907, a large tent was erected (above) and the show began to grow in both scope and attendance. A large stock show pavilion was built on the same site (right and below) and with the show sheltered from the January weather, it continued to expand in popularity. Today, the rodeo and many displays are held in the new Denver Coliseum across the street from the original building, which is also still in use. The Rio Grande and other railroads soon offered special train service and lower fares to attract visitors to the show and today, sixty years later, a special train on the Union Pacific from Cheyenne is still a highlight of Stock Show Week.—*Photos, Denver Public Library, Western History Collection; poster, Colorado Railroad Museum*

Now almost legendary, the Festivals of the Mountain and the Plain ("the" is often omitted from the name) were probably the most spectacular events that Denver has ever witnessed on a regular basis. After considerable discussion, a general consensus developed that the city should have some type of yearly show which could attract visitors from all parts of the state; from this came the idea for the Festival of Mountain and Plain. The first Festival opened on October 16, 1895, and proved such a success that they were held in succeeding years until just before World War I. The Festivals were held out of doors in a spacious stadium at the northeast corner of Broadway and East Colfax Avenue, as seen below, during the 1901 show. The yearly competition to build the most elaborate and beautiful parade float resulted in such fine ones as seen on the opposite page. A highlight of each year's show was the selection of the Queen of the Festival. In the photo at the upper right (opposite page) Ruth Boettcher, daughter of Charles Boettcher I, is reigning as Queen in 1912.—*Program, Denver Public Library, Western History Collection; upper left-opposite, University of Colorado Historical Collections; others, State Historical Society of Colorado*

RUTH BOETTCHER, QUEEN—1912

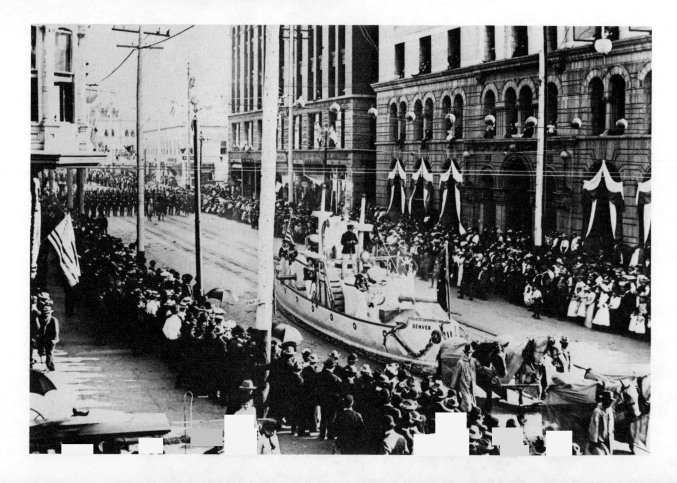

BICYCLES

The bicycle craze hit Colorado in the 1880's and Denver soon boasted several very active "wheel clubs." Members of the Denver Ramblers Wheel Club are seen on the left, in Mt. Vernon Canyon in 1888, while in the bottom photo they pose in a Denver park. Races became very popular and were sponsored by a wide variety of groups and clubs. A group of Denver barbers sponsored the Barber's Road Race in 1896, and a ticket such as the one at the right (opposite), not only admitted you to the race but also included refreshments and dinner—all for $1.00.

No bicycle team was much more unusual than the Fowler Sextet, seen below, on their bicycle built for six. A bicycle was even a good prop for picture taking as in the photo at the upper right (opposite page). The bicycle is an 1888 model, solid tire three seater.—*Photos, State Historical Society of Colorado; ticket, Denver Public Library, Western History Collection*

On a bicycle built for two . . . or SIX!

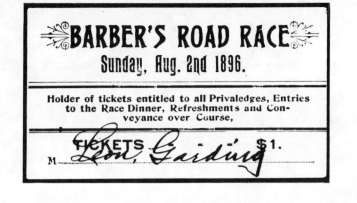

Not everyone used a bicycle to enjoy the countryside. Members of the Bit and Spur Club are posed (left) as they prepare to begin a Sunday outing. Another favorite way to enjoy the scenery was, and still is, by train. In the lower photo, members of the Colorado Camera Club stand beside their special car on a narrow gauge train of the Union Pacific, Denver and Gulf Railway. The man in the second window from the left is William H. Jackson, one of the West's most noted photographers. His son is wearing the wide brimmed hat and seated on the rocks. A number of Jackson's photos appear in this book.—*Left, State Historical Society of Colorado; below, Denver Public Library, Western History Collection*

B A S E B A L L

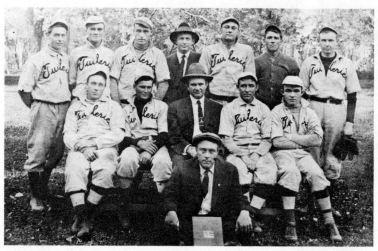

Almost as soon as the first settlements were established along Cherry Creek, the game of baseball began to be played. At first the playing field and the rules were perhaps a bit unconventional but within a few years a number of amateur teams were organized and playing at several fields around the city. On the left, the Tuileries Gardens team is posed after a winning game, while above is seen the Denver Tramway team. Baseball was quite popular with women and in the photo below, the fair ladies of the Ladies Base Ball Aggregation is seen in Denver on September 13, 1892, while on tour across the country.—*Above, E. S. Payne Collection; left, Denver Public Library, Western History Collection; below, State Historical Society of Colorado*

Denver has had several baseball parks but the first large facility was located at West 6th Avenue and South Broadway and known as Broadway Park. The grandstands were heavily damaged by the weight of snow during the great blizzard of December, 1913, and they were also several times damaged by fire. In 1901, Union Park was built at South Broadway and West Center Avenue and in 1922, this facility was enlarged and remodeled with a large donation of funds by the Merchants Biscuit Company. The park (above) was then renamed Merchants Park and served until Bears Stadium (below) was opened on August 14, 1948. The Merchants Park Shopping center was built on the old stadium site in the early 1950's. Bears Stadium was recently purchased by the City of Denver and after being enlarged to hold the large crowds which often attend the Denver Broncos football games, the facility has been renamed Mile High Stadium.—*All, Denver Public Library, Western History Collection*

The University of Denver's Hilltop Stadium was built in 1925 and is seen on the right, during a football game soon after completion. For many years the highlight of the football season was the game between Denver University and Colorado University as advertised at the far right, from *The Denver Post* of November 16, 1946. The stadium served many functions including conventions, fireworks displays, and daredevil racers such as the one below in mid-air leaping over a Denver Tramway bus on July 4, 1946. For a short time the stadium was also used by the Denver Broncos, but after D. U. dropped football in 1961, the school could not justify the high maintenance costs of the aging stadium and it was razed in 1971.—*Both, State Historical Society of Colorado*

Basketball became very popular in Denver at the turn of the century and interest was especially spurred when Dr. James Naismith, the game's inventor, spent the year 1898 at the Denver YMCA. During this time he did much to perfect the game of basketball and to spark interest in the new sport. A host of teams sprang up and many were sponsored by businesses and industries, such as the proud team on the right, sponsored by the Tivoli Brewing Company.—*State Historical Society of Colorado*

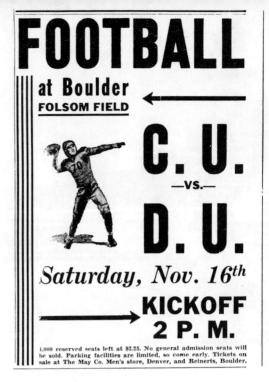

FOOTBALL

at Boulder
FOLSOM FIELD ←

C. U.
—VS.—
D. U.

Saturday, Nov. 16th

**KICKOFF
2 P. M.**

→

1,000 reserved seats left at $2.25. No general admission seats will be sold. Parking facilities are limited, so come early. Tickets on sale at The May Co. Men's store, Denver, and Reinerts, Boulder.

DENVER'S MISS AMERICAS

SHARON KAY RITCHIE—1956
Miss Ritchie came to Denver from Grand Island, Nebraska, in order to attend Colorado Woman's College. While a student there she won the Miss Colorado title and then went on to Atlantic City and won the Miss America crown; she was the first Colorado girl to win the contest.—*Denver Public Library, Western History Collection*

MARILYN ELAINE VAN DERBUR—1958
Miss Van Derbur graduated from Denver's East High School and while attending the University of Colorado, she became Miss Colorado and went on to be selected Miss America of 1958. Miss Van Derbur is seen advertising the 1959 "Rush to the Rockies" celebration which marked the 100th anniversary of the gold rush that opened the state to settlement.—*Denver Post photo, Denver Public Library, Western History Collection*

Denver's beautiful City Park is seen in this panorama of photographs. The Dennis Sullivan Gateway (top-opposite page) is at the south end of the esplanade leading from East Colfax Avenue and is one of the entrances to City Park. Donated in 1917 by John Mitchell, the gate is a memorial to pioneer businessman Dennis Sullivan. The park's race track (opposite) was built in 1898 and was the site for hundreds of races until razed in April 1950, after falling into disuse. The Denver Zoo was begun in 1896, with the first animal being a bear cub. The present zoo facility was started in 1918 and in order to make the animal enclosures realistic, castings were made of actual rock formations in the mountains and used as patterns for construction of the bear pens seen at the lower right (opposite). The two park lakes were built in 1897 and the larger lake is seen in these summer and winter scenes. The electric fountain was built in 1908 and continues to operate every summer evening while the music of the band concert drifts across the lake. The fountain sprays 4000 gallons of water from 2000 nozzles while colored lights are constantly changed from the control tower in the pavilion at the west end of the lake (building at center of photo at lower left).—*Above and upper right (opposite); State Historical Society of Colorado; others, Denver Public Library, Western History Collection*

As the city crowded the banks of Cherry Creek, the once picturesque stream became a cluttered eyesore and posed a constant threat of flood. During the administration of Mayor Robert Speer, the creek was walled and Speer Boulevard built along its route. The creek is seen above, looking east from the Broadway bridge, between 6th and 7th Avenues, in 1897, with the Jacques Brothers Monuments Company at the left. The photo at the right was taken about twenty years later from the same location but facing west after the project had been completed.

The Pioneer Monument (below) was the first segment of the present Civic Center and occupies the former site of Engine Company No. 1 on a triangle bounded by Colfax, Broadway and Cheyenne Place. Built in 1910, the monument marks the end of the historic Smoky Hill Trail.

After removal of the old Arapahoe County Court House, the site, bounded by 15th and 16th Streets and Tremont and Court Places, became a park. After World War II the park became a parking lot and eventually was sold for construction of the May-D&F store. —All, Denver Public Library, Western History Collection

Denver's mountain parks and the city park system are a result of far-sighted planning and much of the credit goes to George Cranmer and Saco R. DeBoer. Cranmer was Manager of Parks and Improvements from 1935 until 1947 and led the development of Red Rocks amphitheater (seen above while under construction in the lae 1930's), Winter Park ski area, and the Valley Highway system. In 1959, Mt. View Park at East 3rd Avenue and Bellaire Street was renamed Cranmer Park; a fitting memorial to a pioneer environmentalist. De-Boer served as City Planner during the 1930's and was responsible for the planning on Cherry Creek Reservoir, Washington Park, Speer Boulevard, and Buchtel Boulevard. DeBoer is seen in the photo at the right, taken at the opening of Echo Lake Lodge in 1926. De-Boer is at the far left, Mayor Ben Stapleton is third from the left and on his left is Charles D. Vail, Manager of Parks and Improvements during the 1920's. Vail, for whom Vail Pass is named, became State Highway Engineer in 1930 and was responsible for highway improvements over Floyd Hill, Wolf Creek Pass, Loveland Pass, and numerous other projects. Second from the right is Frederick R. Ross, active in parks and planning and member of both the Water Board and the Public Library Board of Commissioners.

Typical of Denver parks are Sloan's Lake Park (below) and Berkeley Park (lower right) seen about 1915. —*Below, West. Hist. Coll., Univ. of Colo.; others, D.P.L., West. Hist. Coll.*

For ninety years, one of Denver's favorite recreation areas has been Overland Park. In 1931, the park became a golf course but in earlier years it accommodated a wide range of activities as seen in the historic photos on these pages. The park, first known as Jewell Park, was begun in 1883, by the owners of the Denver Circle Railroad as an attraction to bring passengers to their trains. The ownership went to Henry Wolcott in the late 1890's and the name was changed to Overland Park. The race track was used first for horses and later for auto races as in the scenes on the opposite page, dating to the 1920's. In the early days of flight, the park was a favorite location for both airplanes and lighter-than-air craft such as the one owned by Roy Knabenshue and shown below in about 1907.

In the 1920's the city purchased the park and converted part of it into a tourist camp with the main entrance (above) on South Santa Fe Drive at Colorado Avenue. Thousands of tourists, such as those at the right and lower right, enjoyed the park's facilities during the 1920's and early 1930's.—*Below, State Historical Society of Colorado; others, Denver Public Library, Western History Collection*

O
V
E
R
L
A
N
D

P
A
R
K

The Sells-Floto Circus is now almost forgotten, but early in the century it was well on the way to becoming one of the nation's top circuses. The show was begun by Harry Tammen, co-owner of the Denver Post, and began as the Floto Dog and Pony Show. Tammen and his partner, F. G. Bonfils, built the show with top acts and added Buffalo Bill after his own show went broke. The Sells-Floto winter quarters were at West 27th Avenue and Hazel Court, allowing Tammen to keep a close eye on the show, including the elephants of which he was especially fond. In the bottom photo one of the baby elephants is seen with Fred Bonfils, standing at the left, taking part in a publicity stunt. The show was sold in 1921, to the American Circus Corporation but continued under the original name for several more years. It is seen in another advertising stunt (below) in front of the Denver Post on Champa Street in 1943. —All, D.P.L., Western History Collection

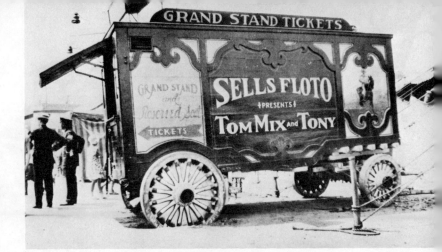

S
E
L
L
S
·
F
L
O
T
O

WILLIAM FREDERICK CODY
"BUFFALO BILL"

RIVER FRONT PARK
During the 1880's, River Front Park was developed by John Brisbane Walker along the Platte River, between 16th and 19th Streets. The park included a race track and a massive gray stone building known as the Castle of Culture and Commerce. The building housed displays of art, minerals and agricultural products, and is seen at the right in the 1930's, when in use by the Denver & Salt Lake Railway. The race track is visible in the photo above, taken as numbers of unemployed men were building boats on which to float down the river in search of jobs in eastern cities. Part of the group later joined Coxey's Army.

THE TUILERIES GARDENS
The Tuileries Gardens, at South Broadway and Hampden Avenue, were built in the late 1890's and featured gambling, vaudeville, boating, ice skating in winter, and in later years, bicycle and motorcycle racing. The park closed soon after World War I and during the 1920's was the site of Alexander Aircraft Company. The area is now part of the Cinderella City Shopping Center.
—*All photos this page, Denver Public Library, Western History Collection*

MANHATTAN BEACH

This artist's conception of Manhattan Beach (above) was never brought to reality. Plans laid down in the 1890's visualized a large resort and amusement park, and while partially completed, the park never approached the planner's dream. Located on the north shore of Sloan's Lake, near what is now the corner of West 25th Avenue and Sheridan Boulevard, the park opened in the summer of 1891 and included a hotel (left) and a summer stock theater. The theater is seen at the right (opposite page), and the 1891 season stock company players are shown at the lower right. The theater burned in 1906 and was not rebuilt. The park is seen below, from Sheridan Boulevard, in the summer of 1898, with two trolleys of the West End Electric Railway visible in the distance.—*Left and lower right (opposite), State Historical Society of Colorado; others, Denver Public Library, Western History Collection*

In 1909, Manhattan Beach was renamed Luna Park and operated under this name for several years, returning to its original name shortly before finally closing about the time of World War I. The Park is seen above, in 1912, looking toward the north from across Sloan's Lake.—*Denver Public Library, Western History Collection*

THE *CITY OF DENVER*

The ill-fated *"City of Denver"* is seen below, about 1900. The boat offered cruises on Sloan's Lake but sank a few years later during a winter storm.—*Denver Public Library, Western History Collection*

The City at Play

On May 30, 1908, crowds of Denverites rode the trolley out to the northwest limits of town to see a fabulous new amusement park—White City. Today the park, better known as Lakeside, is a Denver landmark which still provides thrills to thousands of fun seekers each summer.

These two historic photos were taken by L. C. McClure shortly after the park opened. On the right, the park's main entrance is seen much as it appears today, while below, the view is from the center of the park looking north with Inspiration Point in the background. The advertisement at the top is one of the very first and appeared in June, 1908.

On the opposite page (above) the park is seen in an aerial view taken in the late 1920's, with the lake in the background. The lake was later named by the park manager, Ben Krasner, for his daughter, Rhoda Krasner, who now manages the park.

Swimming has always been popular at Lakeside as seen in the two center photos (opposite). In the park's early years swimmers enjoyed the lake but soon the indoor pool was completed and proved much more popular than the rather cool lake waters. One of the oldest park rides, the Star, is visible behind the swimmers in the outdoor scene. The ride was rebuilt in 1972 and will continue to thrill riders and provide a wonderful view of the park.—*All, Denver Public Library, Western History Collection*

Lakeside

AMUSEMENT PARK

West 46th & Sheridan at I-70

One of the all-time most popular rides at Lakeside is the miniature train. Powered by actual steam locomotives, built in 1903, for the St. Louis Exposition, the trains circle Lake Rhoda. At night the reflection of the park lights on the waters of the lake makes the park seem almost a fairy land. Below, dancers enjoy themselves on the floor of the Casino Theater, which for many years also presented plays and in later years was once used for a walkathon contest.—D.P.L., *Western History Coll.*

MARY ELITCH LONG

A turn of the century poster (above) tells of the wonders of Elitch's Zoological Gardens.

Ivy Baldwin, famed balloonist and aerialist, was a regular performer at Elitch's as early as 1892. On the right, his balloon is prepared for launching from Elitch's in 1910, in conjunction with the Colorado National Guard.—*Upper left, Denver Public Library; others, State Historical Society of Colorado*

The entrance to the Zoological Gardens was first located at what is now West 36th Avenue and Tennyson Street. A short time later it was moved to West 38th Avenue near Vrain Street, and by early in the century it was located at the corner of West 38th Avenue and Tennyson Street where it remains. The main entrance is seen above, about 1905, with a trolley in the background. For many years the trolley was the most popular way to reach the park and in summer the cars were jammed with fun-seekers as they rolled west from downtown. The same entrance is seen (lower left) from inside the park. In 1909, the famous "gate with the angels" was built at the same location and is seen below (right) soon after completion. The widening of West 38th Avenue in 1958, forced the removal of the gate as it was replaced by the present graceful arch.—*Above, Authors' Collection; lower right, Denver Public Library, Western History Collection; lower left, State Historical Society of Colorado*

The Trocadero (above) is known as the "Summer Home of America's Biggest Bands." Built in 1902, it was first used for dance clubs but opened to public dancing after World War I. Two popular park rides are seen on the left, the "Old Mill" and the "Tour of the World." The "Old Mill" was the scene of tragedy when fire swept it and took six lives on July 16, 1944. Over the years, however, the park has had an excellent safety record. The two bottom photos are of the always popular miniature train. The first train (right) was built in 1899 and circled the theater. The larger train (left) threaded its way through much of the park, and one of its two engines is now preserved at the Colorado Railroad Museum in Golden.

In the summer of 1897, the first series of summer plays was presented at the Elitch Theater. Three quarters of a century later it is the oldest summer stock theater in America and growing in popularity. The theater is seen on the right in a 1950's photo and except for a new backstage area, is little changed from its appearance when the photo below was taken half a century ago. The original curtain (bottom) is still in use and displays this verse below the cottage:

> Ann Hathaway's cottage
> A mile away
> Shakespeare sought
> At close of day.

In the years before the start of the summer plays, a wide variety of entertainment was presented in the park, as listed on the program (lower right) for the week of September 6, 1892.—*Top (opposite page), Elitch Gardens; lower right (opposite), State Historical Society of Colorado; all others, Denver Public Library, Western History Collection*

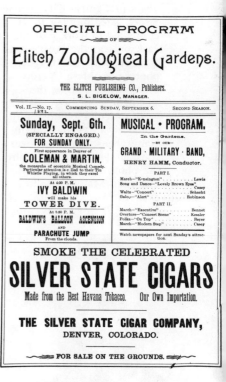

DENVER
"Queen City of the Plains"

Behold "Queen City of the Plains,"
  Gateway to Rockies near,
Where from all quarters, western trains
  Are bringing travelers here!

They journey to the Golden West
  To learn the wealth and sights
Of our great country, richly blest
  With health from mountain heights.

Now Denver lies twelve miles from hills
  Of Rocky Mountains grand.
The wondrous sight with rapture thrills
  The traveler in the land.

One mile lies Denver 'bove the sea,
  At mouth of Cherry Creek,
Which joins the Platte that flows so free,
  As fed by streams from peak.

A fertile valley leads the way
  If northward you would go;
For products wonderful they say,
  From Platte's rich soil do grow.

You see green fields outspreading here,
  With many farms below
And all around the city near,
  Which you should see and know.

Afar to eastward, Plains appear
  And rich horizon vast;
For countless miles the vision's clear
  To where once "schooners" passed.

And to the State House here so great,
  The travelers wend their way,
From Station through the "Welcome Gate,"
  Where *welcome* waits each day.

Two hundred miles of Rocky Range
  Are viewed from Fisher's Tower—
The Peaks so wonderful and strange,
  Which speak unmeasured power.

South, sixty-four miles, lies Pikes Peak,
  Across the country here;
Longs, Evans, James, each one unique,
  At other spots appear.

There's education, culture rare,
  In schools the very best;
Oh, come the wondrous gifts to share,
  Of this far Golden West!

Once here in Denver, you will stay
  For Colorado's air;
To bring you wealth along your way
  And health beyond compare.

"Queen City of the Plains," proclaim;
  For all delight to dwell
In Denver of illustrious fame—
  Beneath her magic spell!

—Reprinted from "Colorado in Verse and Picture, 1916-1928" Copyright 1928 by Laura S. DuVall

THEY CAPTURED THE WEST ON FILM

Four noted western photographers are seen in these photos. William Chamberlain came to Denver in 1861 and for many years operated a studio at 15th and Larimer Streets. His photos provide us with a fine record of the city during its pioneer years. Joseph Collier came to America from Scotland and after a few years in Central City, opened a studio at 415 Larimer Street, later moving to 1643 Larimer Street, where he continued to work past the turn of the century. William Jackson was the West's most famous photographer. He traveled with the Hayden Survey and made the first photos in Mesa Verde and Yellowstone. He took hundreds of photos throughout the West, often on assignment from railroads, and in later years did pioneer work on color photography. Louis McClure opened his studio in 1909 and during the next 25 years made a comprehensive photo coverage of Denver. He also did considerable work for railroads, as was the case when the photo on the right was posed at Hell Gate on the Colorado Midland Railway. Strangely, very few photos exist of Mr. McClure.—*All, Denver Public Library, Western History Collection*

LOUIS CHARLES McCLURE 1872-1957 (standing with camera)

WILLIAM GUNNISON CHAMBERLAIN
1815-1910

JOSEPH M. COLLIER
1836-1910

WILLIAM HENRY JACKSON
1843-1942

Denver: A Pictorial History

BIBLIOGRAPHY

This bibliography is not a complete listing of all published materials on the history of Denver. It is, however, a selection of references which can provide the reader with additional information on the various aspects of Denver history. Certain titles are out of print but are likely to be available in the libraries listed below and in many public libraries.

LIBRARIES

Colorado State Historical Society Library
14th Avenue and Sherman Street
Denver, Colorado

Denver Public Library, Western History
  Department
14th Avenue and Broadway
Denver, Colorado

Norlin Library, Western Historical Collection
University of Colorado
Boulder, Colorado

PERIODICALS AND NEWSPAPERS

Cervi's Rocky Mountain Journal, Denver, Sept. 22, 1949-Present.

City of Denver, The, City of Denver, 1912-1914.

Colorado Magazine, State Historical Society, Denver, 1923-Present. Vols. 1-49.

Denver Express, Denver, April 26, 1906 to Nov. 20, 1926.

Denver Municipal Facts, City of Denver, 1909-1912.

Denver Post, Denver, June 22, 1894-Present. Between Jan. 3, 1927 and Nov. 5, 1928, the *Denver Morning Post* was published as a morning companion paper to the *Denver Post*. The *Denver Post* is now Denver's evening paper.

Denver Republican, Denver, June 4, 1879 to Aug. 11, 1884. Became the *Denver Tribune-Republican*.

Denver Republican, Denver, Jan. 1, 1887 to Oct. 26, 1913. There was also a weekly from 1887 to 1912.

Denver Times, Denver, April 1, 1872 to Nov. 22, 1926. Became the *Denver Evening News*.

Denver Tribune, Denver, Jan. 20, 1871 to Aug. 11, 1884. Merged with the *Denver Republican*.

Denver Tribune-Republican, Denver, Aug. 11, 1884 to Dec. 31, 1886. Became the *Denver Republican*.

Municipal Facts, City of Denver, 1918-1931.

Rocky Mountain News, Denver, April 23, 1859 to present. A weekly paper until August 27, 1860, the *News* has been on a daily basis since that time. Between Nov. 23, 1926 and Nov. 5, 1928 the *Denver Evening News* was published as an evening companion paper to the *Rocky Mountain News*, which is now Denver's morning paper.

BOOKS

COLORADO—GENERAL HISTORIES

Bancroft, Caroline, *Colorful Colorado: Its Dramatic History*, Boulder, Johnson Pub. Co., 1959.

Barney, Liebus, *Letters of the Pikes Peak Gold Rush*, San Jose, Calif., Talisman Press, 1959.

Bartlett, Richard A., *Great Surveys of the American West*, Norman, University of Oklahoma Press, 1962.

Bauer, William and Ozment, James and Willard, John, *Colorado Postal History: The Post Offices*, Crete, Nebraska, J-B Pub. Co., 1971.

Colorado State Historical and Natural History Society, *History of Colorado*, James H. Baker, ed., LeRoy R. Hafen, associate ed., Denver, Linderman Co., 1927. 5 vols.

Colorado Year Book, Denver, Colorado State Planning Commission, 1918-1964.

Denver Posse of the Westerners, *Brand Book of the Denver Westerners*, Denver, 1945 to Present. The Brand Books are published yearly and include short articles on a wide variety of subjects concerning Denver and Colorado.

Federal Writers Project, *Colorado—A Guide to the Highest State*, New York, Hasting House Pub., 1970. The original work was done in 1941 and has been revised in 1970.

Hafen, LeRoy R., *Colorado and its People: A Narrative and Topical History of the Centennial State*, New York, Lewis Historical Pub. Co., 1948. 4 vols.

Hall, Frank, *History of the State of Colorado*, Chicago, Blakely Printing Co., 1889-1895. Second edition 1890-1897. Both 4 vols.

Kenehan, Katherine, *Colorado, The Land and the People*, Denver, Denver Public Schools, 1957.

Stone, Wilbur Fisk, *History of Colorado*, Chicago, S. J. Clarke Pub. Co., 1918. 4 vols.

Westermeier, C. P., *Colorado's First Portrait*, Albuquerque, Univ. of New Mexico, 1970.

Wilcox, Virginia Lee, *Colorado—A selected Bibliography of its Literature 1858-1952*, Denver, Sage Books, 1954.

DENVER

Arps, Louisa A. W., *Denver in Slices*, Denver, Sage Books, 1959.

Bancroft, Caroline, *Augusta Tabor: Her Side of the Scandal*, Denver, Golden Press, 1955.

Bancroft, Caroline, *Brown Palace in Denver, The*, Denver, Golden Press, 1955.

Bancroft, Caroline, *Denver's Lively Past*, Boulder, Johnson Pub. Co., 1959.

Bancroft, Caroline, *Melodrama of Wohlhurst, The*, Denver, Golden Press, 1952.

Bancroft, Caroline, *Mile High Denver*, Denver, Golden Press, 1952.

Bancroft, Caroline, *Silver Queen: The Fabulous Story of Baby Doe Tabor*, Boulder, Johnson Pub. Co., 1965.

Bancroft, Caroline, *Six Racy Madams of Colorado*, Boulder, Johnson Pub. Co., 1965.

Bancroft, Caroline, *Unsinkable Mrs. Brown, The*, Denver, Golden Press, 1956.

Barker, Bill and Lewin, Jackie, *Denver,* New York, Doubleday and Co., 1972.

Bluemel, Elinor, *Opportunity School and Emily Griffith,* Denver, Green Mountain Press, 1970.

Bollinger, Edward and Bauer, Frederick, *Moffat Road, The,* Denver, Sage Books, 1962.

Boner, Harold, *Giants Ladder, The,* Milwaukee, Kalmabach Pub. Co., 1962.

Breck, Allen, *W. G. Evans, 1855-1924; Profile of a Western Executive,* Denver, University of Denver, 1964.

Casey, Lee Taylor, *Denver Murders,* New York, Duell, Sloan and Pearce, 1946.

Charter of the City and County of Denver, Denver, 1972. City Clerk's Office.

Coleman, Alice, *The First Sixty Years, Edgewater's 60th Anniversary of Incorporation, 1901-1961,* Edgewater, 1961.

Colorado Cattlemen's Centennial Commission, *The Co-operative Century,* The Commission, Denver, 1967.

Cook, David J., *Hands Up: or Twenty Years of Detective Life in the Mountains and on the Plains,* Denver, Republican Pub. Co., 1882.

Dallas, Sandra, *Cherry Creek Gothic,* Norman, University of Oklahoma Press, 1971.

Dallas, Sandra, *Gold and Gothic,* Denver, Lick Skillet Press, 1967.

Davis, Elmer O., *First Five Years of the Railroad Era in Colorado, The,* Golden, Sage Books, 1948.

Davis, Sally and Baldwin, Betty, *Denver Dwellings and Descendants,* Denver, Sage Books, 1963.

Eatwell, John M., *Denver's Golden Days and Apothecary Palaces,* Denver, Antique Bottle Collectors of Colorado, 1972.

Etter, Donaldo D., *Auraria, Where Denver Began,* Colorado Associated University Press, 1972.

Fallis, Edwin, *When Denver and I Were Young,* Denver, Big Mountain Press, 1956.

Ferril, Thomas Hornsby, *Rocky Mountain Herald Reader,* New York, Morehouse-Barow, 1966.

Ferril, Thomas Hornsby, *Words for Denver and other Poems,* New York, Morrow, 1966.

Fowler, Gene, *Timber Line: A Story of Bonfils and Tammen,* New York, Covici Friede, 1933.

Hicks, Dave, *Englewood From The Beginning,* Denver, A-T-P Pub. Co., 1971.

Johnson, Charles, *Denver's Mayor Speer,* Denver, Green Mountain Press, 1969.

Johnson, Forrest, *Denver's Old Theater Row,* Denver, B. Lay, 1970.

Jones, William and Wagner, F. Hol, Jr. and McKeever, Gene C., *Mile-High Trolleys,* Denver, The Intermountain Chapter of the National Railway Historical Society, 1965. (New edition available from Pruett Publishing Company, Fall, 1973).

Karsner, David, *Silver Dollar: The Story of the Tabors,* New York, Covici-Friede, 1932.

Kelsey, Harry E., *Frontier Capitalist, Life of John Evans,* Boulder, Pruett Pub. Co., 1969.

Kohl, Edith, *Denver's Historic Mansions,* Denver, Sage Books, 1957.

Larsen, Charles, *The Good Fight, The Story of Judge Ben Lindsey,* New York, Quadrangle, 1972.

Miller, Max and Mazzulla, Fred, *Holladay Street,* New York, Ballantine Books, 1962.

Mumey, Nolie, *Clark, Gruber and Company, A Pioneer Denver Mint,* Denver, Artcraft Press, 1950.

Mumey, Nolie, *Professor Oscar J. Goldrick and His Denver,* Denver, Sage Books, 1959.

Parkhill, Forbes, *Wildest of the West,* New York, Holt, 1951.

Perkins, Robert L., *The First Hundred Years: An Informal History of Denver and the Rocky Mountain News,* Garden City, Doubleday & Co., 1959.

Robbins, Sara E., *Jefferson County, Colorado,* Lakewood, Jefferson County Bank, 1962.

Seybert, Olga and Marshall, Helen L., *Have You Ever Seen Denver?,* Boulder, Johnson Pub. Co., 1971.

Smiley, Jerome C. ed., *History of Denver, With Outlines of the Earlier History of the Rocky Mountain Country,* Denver, The Times-Sun Pub. Co., 1901. Note: This work has been reprinted and is available from the State Historical Society of Colorado.

State Historical Society of Colorado, *Colorado Volunteers in the Civil War,* Boulder, Pruett Press, 1963. Reprint of the 1906 edition.

Spring, Agnes Wright, *Denver's Historic Markers, Memorials, Statues and Parks,* Denver, State Historical Society of Colorado, 1960.

U. S. Geological Survey, *Floods of June 1965 in the South Platte River Basin, Colorado,* Water Supply Paper 1850-B, Washington, D. C., Supt. of Documents, 1969.

Van Cise, Philip S., *Fighting the Underworld,* Boston, Houghton Mifflin, 1936.

Vickers, William B., *History of the City of Denver, Arapahoe County and Colorado,* Chicago, O. L. Baskin and Co., 1880.

Wagner, F. H., *The Colorado Road,* Boulder, Johnson Pub. Co., 1971.

Wharton, J. E., *History of the City of Denver from its Earliest Settlement to The Present Time,* Denver, Byers and Dailery, 1866.

Zamonski, Stanley W. and Keller, Teddy, *The Fifty-niners,* Denver, Sage Books, 1961.